The Sh

RAGE

The Shape of

THE FILMS OF
DAVID CRONENBERG

A Publication of the Academy of Canadian Cinema

General Publishing Co. Limited/*Toronto, Canada*

New York Zoetrope, Inc./*New York, U.S.A.*

The Shape of Rage — The Films of David Cronenberg was published with the support and financial assistance of the Canada Council. The Council's unique involvement in projects such as this one underlines its serious and long-standing commitment to film and filmmakers in Canada. For this the Academy is sincerely grateful.

In addition, this book also received financial support from the World Film Festival of Toronto Inc. (Festival of Festivals) and their funding agency, the Department of Communications — Cultural Initiatives Fund. It was launched in conjunction with a retrospective of the films of David Cronenberg at the 1983 Festival.

The Word, The Flesh and David Cronenberg by John Harkness was reprinted by kind permission of *Cinema Canada*.

The Image as Virus by Timothy R. Lucas © 1983 Frederick S. Clarke, was excerpted with permission from material to be published in a forthcoming issue of *CINEFANTASTIQUE* magazine.

A publication of the Academy of Canadian Cinema
Published in Canada in 1983 by
General Publishing Co. Limited
30 Lesmill Road
Don Mills, Ontario
M3B 2T6

Published simultaneously in the United States by
New York Zoetrope Inc.
Suite 516
80 East 11th Street
New York, N.Y. 10003

ISBN: 0-7736-11371
Printed and bound in Canada

Cover photograph and all chapter photographs by Nigel Dickson
Cover design by Janis Bowley

Contents

Introduction   vii

The Visceral Mind: The Major Films of David Cronenberg   1
William Beard

The Comedy of Cronenberg   80
Maurice Yacowar

The Word, The Flesh and David Cronenberg   87
John Harkness

A Canadian Cronenberg   98
Piers Handling

Cronenberg: A Dissenting View   115
Robin Wood

Cronenberg Tackles Dominant Videology   136
Geoff Pevere

The Image As Virus: The Filming of Videodrome   149
Tim Lucas

The Interview   159
William Beard and Piers Handling

Filmography   199
Established by D. John Turner

A Select Bibliography   211

Acknowledgements

The Academy of Canadian Cinema wishes to express its sincere thanks to editor Piers Handling whose extensive background and experience helped make this book possible. Alison Reid deserves a special mention for her invaluable editorial assistance. The fine job of typesetting, design and layout is due to the patience and competence of Debbie Young of Altype who worked long hours under great pressure to produce this book.

We would also like to express our appreciation to Françoyse Picard of the Canada Council and Wayne Clarkson, Director of the Toronto Festival of Festivals for their contributions to this book. Peter Mortimer, Paul Audley, Lorraine Durham, Peter Harcourt, Nelson Doucet and James Monaco offered invaluable advice, guidance and support. Carol McBride was indefatigable in her efforts on our behalf. Pat Mycyk of the Canadian Film Development Corporation, Martin von Mirbach of the Canadian Broadcasting Corporation and Paul Gratton of Superchannel were most cooperative in arranging screenings and lending facilities. D. John Turner of the National Film, Television and Sound Archives extended his help whenever it was needed. Pierre Véronneau of La cinémathèque québécoise and Barbara Mainguy of the Festival of Festivals graciously provided help and support, as did Gerald Pratley and the staff of the Ontario Film Institute. Sue McKenna and Marie-Claude Hecquet typed portions of the manuscript. New Cinema Limited were most generous in lending some of the contributors prints. The staff of the Academy of Canadian Cinema were also extremely helpful.

Nigel Dickson and Rick Porter made their stills collection available to us as did the distributors of David Cronenberg's films, and we are most grateful for their assistance. Connie Tadros of *Cinema Canada* and Frederick S. Clarke of *CINEFANTASTIQUE* were also very cooperative. We would like to thank David Chute and Paul M. Sammon for the interest they took in the project. The staff of the National Film, Television and Sound Archives provided invaluable assistance and special mention should go to Andris Kesteris and Sylvie Robitaille. Ebe-Rita Leone of Cineplex Inc. generously provided photographs.

Finally, we would like to extend our gratitude to David Cronenberg who made himself and his material available to us and was extremely generous with his time.

MARIA TOPALOVICH
Director of Communications
ANDRA SHEFFER
Executive Director

August, 1983

Introduction

It gives me great pleasure to introduce this book by noting that this collection of essays on the films of David Cronenberg marks the first in a series of books by the Academy of Canadian Cinema. Through the Academy's annual film awards, the Genies, and its various other programmes, it is working to create a wider visibility for Canadian cinema. The Academy has made great strides over the past five years, and this book is an important step in the extension of its goals. It is indeed a logical one.

Most of us who think and write about Canadian cinema are extremely concerned with the problem of visibility. Our films are not seen and our directors and stars are not known. Work of the kind found here has a double purpose — of interpreting so that viewers gain more of a sense of what the films are saying to us, and also promoting a major filmmaker who has long been consigned to the periphery of our cinema.

The films of David Cronenberg have split critical opinion into two. They are either adored or reviled. It is difficult to remain indifferent to the films; on the whole they provoke strong reactions in their viewers. But there is no question that Cronenberg is one of our major filmmakers. Regardless of which side of the critical spectrum you support, his films cannot simply be ignored.

The publication of a book on a director who is still actively working is a hazardous endeavour. But the essays that comprise this book have come at an opportune time. It is not too early to tell what Cronenberg's thematic concerns will become, nor is it too late to intervene actively with the future work that he will produce. Critical work on Cronenberg has been sporadic at best. This book is a compendium of differing perspectives and ideas on the films. If much of the critical establishment in this country has ignored him, then these essays show how myopic this attitude has been. For, despite the apparent sensationalism with which his work is viewed, it becomes evident after reading the articles gathered here that Cronenberg is a serious and concerned artist, providing us with a measured, thoughtful view of the world.

No artist's work can be interpreted or viewed in just one way. The merits of this book lie in the diversity of critical approaches that explore the films in differing ways. This kaleidoscope of ideas can be distracting but what is intriguing is how much common ground is found by the various contributors.

Yet, this book is not meant to be simply a paean to David Cronenberg and his films. It has tried to engage the films with the degree of seriousness that they warrant. We leave the validity of our observations to the reader, who we hope will take away a broader sense of what it is exactly these films are saying to us.

Piers Handling

Biography

David Cronenberg was born in Toronto on March 15, 1943. Raised by a writer-father, who also edited "True Canadian Crime Stories", and a musician-mother, Cronenberg's primary interests were music, science, literature and, of course, movies of all kinds. Also intrigued with writing from an early age, he submitted fantasy science-fiction stories to magazines and although none were accepted, he received encouraging letters from editors urging him to keep writing.

Cronenberg received his early education at Dewson Street Public School, Kent Senior School, Harbord Collegiate and North Toronto Collegiate, before entering the Honours Science program at the University of Toronto as an Ontario scholar in 1963. Switching a year later to Honours English Language and Literature, after a short story of his won the prestigious Epstein Award, Cronenberg was subsequently awarded the Gertrude Lawler Scholarship for finishing first at University College. He interrupted his studies briefly in 1965 to travel in Europe, returned the next year and graduated with a General B.A. in 1967.

Cronenberg made his first short film, *Transfer* in 1966. Immediately before shooting his first feature film *Stereo*, he decided to resume his studies towards an M.A., but shortly after chose to devote his energies totally to filmmaking.

After completing his second feature, *Crimes of the Future*, Cronenberg went to Europe on a Canada Council grant in 1971. Returning to Toronto in 1972, he spent the next two years writing and preparing *Orgy of the Blood Parasites*, which would later be retitled *The Parasite Murders* and *Shivers*. Its success led to him making a second low-budget feature film *Rabid*, which consolidated his growing reputation as an emerging 'horror' filmmaker. The films that followed confirmed his stature and *The Brood*, *Scanners* and *Videodrome* marked him as one of Canada's major directors. He has just finished shooting *The Dead Zone*, an adaptation of Stephen King's novel. Apart from this and *Fast Company*, he has written the screenplays to all of his other feature films.

Over the years, Cronenberg has directed dramas for the Canadian Broadcasting Corporation and his films have won awards at film festivals around the world, including the Grand Prix at the International Festival of Horror and Fantasy Films in Sitges, Spain. He is currently living in Toronto with his wife and two children.

The Visceral Mind

The Major Films of David Cronenberg

William Beard

To date, David Cronenberg has written and directed for theatrical release two medium - length "art" films (*Stereo* and *Crimes of the Future*), and six commercial features (*Shivers, Rabid, Fast Company*, The Brood, Scanners* and *Videodrome*). These films are known principally for their violence, their horrific visceral explicitness and their twisted sexual aggression. They are notorious for sensationalism and cinematic exploitation. How, then, do they deserve serious critical attention? The short answer to this question is that Cronenberg's work manifests a high degree of consistency in its thematic concerns, distinct trademarks in its subject matter, considerable evidence of artistic self-consciousness, and a notably expressive cinematic technique. As originator, writer and director of his films Cronenberg is plainly a creator, and the movies he creates have a content and a tone of voice unlike any other.

But originality and artistic self-consciousness are not in themselves sufficient reasons to value any filmmaker highly, and Cronenberg's films must still answer to the charges of moral irresponsibility or viciousness laid against them from various sources in the critical spectrum.

---

* I have deliberately excluded any discussion of *Fast Company* because of its very great difference from the remainder of Cronenberg's theatrical films.

In the study that follows I hope, by a detailed examination of each of
Cronenberg's feature films, to demonstrate that although they often
deal with "tasteless" and "offensive" matters, they do so within the
context of a considered, even philosophical, structure of ideas and
attitudes; and that they are not dangerous examples of base instinct
run wild but are rather *about* (amongst other things) the dangers of
the explosive unconscious forces that lie within everyone.

Much of the objection to Cronenberg's work is simply an
objection to horror movies as such — or at least to the horror movies
of the 1970s and '80s, with their escalated levels of sex and violence.
The standard critical view of these films is that they are superficial,
morally suspect attempts to cash in on debased attitudes without
scruple or artistic purpose, that they represent indulgence for the sake
of indulgence to the same degree as a Roman banquet and with
possibly more degrading results. The notion that it might be possible
to speak of a philosophy of the horror film or to claim for it any kind
of meaning would be regarded in many quarters as laughable.

Yet it can be argued (and has been, persuasively, in the collection
of essays *The American Nightmare*) that the horror genre has at its
base a symbolic action that articulates ordinary psychological tensions
— tensions resulting from a conflict between repressive social norms
and the innate desires of the human animal. Wishes unacceptable to
society are repressed. But repressed wishes do not cease to exist —
especially not when they are being renewed constantly in the unconscious mind. They are merely forced into new shapes or stored in the
form of frustration, resentment and hostility. In the horror film the
repressed returns in the form of a "monster" (a deranged human, an
alien creature, or some other manifestation) to wreak destruction in a
release of dammed-up feeling, twisted into violent aggression by its
period of imprisonment and denial. The viewer beholds what he fears
but also what he desires, and together with horror he experiences a
feeling of liberation.

The emotional forces involved here are very powerful, springing
from the deepest wells of the unconscious, and they are not only by
their very nature inarticulable but also completely unmediated by
reason or ethics and quite repugnant to the conscious mind. It is the
generic aim of the horror film to tap this cauldron of explosive feelings and give expression to them — and since they *are* "unacceptable" it is (apart from anything else) necessary for them to be
expressed in "unacceptable" forms: unrestrainedly sexual, violent.
The concept of *violation* is central to the genre. Those things that are
found most objectionable in the horror film are the most central to its
existence — it is not sufficient merely to refer to such feelings, to
observe them from a distance or to encounter them only in their

sublimated forms, because as anything other than direct, audience-shared feeling they are simply unavailable to the conscious mind. Nevertheless, it remains possible to condemn the horror film, to feel that the experience it evokes is unhealthy and potentially destructive. But judgement cannot be rendered one way or the other in ignorance of the mechanism that structures and sustains the genre, and any condemnation must be preceded by an understanding that few critics of the form have displayed.

Cronenberg's place within the horror genre is in some respects a peculiar one. The basic dualism of the genre (as Robin Wood has shown in *The American Nightmare*) pits the "normal" against the "monstrous," and a number of Cronenberg's films — especially *Shivers*, *Rabid*, and *The Brood* — explore this opposition. In these works society (and in *The Brood* society's extension, the family) is presented as believing itself to be rational, ordered, coolly functional, under control. These qualities are signalled by architecture and decor, by the social behaviour of the characters and by the ambitious optimism of the high priests of modern society, the scientists. There is a denial here of instinct and appetite, of the irrational and the uncontrollable: these are repressed. And having been denied and ignored, they erupt with a destructive force that smashes habitual order, confounds all assumptions and rages with a wild energy. This simple model applies most clearly to *Shivers*, but with each film Cronenberg has moved further away from the basic genre structure, until in *Scanners* and *Videodrome* it is almost unrecognizable, and the terms of the underlying opposition are cast in a more purely personal and self-referential form.

The most idiosyncratic aspect of Cronenberg's work is certainly his obsession with the dichotomy of, and relationship between, mind and body. This is a dominating element in every one of his films, from the early *Stereo* and *Crimes of the Future* onwards, and it represents the major difference in content (and ultimately in theme) between Cronenberg's horror films and those of any other practitioner. Generally speaking, body may be equated with the passions, instincts, and unacknowledged desires of the central horror genre dualism, but a simple equation is not adequate to explain the grim enthusiasm and inventiveness of Cronenberg's regurgitative version. His depiction of the body as an anarchic domain of its own is the most vivid, startling and horrific characteristic of his movies, and is undoubtedly the first thing people recollect when they think of his work: congealing goo seeping from ears and noses, squirming fleshy parasites inhabiting people's abdomens, strange growths, new organs, bizarre changes occurring in the body and explosions of blood and flesh. These and other spectacular expressions of the body's will constitute an insistence on the physical, unknowable, untameable half of the human animal — an aspect that forever lies in wait beneath the bland assumptions of control and the airy cerebrations of the conscious mind.

If all goes well, a precarious balance between rationality and instinct may be maintained. But the body may be goaded into unstoppable revolt if its mysterious needs and mechanisms are tinkered with or denied or ignored. The principal villain here is an overweening Cartesian rationalism of the mind that Cronenberg sees as a recurring tendency. This quality is most overtly represented by the steady stream of mad scientists in his films, whose attempts to make everything work perfectly inadvertently knock the delicate balance askew, sending the body on its rampages. Scientific experiments in telepathy, cosmetics, organ substitution, plastic surgery, radical psychiatry, tranquillizers and subliminal video signals are among the metaphors for hubristic rationalism in Cronenberg's work, and the scientists engaging in these practices are older males (often father figures) who believe unquestioningly in their ability to improve mankind. Their faith — and that of society in general — in the power of consciousness and reason to control human nature is confounded by the appearance of eruptive side effects whose force utterly overturns reason, morality and every other form of civilized order. For Cronenberg the mind/body dichotomy is, so to speak, a two-way street: when the confident head tries to manipulate the gut, it not only fails but also provokes the gut to rise up and have its way with the head — often literally.

While the terms of this violent opposition/connection, despite their very personal nature, fit for the most part quite comfortably into the conventions of the horror genre (i.e., there is no doubt that *Shivers, Rabid, The Brood* and even *Videodrome* are horror movies), they are actually used to express a philosophy somewhat at odds with the genre as a whole. The pattern of repression and release is presented by many horror films in a straightforward way, which endorses the outburst of violence, or at least demonstrates its necessity in the given environment. There is only one Cronenberg film that assumes this form at all closely: *Shivers*. In that film the sterile apartment complex where the action takes place is both architecturally and in the normal, "safe" lives of its inhabitants a symbol for the repression and denial of instinct; and when the parasites invade the building and turn its bland middle-class residents into raving sex maniacs there is a sense of justice as complacency is destroyed. But in his subsequent films (and even to a degree in *Shivers*), Cronenberg concentrates to a greater extent on the problem of *balance*. The arrogance of rationalism is not a good thing, but the eruptions of the body are even worse. They pervert and maim and kill, and if they bring a measure of liberation, that is often not nearly enough to compensate for what is lost. This is definitely the message of *Rabid* and *The Brood*, where people we care about have their lives tragically destroyed. In these films Cronenberg watches the loss of control with an air of clinical detachment and (especially in *Rabid*) even a wry sense of irony. But he is not really amused and not really detached either. He merely regards the burgeoning horrors from the perspective of one who knows what happens when the intricate balance of human nature goes awry; and his attitude to the cycle of repression and release is not simply one of revenging enthusiasm at the overthrow of unhealthy restraint (the genre's central model), but is, rather, much more analytical and ambivalent.

In short, Cronenberg offers in these films a more considered — and much more pessimistic — model of the repression/release dialectic than the "therapeutic" one advanced by Robin Wood in *The American Nightmare*, and one that sees no clear path, even in theory, to wholeness and health. The simple release of repressed impulses is no more viable than simple repression, and all that can be sought is a

Candy with Nola's "brood" guarding her protectively in *The Brood*

fragile balance of opposites. In *Scanners* and *Videodrome*, it is true, there is a suggestion of an apotheosis or transformation of human beings into new forms of life freed from the need to juggle contending forces. But if transformation is cheerfully tried on for size in *Scanners*, the much more agonized return to the subject in *Videodrome* is mired in the bog of subjectivity, and full of torturing doubts and questions.

It may not be too much to claim that Cronenberg is essentially a *philosophical* filmmaker, an artist conducting an inquiry into human nature by way of his own personal concerns. This, again, has tended to take him away from the socially (and politically) oriented model advanced by Wood, and towards an exploration of the mutual responsibility of society *and* the individual for the problems of human life — until *Videodrome* raises the purely philosophical question of perception itself. If *Shivers* is a comparatively straightforward horror film that delineates collective social repression overturned by frustrated inner desires (also collective, or at least universal), then each of the later films displaces the struggle further away from the social arena and rephrases it in increasingly individual terms. *Rabid* certainly does contain a wildly spreading social epidemic, but it also contains, unlike *Shivers*, a central character who communicates the disease and must face the problem of responsibility. In *The Brood* the wider social perspective is replaced by the microcosm of the family, and the pattern of repression and release finds a new, quite undisguised, expression in a Freudian drama of stifled parent-child hostilities that break out into literal enactment.

Scanners leaps energetically in a quite different direction: the mind/body split is clearly signalled in the telepathic-telekinetic scanners, but the inner powers accidentally aroused by science are here polarised into good and bad (there are good scanners and bad scanners), while the question of balance is recast as a question of *control*. The possibility is raised of controlling inner forces and using them for good, and the locus of the drama is more clearly than ever the self. Finally, *Videodrome* is the most inner-directed of all: a "first-person" movie in which the hero's impulses and body get out of control, and in which the borders between hallucination and reality, fantasy and objective fact, and even the individual and society are smudged to the point of solipsism. If *Scanners* is philosophically the most optimistic of Cronenberg's films, *Videodrome* is philosophically the most self-questioning and in a way pessimistic: how can one maintain a balance if none of the information coming in is trustworthy? Because of the absence of a "monster" in *Scanners* (in effect he is only a bad guy), it is probably not even a horror film. And *Videodrome*, though many characteristics mark it as a horror movie, can be seen basically as an impressionistic analysis of the imaginary and real monsters inhabiting the self; thus the film is conceptually very far from the society/self or other/self dichotomy of the typical horror film, and the clearest expression of Cronenberg's ambivalence towards the question of control and repression.

Furthermore, the ironic humour that is so much a part of the early films — *Stereo, Crimes of the Future, Shivers* and *Rabid* — abates as the thematic movement turns inward; *Scanners* and *Videodrome* are almost without humour. This is quite in keeping with the gradual shift in perspective from a relatively detached observation of the incongruities of the human situation to involvement in intense struggles between individuals and within the personality itself. Also, for Cronenberg as for so many other artists dealing with violent and potentially threatening subject matter, humour constitutes a kind of defence mechanism — a refuge of detachment and perspective amidst the war between blind rationalism and blind instinct. Its relative absence in *The Brood* and its virtual disappearance in *Scanners* and *Videodrome* are indications of Cronenberg's growing engagement with his material and his willingness to explore feeling and experience more directly without the protective but limiting shield of irony.

Apart from the unique nature of Cronenberg's specific thematic concerns, the consistency and complexity of their development, and the very personal terms of their expression, there are many other unmistakable marks of artistic self-consciousness to be found in his films. In the earlier films, these often take the form of a lighthearted and mischievous wit — the ironic humour just mentioned: the tone of languid sententiousness in the voiceover narrations of *Stereo* and *Crimes of the Future*; details of decor and costume such as background posters or T-shirt maxims in *Shivers* and *Rabid*; the deliberate pursuit of ironic incongruities between normality and unseemliness in those two films; the colourful and meaningful names given to characters and institutions throughout his work. These and other elements all constitute a private reference the viewer is privy to if he is alert enough and that amuses him by flattering his intelligence and perceptiveness. In the succeeding films, as the tone grows darker and the mood more overtly serious (though *Scanners* is something of an exception here), there is more straightforward and less ironically detached evidence of a controlling artistic mind. The detailed intensity of the psychiatric sessions and the reverberant complexities of inter-generational relations in *The Brood*, the nightmarish power and conviction of Tom Coulter's commissioned sculptures in *Scanners*, and, most remarkable of all, the dense, proliferating web of connective imagery in *Videodrome* are examples of this shift.

Then there is Cronenberg's visual style, which in itself is sufficient to mark him as an artist. *Stereo* and *Crimes of the Future*, which he photographed and edited himself, are immediately striking to the eye, in large part because of their overwhelming emphasis on cold, modern, almost depopulated settings beheld by an alienating and alienated camera. The simplicity and restraint of this basic approach, the clear tendency to visual formalism and even abstraction and the instinctive grasp of how to make elements of the image (setting, decor, composition, etc.) essential features of the meaning all show Cronenberg to be a classicist by inclination in the matter of visual style. The addition of spectacular violence, sexual excess and bloody visceral mess in *Shivers* and *Rabid* in no way diminishes this classicism of technique — indeed, these aspects serve only as counterpoint to the cool detachment of Cronenberg's camera and produce a dialectic of style and content that mirrors the thematic dialectic of conscious rationality and unconscious bodily instinct informing his whole work. In *Shivers* and *Rabid* the clean, dehumanized settings (and the camera's corresponding formalist presentation of them) are transplanted from the abstract avant-garde world of the art film to the conventional narrative world of the commercial feature, where their effect is not so overpowering, but where they continue to operate in an equally important, if more naturalistic and subtle, way. Surveying the chaos and ruin brought about in these films with a calm and objective eye, Cronenberg remains a visual purist.

In *The Brood* there is a change. Many of the locations are older, more lived-in, more organic. Although there are still some notable moments of contrast between clean, bright order and bloody destruction, the film as a whole looks darker and more roughly textured — a tendency that culminates in the crude wooden shack that houses the brood itself, the most concentrated locus of destruction in the film. This darkening and coarsening of the pallette is appropriate to the greater inwardness and the increased emphasis on psychology and private drama.

Scanners, by contrast, is a more "exterior" film, with its exuberant adventure-movie structure and its relative polarization of good and evil. And these characteristics are reflected in a return to clean lines and antiseptic neatness in a number of scenes in the film. Still, the look remains muted in comparison to the sharp contrasts and primary colours of *Crimes of the Future*, *Shivers* and *Rabid*. Unpainted concrete, dark brick and grey metals are much in evidence; and in the mad sculptor Ben Pierce's rural studio, there is a natural mess and clutter virtually unprecedented in Cronenberg's work.

With *Videodrome* the development begun in *The Brood* comes to a head. Almost wholly trapped inside the private mind by the ungover-

Some of the apartment dwellers in *Shivers* attack their next victim

nableness of the senses and the treacherous uncertainties of perception in general, *Videodrome* is the most interior of Cronenberg's films. Its visual style has moved to the opposite extreme from the obsessive neatness of the early films. The art direction and choice of locations throughout emphasize a disorder ranging from mundane untidiness to outright seediness and dereliction. Moreover, the colour scheme of much of the film has shifted radically into a spectrum of dull oranges, reds, and browns — visceral colours in fact, for here the privately instinctual has triumphed so completely that the visceral has overrun the outward visible world. Yet even here there remains an underlying element of classicism in the visual style: no perspective-distorting zooms, no friezelike telephoto shots for impact, no handheld *cinéma-vérité* messiness, always an awareness of the formal properties of the image and, for the spectator, a sense of the firm controlling eye of the director. While Cronenberg's thematic concerns have developed from film to film, his visual style has developed with them; but what has remained constant is his ability to speak a coherent visual language, to translate thoughts and feelings into clear images. And it is this quality that makes Cronenberg something more than just a filmmaker with interesting and sophisticated ideas — it makes him a cinematic talent.

It does Cronenberg no favours to claim too high a place for him. He is not — or at any rate not yet — a Hitchcock or a Sternberg (to name at random two masters who also worked almost exclusively within the realm of "commercial" pictures). But the more one examines his films the more extraordinary their tissue of references and continuations becomes, and the more deeply is the filmmaker's originality confirmed. This remains true despite the presence of flaws and limitations in his work. The very least one can claim for Cronenberg is that he is an extremely *interesting* filmmaker — certainly the most interesting in English-speaking Canada by a wide margin.

*

In the main body of this essay, which is made up of separate sections devoted to each of the features, it is my aim to convey something of the complexity of Cronenberg's work and to examine the individual films to understand how each one operates, as well as how it connects with the others. For various reasons (partly the difficulty of getting hold of the films to study them at length), the sections on *Stereo* and *Crimes of the Future* are less detailed than the others, and also the sections on the later films are fuller than those on the earlier ones, owing largely to the accretion of implications from one work to the next and to the growing context for each new statement. The much more extensive section on *Videodrome* is simply due to the great density of that film, far in excess of anything previously visible in Cronenberg's work. I have tried to make all the sections to a degree self-contained, in the hope that they can serve as general introductions to each of the films for those readers wishing to use the essay for reference purposes.

Stereo (1969)

Going back to Cronenberg's early short features clarifies certain aspects of his work that may be harder to see amidst the more sensational distractions of his later films. The 63-minute *Stereo* was shot for $8500 in 35mm black-and-white without direct sound; a voiceover narration was added (indeed written) later. Its most striking features are its highly formalized, almost abstracted visuals and the confident tone of its extremely strange and idiosyncratic "plot." In this first feature we find some of Cronenberg's distinctive themes already present in sophisticated form. The dreamlike and disconnected action takes place in some unspecified future at an institution devoted to experiments in telepathy (a subject the director was to return to much later in *Scanners*). Amidst cool, sterile, inhumanly perfect surroundings — a deserted Scarborough College in Toronto — figures perambulate listlessly, dressed in stylized costumes, constantly framed and defined by the architecture and decor. On the soundtrack, in a tone purged of all emotion or even interest, a series of voices "describe" what is going on in terms both rational/ scientific and unintelligibly disconnected. They speak of "human social cybernetics," "biochemical induction-extension of the mind to telepathic communication," "psychic addiction to the telepathic object," "existential organic fields," "psychophysiology" and "schizophrenetic intrusion." Obscure ritual-experiments are enacted with an apparent blandness belied by the news that one of the subjects became so disturbed that he attempted to drill a ¼-inch hole in his skull ("an act," as the narrator tells us, "of considerable symbolic significance").

The language of the narrators' comments and the air of intense seriousness with which the unidentified characters perform the absurd and arcane actions of the film are clear indications of *Stereo*'s wicked, straightfaced satire of scientific jargon and experiment. These "researchers," floundering neurotically amidst the elaborately inflated language and practices of their profession, motivated alternately by a hubristic Faustian idealism or by a sheer love of power, and maintaining an attitude of perfect detachment towards their "subjects" are the ancestors of all of Cronenberg's later mad scientists. Indeed, the scientists of *Stereo* are perhaps the most clearly defined of all in their combination of coolly competent appearance and actual twittering ignorance. They think they are in control of the telepathic experiments; in fact they merely set in motion something they can neither understand nor influence.

Stereo's satire is often very amusing in a dry sort of way, but humour is not the film's principal aim. More important is the pervasive sense of sophisticated unease springing from the alienating settings, the unexplained events, the emotional coldness of the narration and the occasional outbursts of violence. *Stereo* is an extremely introverted film, invoking, retreating into and hiding behind the unknowable reaches of the human mind. The alienation imposed by the setting is a strong inducement to silence, disconnected activity and random explosions of feeling. Under these circumstances

One of the telepathic patients in *Stereo*

telepathy becomes a way of bypassing the isolation imposed by the environment. It is strongly associated with the instinctive, the unconscious, the sexual. The process of telepathy, once undertaken, is unpredictable and uncontrollable, its effects ranging from the addictively pleasurable to the intensely painful. It is based on a relation of power (the dominance of one mind over another) and carries with it the danger of corruption and mental imbalance, as well as the prospect of an entirely new and dazzling form of human cooperation. (*Scanners* later takes up these notions in greater detail.)

None of these ideas is stated clearly or explained fully. Instead, there is a drifting series of partial descriptions and brief, unconnected generalizations — vivid, and at times startling, but hardly coherent or whole as a theme. What remains in the mind after seeing *Stereo* is not its ideas as such, but rather a diffuse atmosphere and several striking individual moments. It is hard *not* to be struck by, for example, the scene in which a bare-breasted girl sits blindfolded on a laboratory table while her telepathic partner erotically caresses the viscera of a medical instructional model torso; or by the scene in which a couple makes love in a laboratory while the camera cuts to various technical fixtures of the room. In the light of Cronenberg's subsequent work, harbingers of things to come are to be found everywhere. For example, *Shivers* is directly foreshadowed by the notion of "omnisexuality" and a human community that has sexually "demolish[ed] the walls of psychological restraint and social inhibition." Many of the features of the telepathic experiments, including the maddened subject who drills through his head, reappear in *Scanners*.

Thematically, *Stereo* is important because it establishes the filmmaker's special attitude towards the relationship of mind and body. Hubristic science here attempts to aggrandize the mind, only to discover that the delicate balance of forces within the human animal will not tolerate interference without disturbing consequences — the relation between mental and physical, rational and instinctive, is far stronger and more unpredictable than science imagines. In *Stereo* the consequences of tampering with in-built balance are, as ever in Cronenberg's work, dismal. Various subjects at the institute suffer "self-encapsulation" leading to suicidal behaviour or "the development of a false telepathic self" while "the true, oral, verbal self" broadcasts "morbid telepathic images of decay and vampirism." The telepathic experience itself is described as "overwhelming, exhausting, akin to pain." Although these symptoms are destructive to the subjects of the experiments, and the whole activity is vaguely distressing to the viewer — especially amidst the film's cold, alienating physical environment — the horror in *Stereo* (and in *Crimes of the Future*) remains on the level of unease. Not until *Shivers* and *Rabid* do the forces invoked in *Stereo* rise up and join together in a general apocalypse. But the roots of that apocalypse may be clearly seen in Cronenberg's first major film.

Crimes of the Future (1970)

Crimes of the Future is very similar to *Stereo*, except for a rather more "plotted" scenario, the use of colour and an enterprising soundtrack filled with buzzing, chirping and clicking noises. But in their essentials the two films are virtually interchangeable. *Crimes of the Future* manifests the same formalist approach to mise-en-scène, the same dreamlike action, the same involuted, impenetrable, pseudo-scientific voiceover narration, even the same central actor (Ronald Mlodzik, giving another memorably fey and neurotic performance). As in *Stereo*, it is impossible to work out just what is going on at many moments. What is clear is that the action takes place in a future that has been devastated by a mysterious disease caused by cosmetics. The disease is called "Rouge's Malady," after its discoverer, the mad dermatologist Antoine Rouge, and it is particularly virulent amongst post-pubertal females. Its symptoms include a gooey coloured effluence, which runs from ears, nose and mouth and is strangely attractive to the senses. People are drawn to smell and lick it. The hero, Adrian Tripod, an erstwhile disciple of the now-vanished Rouge, wanders in existential mists from institution to institution (they have names like the House of Skin, the Institute for Neo-Venereal Disease, the Oceanic Podiatry Group, the Gynecologist Research Foundation and Metaphysical Import/Export) in search of some solution.

The scenario clearly foreshadows that of *Rabid*, where again a disease triggered by cosmetic activity (plastic surgery) devastates society and produces in its victims a foamy discharge from the mouth. The compulsion felt by people in *Crimes of the Future* to lick and eat this substance is an early indication of Cronenberg's insistence on, and fascination with, the fact of our bodies — a fact we cannot escape no matter how much we might like to. The conjunction of this eating of bodily goo with the denial of the instinctive and the bodily represented by the architecture and decor in the film is a particularly striking one, and does much to create the special, peculiar atmosphere of *Crimes of the Future*. The film indeed centres around the familiar Cronenbergian mind/body problem. The mind's attempt to remodel the body (cosmetics) results in the body's revolt (Rouge's Malady), which in turn begins to affect the mind (the solitary metaphysical angst of the narrator Adrian Tripod). One patient at the Institute for Neo-Venereal Disease "was once a fierce sensualist; now he has become a pure metaphysician. . . his body has begun to produce puzzling organisms — complex, perfect, but essentially without function. . . his disease is possibly a form of creative cancer." At the Gynecologist Research Foundation "the concierge speaks of a rootlike excrescence growing from one of his nostrils — he believes it to be an extension of certain cerebral nerves." These developments are strikingly prophetic of the central events of *The Brood*, in which psychological pressures have direct consequences upon the bodies of the subjects. As in *Stereo*, the future seems to hold "a novel sexuality, a new species of man, a new form of biochemistry, a new mode of reproduction," and the film ends with Adrian's experimental coupling with a pre-pubertal girl in an attempt to bypass Rouge's Malady. Here we may also see a distant anticipation of *Scanners* and *Videodrome*, with their transformational endings wherein "a new species of man" is again suggested.

Adrian continually emphasizes his alienation, his isolation, his inability to understand or communicate anything. As in *Stereo*, the obscure verbal meanderings of the narration are presented with amused detachment — Adrian especially seeming like a forlorn, caricatured sufferer from Antoniennui — and humour once more goes hand in hand with profound alienation. However, developments like the diffident/ecstatic foot massage practiced by the Oceanic Podiatry Group, or the little plastic bags full of odd clothing articles that various candidates for executive office in Metaphysical Import/Export are asked to lay out in wierd Rorschach fashion have a charm more surreal than comic. And the lingering suggestion of violence (sinister figures in coats projecting Pinteresque menace) adds to the sense of unease. Even more than *Stereo*, *Crimes of the Future* is a tiny masterpiece.

Crimes of the Future surpasses *Stereo* visually if only because of Cronenberg's sensitivity to the use of colour in the decor of his chosen locations (again, very similar in appearance to those of *Stereo*). The rich-hued velvety fixtures and subtle coloured lighting add a great attractiveness to what remains a cool, formalist and dehumanized style of architecture, and the abstract art and sculpture in the "conspiracy" scene is splendidly attractive. Both *Stereo* and *Crimes of the Future*

Crimes of the Future is striking in its use of space and architecture

recall Godard's *Alphaville* in their ability to convert present-day locations into the landscape of an imagined future by skillful control of the camera, and both filmmakers are making essentially the same point about the emotional coldness and attractive/frightening rationality of our physical surroundings.

In both *Stereo* and *Crimes of the Future*, Cronenberg employs his avant-garde obscurantism deftly, using it to try out all kinds of odd inspirations and defusing its potential pompousness and opacity by deliberately making fun of these aspects himself. These are clever films in their ability to play with ideas and settings in a free-associative, almost abstract way, while remaining detached from the implications of what is shown, and in particular resolutely declining to say anything overtly or clearly. They are both neater, less problematical works than Cronenberg's subsequent full-fledged horror films, if only because they are easier and safer in their attitudes. They are sanctioned by the respectable tradition of ellipsis, fragmentation and obscure symbolism in twentieth-century art, and they demonstrate their sophisticated awareness of that tradition by sweetly mocking it. The psychic malaise depicted in both films is part comic and part self-indulgent, so that despite its disturbing overtones it encourages in the viewer a detached and ultimately comfortable standpoint. *Shivers*, is most ways a crasser film than either of its predecessors, is an artistic step forward for Cronenberg simply because its feelings are stronger, more real, more focused and finally more responsible.

Nevertheless, both *Stereo* and *Crimes of the Future* are perfectly acceptable films, entirely successful in their own inventive, slightly precious terms. They unmistakably document not only Cronenberg's recurring themes and obsessions but also his formalist and symbolic approach to mise-en-scène — a crucial element of the later films, but one seldom noticed because of their escalated violence and horror.

Shivers (1975)

Cronenberg's first mainstream commercial film, *Shivers*, is a horror movie in every sense of the word. Even among his subsequent films it is notable for its extreme preoccupation with the visceral and the sexually violent. Both of these qualities are united in the parasite-creature, "a combination of aphrodisiac and venereal disease," which crazy Dr. Emil Hobbes develops both for medical reasons and to counteract man's excessive cerebralism and estrangement from his body, and which then proceeds to run amok in a modern apartment complex on a Montreal island.

The film documents the gradual spread of the parasite "disease" from Hobbe's first experimental patient, Annabelle, to the rest of the inhabitants of the complex. The parasites, originally conceived as a substitute for ailing body organs, and then converted into stimulators of desire, transform their hosts into raving sex maniacs. The central character is the apartment's resident doctor, Roger St. Luc, who investigates the incidents and later becomes, together with his nurse/girlfriend, the last target for the parasites. Although St. Luc has a certain protagonistlike function, most of the movie's time is spent with the many secondary characters affected by the plague. In this respect *Shivers*'s real protagonist is collective — the inhabitants of the complex and, by extension, people in general.

The parasites are as suggestive as anyone could wish, simultaneously evoking the phallic and the excretory. They grow in people's abdomens and are passed through mouth-to-mouth contact; they also fly at faces and attach themselves, leechlike, to bare flesh, leaving massive blotches and burns. In one scene a parasite slithers up the drain into a woman's bath and crawls into her vagina (the phallic suggestion made explicitly); in another, a man slowly extrudes one through his mouth (the excretory); and in a third, the most bloody in the film, a character has his face covered by them, and, screaming amidst the gore, tries to pry them off with pliers. Scenes such as these led Robert Fulford, in a frequently quoted remark, to call *Shivers* "the most repulsive movie I have ever seen," and provoked an outcry of disgust from reviewers across Canada, including expressions of shock that taxpayers' money (via the Canadian Film Development Corporation) had helped to produce the film.

There is no doubt about the grossness of *Shivers*'s assault on the sensibilities of the viewer and on the canons of "good taste" in general. The parasites represent by far the most graphic and extreme example of Cronenberg's thematic polarity of body, and their impact cannot be explained away by pointing to their parodic excess, nor to the stance of witty detachment that characterizes much of the film. Furthermore, sex is constantly related not only to violence and blood, but also to the visceral and the excretory. To say that Cronenberg is accepting of the latter aspects of the human being in a society that regards them as repulsive (and thus that the grossness and shock are in the viewer's mind, not the filmmaker's) would not exactly be accurate. Cronenberg is, here and elsewhere, genuinely fascinated with the visceral, the sexual and the violent — even obsessed by them.

Of course it is not enough simply to show something — anything — that is disgusting or shocking and then claim that what is going on is the beneficial release of repressed feeling. But *Shivers* does not do this. Its violation of moral codes governing sexuality and violence is systematic — and it is connected precisely to the deadening effects of an overly rational and antiseptic way of life. The raw expression of impulses ranging from the naughty to the murderous takes on real significance in the context of the specific environment depicted in the film. Like *Stereo* and *Crimes of the Future*, *Shivers* takes place in surroundings of smooth, coolly attractive, dehumanized perfection. Starliner Towers, on its own island "far from the noise and traffic of the city" (as the promotional voiceover that begins the film proclaims) is a citadel of twentieth-century Cartesian order. Laid out in architecture of rectangular functionalism and decorated in the ultimate tasteful elegance, it is indeed a microcosm of modern urban values in an upwardly mobile society. All rough edges have been removed, all feeling subsumed into an atmosphere of clean, detached blandness. It is, in the terms of Cronenberg's vision, a perfect denial of body, of instinct, of the unconscious, of death.

Cronenberg's camera treats this environment, and to a degree also the people who inhabit it, with the detachment it deserves, creating endless compositions of great formal attractiveness. Right from the beginning he sets himself the task of establishing the film's dialectic: bringing an environment expressing rational values into violent confrontation with the messy, anarchic subsurface of the human animal.

The first post-credit sequence intercuts the apartment manager's cooing sales talk to a cozily domestic couple with the murderous assault on Annabelle (presented to the viewer with no explanation at all), and swiftly follows with a parallel montage of Hobbes's graphic operation on the half-naked unconscious girl juxtaposed with a man staring into his bathroom mirror using a Waterpik on his teeth. The latter sequence is immediately complicated when the man, Nicholas Tudor, has a brief, violent abdominal seizure and then blithely goes in to breakfast amidst smooth, colourfully decorated surroundings and proceeds to treat his solicitous wife with an indifference bordering on contempt. We are at once thrown into the conflict of everyday contemporary lifestyles versus unexplained and disturbing violence — a conflict that escalates in intensity and complexity throughout the film until the orgiastic, nihilistic surrender of the final climax when the last remaining "rational" survivor goes down under a sea of arms and mouths. The quiet coda ironically re-establishes the appearance of order as the parasite people drive away from the island to spread the mania abroad.

Thematically speaking, the parasite plague (or parasite liberation) is also based in the excesses of reason. Although Cronenberg denies that any animus towards or even criticism of science is to be found in his films, it is more than coincidence that the telepathic experiments in *Stereo*, the cosmetics in *Crimes of the Future*, the parasitology in *Shivers*, the plastic surgery in *Rabid*, the physiological psychology in *The Brood*, the drug research in *Scanners* and the television "breakthroughs" in *Videodrome* all have unpleasant results ranging from the personally destructive to the socially cataclysmic. Science here must stand as a representation of human reason in general. And in Cronenberg's films catastrophe arises from the rational attempt to improve the human animal. Given the destructive consequences of instinct (especially when suppressed) and the spectacular failures of reason, one much conclude that Cronenberg is (at least excluding *Scanners*) a pessimist. *Shivers*, despite the comic distance from many of its characters and the black humour of its scenario, offers a disturbing view of humanity unstably polarised between cold control and voracious appetite with nothing in between capable of surviving the withering crossfire.

This is not at all to deny the massive presence in the film of "a certain savage joy" (to use Cronenberg's own words). The parasites may be stomach-turning and frightening, but their effect on people is not simply to turn them into monsters. People as well as architecture and decor can function as temples of rational control and emotional denial, and their transformation by the disease is as important dramatically as the transformation of Starliner Towers is iconographically. Minor characters, such as the smarmy apartment manager (Ronald Mlodzik again), the tuxedoed waiter, the diffident and fastidious old French-speaking couple and the mother and child in the elevator are clear symbols of ordered normality sent resolutely, even gleefully, to the wall. The overthrow of reason, conventions, standards, good taste and everything that is part of the machinery restricting human animality is accompanied by an exhilarating and terrifying sense of liberation as the bonds of restraint are sundered. Of course this is a central feature of horror movies in general, but in *Shivers* the liberation is made explicit by the "savage joy" on the faces of the marauders, and especially by the orgiastic slow-motion climax, in which the last man is initiated into the fraternity of excess.

The ironic sophistication of *Shivers* is nowhere more evident than in the treatment of the hero, Dr. Roger St. Luc. His relaxed manner and air of confident assurance soon begin to appear not just inadequate, but smug and out of touch. It doesn't take long for his public relations sangfroid to crack, revealing the hard, brittle ego underneath. Although his violence under stress is disturbing (as when he beats an attacker to death with a crowbar), St. Luc is basically a comic figure — a nice send-up of the cool, up-to-date professional who always feels he has things under control. It is fitting that he should be the last to succumb to Cronenberg's wild Eros, especially after his indifferent shrugging-off of his nurse's lazy striptease in an earlier scene. As one after another of the film's characters fall to the parasites, his immunity begins to seem like a perverse willfulness. Why should he survive when all the best people have succumbed? In this way Cronenberg co-opts the viewer's sympathies for St. Luc's eventual destruction. In that final, horrifying/ecstatic climax, he is in some respect getting a richly deserved come-uppance.

Several of the other characters are in fact more sympathetic or more interesting than the "hero." Miss Forsythe, his girlfriend, displays a willowly Veronica Lakeish charm, and in her case the boundaries between normal and pathological sexuality are meaningfully blurred. The dream she narrates towards the end of the film, which postulates an omnisexuality (shades of *Stereo*), serves as the bridge carrying us over from "normal" subconscious sexual chaos to the horrors of parasiteland. But there is something else here as well. In this monologue, delivered significantly in the dirty basement of the complex rather than its antiseptic living area, horror is finely balanced with a positive urge to reach out and accept everything that seems disturbing or frightening:

> Roger, I had a very strange dream last night. In this dream, I found myself making love to a strange man. Only I'm having trouble, you see, because he's old and dying, and he smells bad, and I find him repulsive. But then he tells me that *everything* is erotic, that everything is sexual. You know what I mean? He tells me that even old flesh is erotic flesh, that disease is the love of two alien creatures for each other — that even dying is an act of eroticism. That talking is sexual. That breathing is sexual. That even to physically exist is sexual. And I believe him. And we make love *beautifully*.

This speech expresses a suggestion of tortured emotional ambivalence underlying the action at a deep, otherwise almost unarticulated level. It indicates that Cronenberg is struggling to accept the world of the body, of sex *and* of decay and death — the world of the parasites. Certainly it is an ambivalence, however, since immediately after the speech Forsythe opens her mouth wide, and a parasite horrifyingly appears in it. But Forsythe is also the sexuality that St. Luc stupidly rejects. He immediately binds her mouth, in an image of sadistic eroticism, to prevent the "disease" from escaping to infect him. When she appears in the final swimming-pool orgy, smiling with an evil sweetness, she is a splendid image of *la belle dame sans merci*

Nicholas Tudor has just had a seizure in the bathroom scene in *Shivers*

coming to claim at last, with an open-mouthed kiss, that part of St. Luc that he has vainly attempted to deny.

Another figure of insinuating female sexuality is Betts, the woman in the bath. She is played by Barbara Steele, an icon of the genre after her countless appearances in European horror movies, who brings all kinds of overtones to the character — a cool, potent eroticism, and a sense of sinister knowingness. She fixes her lesbian attentions — successfully in the end — on Janine Tudor, Nicholas's wife, a traditional housewife ignored and sexually humiliated by her husband, in a kind of sardonic radical-feminist allegory.

But it is Janine Tudor who is the real focus of the film's human sympathies — and the best demonstration that *Shivers*, despite its wicked ironic humour and regurgitative violence, is conscious that finally this is no joking matter. Janine's relationship with her saturnine husband, Nicholas, constitutes the movie's most unstylized picture of real-life problems and furnishes a dimension of ordinary human suffering that helps to confer seriousness on the film as a whole. Nicholas (a memorable portrait of almost catatonic self-absorption by Allan Migicovsky) is oblivious to all outside influence, and though his preoccupation with the creatures inhabiting his body is quite understandable, it does not explain the callous indifference with which he treats his wife. Janine, touchingly, is trying to explain his behaviour and symptoms according to her own anxious theory, which is that he has cancer. (His real disease, namely human-nature-à-la-Cronenberg, is endemic and incurable.) Her attempts at cheerful compliance with his moods are offset by her worried confession of her fears to Betts; and the scene in which she discovers Nicholas sprawled in front of an open refrigerator, then finds the spatters of blood attesting to his ailment in the bathroom and finally is brutally rejected in her attempts to comfort him is poignantly realized. Her anguish rises even further in the later scene in which she tries to comply, in tearful and frightened confusion, with his strange and sudden sexual appetite.

These scenes and the ones featuring Nicholas alone in their apartment also provide the basis for some of Cronenberg's finest mise-en-scène. One might say in general that the mise-en-scène is always used to add an extra dimension or create a meaningful context for the action. The stylish elegance of the settings is continuously played against the horrors of the drama, in a dialectic of style and content that mirrors the thematic dichotomy of mind and body. The technique is particularly evident in the brilliant floor-level shot of the clean, antiseptic bathroom into which Nicholas stumbles: retching convulsively into the tub, he dribbles blood onto the toilet seat, pulls down a pair of neat, symmetrically arranged towels to wipe his mouth and finally lurches out again, leaving the shot as it began except for the disarray of towels and a solitary stain of blood against the white porcelain of the toilet. This shot, small and relatively unimportant as it is, can nevertheless stand as an example of Cronenberg's film-making skills. With its fixed Ozu-like camera angle, its beginning and ending in unpopulated space, its use of doorways to frame and conceal the action by turns and its progression from order to disorder within the context of a detached formal composition, the shot is an anthology of cinematic virtues and an index of the director's control and restraint.

Innumerable examples of a similar nature might be adduced, wherein Cronenberg makes good use of the indirectly lit corridors, glass-and-marble lobby, *noir*ish underground garage and elegant apartment furnishings of the complex. Except for the flurries of handheld closeups and staccato editing of shock scenes, and the occasional slow-motion shot, the director's camera is inevitably calm, formally objective and detached. It is a stance that conveys aesthetic distance and a sense of the inability (as well as the unwillingness) to interfere. Cronenberg here stands back from his material, viewing it dispassionately, often curiously, and with a sense of inevitability amounting to pitying serenity. The latter is emphasized especially in the musical score: moments conveying the progress or extent of the damage, or foretelling it, will frequently be accompanied by wistful or melancholy music. Perhaps the most characteristic shot in *Shivers* — and it has its equivalents in *Rabid* and *The Brood* — is a longshot of the exterior of the complex by night, in which the chaos and violence we know to be going on inside are distanced into a formal composition: both the building and the shot itself are clean, balanced, hard-surfaced, with an attractiveness at once ironic, sinister and sad because it is so removed from the realities within.

The moral here, as in so much of Cronenberg's work, is that the film cannot be read accurately without taking account of its mise-en-scène. The action, the dialogue, and the narrative shape may well give a good indication of thematic patterns and central ideas; but the interpretive, inflective function of camera placement and composition, setting and decor, photography and editing, is essential to the actual experience of the film, and to its final meaning.

It should not be forgotten that *Shivers* was Cronenberg's first mainstream commercial film, and that its sheer technical competence (to say the least) is remarkable under the circumstances — particularly considering the miniscule $179,000 budget. Although its structure may recall Don Siegel's *Invasion of the Body Snatchers* (in reverse — this time the pods are the sexually alive ones) and individual scenes bring that and other specific films to mind (*Night of the Living Dead* in the ravenous little girl and the zombie-crowds at the end, *Psycho* in the bathrooms), *Shivers* is a forceful and original movie, which, like all its creator's work, catches the spectator off guard and surprises his expectations. If it lacks some of the depth of most of the later films, it is by no means shallow in itself. In one sense it is the most problematic of Cronenberg's films because of its explicit, not to say sensational, feasting on violence and sex. But in another sense it may well be the least problematic in that its thematic oppositions are so intelligible and formally satisfying. In his subsequent films Cronenberg's picture of the world becomes more complex, more responsive to the dilemmas of the individual, and in general more ambitious. But the very simplicities of *Shivers*'s vision give it a unique coherence.

Rabid (1976)

Cronenberg's next film, *Rabid*, had a bigger budget ($530,000) and a less restricted setting. Its horror is a rabieslike plague, which causes its victims to go berserk and attack others (and thus pass on the disease) before dying. The disease springs from the vampirish attacks of young Rose, the heroine, who has developed a strange organic spike in her armpit as a result of radical plastic surgery performed on her after a near-fatal motorbike crash, and who discovers that human blood is the only form of nourishment her body will accept.

The thematic consistency with Cronenberg's previous work is plain. Once again a medical attempt to restore health (and in this case a much more justified and less crackpot attempt than in *Shivers*) results in a wild and inexplicable rebellion of nature: Rose's life is (temporarily) saved, but the city of Montreal is turned into a nightmarish phantasmagoria of terminally rabid crazies and blunt martial law. It is significant that the clinic where Rose is operated on is devoted to plastic surgery — the co-opting of medical science in the interests of keeping up appearances. The Keloid Clinic performs the same function thematically as the Starliner Towers does in *Shivers*, enclosing the human animal in an envelope of clean lines and attractive proportions, smoothing over unsightly nature and denying the unacceptable warts and messy instincts of the body. This remains true of the clinic despite Dr. Keloid's rejection of a suggestion that he set up a franchise of plastic surgery resorts ("I don't want to become the Colonel Sanders of plastic surgery") and the fact that the radical operation performed on Rose is necessary under the circumstances. Though Keloid appears morally justified in his medical decision, his unthinking confidence in the use of an untried technique, despite warnings, looks very much like another case of rational hubris. In any event, the result is a bodily backlash of staggering and uncontrollable irrationality, which produces a series of proliferating horrors.

As in *Shivers*, the action has a social basis. The characters are many, there are a multitude of cameolike anecdotal episodes, and in general the scenario anatomizes the impact of the problem on a large number of people. In addition, the setting is expanded. The disease spreads almost immediately outside the confines of the clinic (in this respect *Rabid* takes up where *Shivers* left off); Cronenberg's interest in all these scenes is to examine the reactions of society to peril of an unfamiliar kind. The normal activities of eating at a roadside diner, driving a truck, visiting a porno movie, riding the subway and going Christmas shopping are all subjected to the transformations of private mania and civic emergency. In turn private terror and public disarray are converted into banal routine, as soldiers systematically gun down crazies in the streets, white-suited men with disinfectant rush in to mop up, and corpses are tossed into garbage trucks.

The epidemic spread of the disease is a boon to the narrative, since the film can merely latch on to the infectees and watch them carry the malady abroad. The number of possible dramatic situations increases geometrically, encouraging the use of any number of effective locations and providing a motherlode of potential parallel montage to be mined whenever required. Each manifestation of the disease carries within it the seeds of dramatic consequences down the line, as the victim rises to become a predator. This is a situation familiar from Siegel's body snatchers and especially Romero's living dead, as well as from *Shivers*; but in *Rabid* it is played off against the heroine's private and different drama and also catapulted out into society at large, in contrast to the claustrophobic confinement of the other films. The result is a blueprint for a mushrooming action of great forward drive: the epidemic as plot becomes the plot as epidemic.

Even more important than the expansion of locale relative to *Shivers* is the film's grounding in the lives of its two principal characters, Rose and her boyfriend, Hart. Whereas *Shivers*'s central couple isn't all that central, and their characters relatively un-examined, Rose and Hart are taken seriously as people and granted the kind of complex humanity that in *Shivers* is restricted to the secondary character of Janine Tudor. The fact that we really care what happens to Rose and Hart, and that their problems are presented as a parallel and equally important action next to the drama of the plague, adds a dimension quite new in Cronenberg's work — a clear stepping-stone to the essentially private traumas of *The Brood*. In *Shivers* the characters are more often the butts of irony than the vessels of feeling; in *Rabid* the reverse is the case. Secondary characters like Keloid's business parter, Murray, and Rose's friend Mindy are given moments of tenderness, and their deaths beheld more with sorrow than with "savage joy." And the even less important characters of Keloid; the truckdriver, Smooth Eddy; Rose's first victim, Lloyd; Judy, the girl in the swimming pool; and Rose's final pickup (who eventually is the cause of her own death) are accorded a measure of dignity not often to be seen in *Shivers*.

But it is in the treatment of the two central characters, and especially the heroine, that *Rabid* achieves a new complexity. Within the tradition of the horror genre, Rose is the movie's "monster": she preys on people and sucks their blood, she causes death and social disruption. But Rose is basically a scared young woman, waking up after weeks in a coma with an appetite (and a new organ for indulging it) that she can't understand and that she attempts to suppress or displace, trying to avoid thinking about the realities of her bizarre situation as it dawns on her, forced to make agonizing moral decisions she's not equipped to deal with, and finding all her normal resources inadequate to meet this strange and horrifying problem. She is both frightened and ashamed, and her vulnerability is a striking contrast both to her habitual self-confident sexual role-playing and to the strength and violence of her compulsive vampirism.

The presence of Marilyn Chambers, Ivory Soap girl-next-door turned porno queen, in the role adds extra resonance. Whatever her abilities as an actress, Chambers was (and is) certainly best known as a sex object pure and simple — as a body, in fact. And whatever Cronenberg's reasons for using her in the film, he was no doubt fully conscious that one look at the marquee was going to be enough to get his audience automatically thinking sex. To a degree the film plays up to these expectations: a certain amount of the naked Chambers is in fact visible. More interesting, though, is the way in which one's consciousness of the actress as a sexual icon colours the perception of all her behaviour. Rose's appetite for blood, and by extension the plague she spreads, are identified with the libidinous desire for sexual excess (just as in *Shivers*), and the action of *Rabid* is therefore connected with the idea of a compulsive/catastrophic liberation of repressed/destructive sexuality.

But the character of Rose certainly amounts to more than the popular conception of Marilyn Chambers. The surface of the character is that of a nice, normal girl, albeit one who has been around — and this impression operates on the spectator as a denial of preconceived expectations. Cronenberg is interested not so much in the explosions of the id as in the simultaneity of reasoned, compassionate behaviour *and* explosive id within ordinary human nature. What we get in *Rabid* is a three-fold contrast: 1) Marilyn Chambers, sex queen, turns out to be 2) a sweet, vulnerable girl, Rose, but then 3) Rose turns out to be the perpetrator of a raging, destructive passion. The reverberations become almost Pirandellian when Rose visits a porno theatre and subtly encourages a man to make a pass at her, whereupon she strikes for blood. The statuesque assurance of Chambers's carriage, the stylish independence expressed in her wardrobe, and the provocative knowingness of her behaviour around men (all qualities suggestive of power and control) are set against opposite qualities of innocence and human weakness: the angelic simplicity of her face; her childlike, piping voice and a tentativeness in verbal delivery (inexperience as an actress perhaps paying unexpected dividends here); and a need for comfort and aid openly expressed in moments of fear.

Further levels of ambiguity are suggested in Rose's attacks themselves, which carry strong sexual overtones but are less explicit in this respect than those in *Shivers*. In *Shivers* the parasites are essentially passed from body to body by a voracious kiss, whereas in *Rabid* the initial infection comes from Rose's armpit spike, employed in an embrace. Open-mouthed kisses are always sexual, but embraces can be simply affectionate or consoling or loving. In general Rose's method of attack is disturbing because of its suggestion not simply of aggressive sexuality but of emotional need and even human vulner-ability; and if the assaults in *Shivers* resemble rape, Rose's in *Rabid* have an affinity to lovemaking, with overtones of mutual consent or at least a degree of mutual responsibility.

The three attacks we see at length are particularly clear in this regard. The first, on fellow-patient Lloyd Walsh, begins with his discovery of her thrashing around convulsively in her hospital bed, her breasts uncovered. She appeals to him to hold her because she is cold, and when he complies with mixed feelings she strikes, precipi-tating a wild, convulsive embrace, punctuated by gasps and moans, which then subside into quiet whimpers and shudders as Rose soothingly strokes his head with postcoital tenderness. The next attack, on a drunken farmer, is actually in self-defence, as he lurches at Rose with sexual mischief in mind and is rewarded with a spike in the eye for his ogling assault. The attack on Keloid follows the same pattern as the one on Lloyd, except that it is preceded by a scene in

Rose develops a strange organic spike as the result of radical plastic surgery performed on her in *Rabid*

which Keloid comforts Rose in his best bedside manner. When she collapses onto his shoulder in distress, the viewer flinches in anticipation of another attack, only to be met with the fact that this is an ordinary frightened person seeking reassurance, not a vampire on the rampage. This is the scene that best brings out the deep ambivalence of attack-as-embrace latent throughout the film.

When Rose is driven from her girlfriend Mindy's apartment by the need for food (i.e., blood), it is significant that she chooses the denizens of a porno theatre as potential victims, the implication being that if anybody has to suffer it should at least be someone indulging in a sleazy appetite of his own. And when Rose decides to submit herself to a self-punishing "experiment" to discover whether she is the one responsible for the epidemic, it is more than coincidental that she should choose to pick up a man on the loose.

In each of these cases the male victim's sexual appetites have been a factor, and the ensuing embrace has been to a greater or lesser extent voluntary. Rose's phallic spike (achieving penetration) not only becomes an expression of her aggressive sexual-emotional need but also infects the recipient with similar needs — or, symbolically, awakens in him a dormant hunger. The suppressed desires of the body, once aroused, cannot be controlled and moreover give rise to a chain reaction of epidemic proportions. In this respect *Rabid* presents sex, and even sexual love, as a matter not to be toyed with. Marilyn Chambers, icon of easy sex, and the males who seek casual sexual favours from her become tokens of the dangers of assuming that sex can be indulged in as a pure appetite without consequences. One might go further and suggest that *Rabid* allegorically depicts the potential social catastrophe inherent in a culture that encourages sexual impulses without really considering what innate forces are being unleashed. (This is a train of thought that leads directly to *Videodrome*.)

As for Hart, he is seen even more clearly than Rose as a sufferer, and moreover one condemned to passivity. His love for Rose is established as early as the pre-credit sequence, and it is reaffirmed at salient points throughout the film. It is Hart's fate to be separated from the object of his concern and affection for virtually the entire action. He is in Montreal when she awakens from her coma, and by the time he gets to the clinic she has fled to the city while he is restrained on the spot by a quarantine order. When he actually does finally come face to face with her, he finds her bent over the inert form of Mindy, extracting blood, and this, together with the experiences he has undergone in connection with the plague, causes him to burst out at her in a frenzy of reproach. (She responds first with defensive whimpers, then with her own reproach to him for the motorcycle crash; and the two of them end up locked in a paroxysmic embrace of love and hate that encapsulates the contradictions the movie is exploring.) But it is not long before Hart is out of it again, lying unconscious at the bottom of a stairway, and nothing is left for him but to sob and rage futilely over the phone when Rose calls him from her last victim's apartment.

Hart's situation in the film is an extremely painful one, and we as viewers are not spared that pain. But the spectacle of the hero's inability to affect *anything* in the movie is an ironic one; and Hart's enforced impotence deprives him of full dignity as a character and makes him faintly ridiculous even while we are sympathizing with him. Surely it is not mere coincidence that his name should suggest that body organ associated with the tenderer emotions, and hence an encoded message to the effect that love is not enough.

Rabid has been called by some sympathetic commentators (and by Cronenberg himself) a "light" or "fun" movie, and though I cannot at all agree with this as an overall assessment (at least when comparing the film to Cronenberg's earlier work), the movie certainly has its share of wit and humour. Some of the humour seems expressive of the filmmaker's high spirits and zestful irony, but the rest has a deeper relevance to the underlying themes of the film. The more playful examples include the subtle jokes about plastic surgery and health in general; the deft employment of radio and television news announcements in the background (here expanded from their role in *Shivers*); the foreign porno movie's dubbed soundtrack, which serves as a deadpan counterpoint to the scene in the cinema, and even manages to supply dramatic relevance ("reality is like a dream"); and the beautifully executed shopping-plaza scene in which Rose is approached by an absurd young swinger on the make.

More characteristic — and more disturbing — is the appalling humour of the more violent scenes. The rabid farmer attacks an order of fried chicken and then the people in the diner with equal gusto (the horrific as bad manners). Keloid goes berserk amidst the familiar medical rituals of an operation ("give me something to cut with, nurse"). A functionary from the mayor's office is interrupted in the middle of his bureaucratic excuses for not taking the epidemic seriously by a gang of rabid construction workers who assault his car with a jackhammer (civic politics and municipal labour unrest as horror). Mindy's polite embarassment at a sick-looking woman on the subway is subverted when the woman dives hungrily at another passenger. A cop in the shopping plaza accidentally machine-guns Santa Claus. The shooting of the crazy who attacks Hart's car is done with the boredom of casual routine. Their humour is derived from a lunatic exaggeration of ordinary situations, and a contrast between "normal" and "insane." They are disturbing because they make explicit a covert recognition (which we all share to some degree) of the powerful forces lurking beneath the surface of ordinary appearances.

Once again Cronenberg's mise-en-scène functions to enrich the meaning of the film. The settings, far more numerous and varied than in *Shivers*, operate in the same symbolic manner. The Keloid Clinic, with its neat rooms and corridors and sterile medical facilities, the happy-looking home where Hart's confidant, Murray, finds his family destroyed, the bustling festive shopping mall that explodes into violence, the nighttime city street dominated by a colourful neon restaurant sign where a soldier snipes down crazies — all of these and other locations offer an ironic contrast between the decorative expressions of a society that thinks it is in control and the messy and violence evidence that order — and its concomitant aesthetic cleanliness — are precarious things indeed.

When Rose's attack on Lloyd is discovered, the cheerful yellow-and-white abstract painting on the wall of her room in the clinic has been knocked askew from its rectangular "rightness" and is disfigured by an anarchic red smear of blood — now, in effect, a new piece of abstract art more expressive of the real state of things than it was before. The mayhem throughout the city late in the film is intercut with scenes of Mindy affectionately tending Rose with cold compresses and suggestions that she should just rest and not worry; and the melancholy irony of these motherly attentions — so tempting in their offers of escape into childhood and innocent suffering, and so impossible to accept — is subtly emphasized by the clean and pretty pink-checked sheets of the bed Rose lies in. And on a more abstract or philosophical level, the large spherical sculpted head split in two, which adorns the apartment of Rose's last victim, seems to express the film's vision of man as a schizoid creature whose head is at war with his body and is yet inescapably connected to it. (Incidentally this object is a clear foreshadowing of Ben Pierce's powerful sculptures in *Scanners*.)

Cronenberg's increasing skills as a filmmaker also ensure that *Rabid* has the crisp excitement of a well-told story. The control of the narrative impulse via editing (i.e., parallel montage) has already been mentioned, but in addition it might be remarked that the action sequences are filmed with greater finesse and restraint. The spectacular car crash created when Lloyd attacks his cab driver is breathtakingly staged and edited — no more perfect morsel of action cinema exists. In all the details of story construction and cinematic technique, *Rabid* represents an advance in control and refinement over *Shivers*, and is perhaps Cronenberg's most compelling film as pure narrative prior to *Scanners*.

But *Rabid* is a better film than *Shivers* not for these reasons, but because it is a deeper and more serious one, and because for all its humour it reveals a tragic vision of life that seems a recurring feature of Cronenberg's work. *Rabid* is full of characters we care about — even if only a little bit — and they all suffer deeply or die or both. All the plans and adjustments and attempts to cope that the characters make in this film come to grief. This is indeed a trait of many horror movies — and an index of the genre's subversion of the myths of normality. But in *Rabid* there is a particularly inescapable realization that nothing works and everything good perishes. Rose's travail is derisorily compensated by a few moments of strength and power (though all she really chooses is her death), and Hart is left with nothing but his impotence and sorrow. The film's final, unforgettable image is of Rose's body, her face looking more seraphically innocent than ever in death, lying in an alleyway and being tugged at by a dog, before being picked up and thrown unceremoniously into the back of a garbage truck. Her face is turned over into the rubbish, but she is not defiled. Rather there is a sense of tragic waste, and, finally, catharsis and elegy, that sets the seal on *Rabid* as a serious and deeply felt work.

The Brood (1979)

The Brood again represents an upward move for Cronenberg in commercial terms — another increase in budget (to $1.4 million) and two stars with international reputations, Oliver Reed and Samantha Eggar. But in other respects the film is on a much smaller scale than *Rabid* and *Shivers*. For the first time Cronenberg moves out of the social sphere and wholly into the personal one, concentrating on a private calamity. Although all of his films are personal in an artistic sense, *The Brood* has a special reference to Cronenberg's life, since, by his own testimony, it is based on the painful breakup of his first marriage. But the autobiographical elements in the work are irrelevant to a critical reading of it, and they are only of interest in that they go some way towards explaining its depth of feeling and peculiar sense of anguish.

Thematically, *The Brood* is once more rooted in the mutual interdependence of mind and body. But whereas the previous films begin with the tinkerings of physical science that produce predatory *feelings* (lust in *Shivers*, hunger in *Rabid*), *The Brood* begins with the mental science of psychology, whose reductionist logic produces predatory *things*. The Somafree Institute of Psychoplasmics, developed by psychiatrist Dr. Hal Raglan, treats patients by encouraging them to give bodily expression to subconscious anger, and the results vary from sores and cancerous growths to "the brood" of Nola Carveth — actual beings produced by her body that are the walking incarnations of her inner feelings. Raglan encourages his patients to "go all the way through" their emotions of hurt and rage "to the end." "Don't stop," he says to them; and it is this wish to effect a liberation from normal restraint, repression or balance that constitutes his hubristic Cartesian error in the Cronenbergian world. The carrying of psychotherapeutic methods to their logical extreme results once more in the creation of an antirational destructive force that strikes without thought or inhibition, and another form of plague is set loose.

But this time the victims are not randomly chosen. They are either the therapeutic subject himself ("Dr. Raglan encouraged my body to revolt; now I've got a small revolution on my hands, and I'm not putting it down very well," says one patient with psychoplasmically induced cancer of the lymphatic glands), or else, in the most advanced case, the objects of the patient's subconscious hatred — Nola's mother and father, her daughter and her supposed sexual rival. In a literal and significant way, the murderous attacks of the brood and the movie's horror in general is kept very much in the family. The terrible actualization of the process of therapy is enacted against parents by their child and against a child by her parent (with a single exception to encompass sexual, and also domestic, jealousy). The film allegorizes a personal drama, and carries a recognizable private conflict, domestic and generational, into the amplified metaphorical conventions of the horror genre. Furthermore, the use of the self-contained family as the narrative focus and the invocation of Freudian principles give the film a universal dimension, which makes it more than just a case study.

The family relationships in *The Brood* are very complex and suggestive. Virtually every simple description of a relationship, every moral judgement rendered by one character (family member) about another is contradicted or made ambiguous by something else in the film. Nola's accusation that her mother, Juliana, beat her as a child is contradicted by Juliana's testimony that she didn't, that Nola "would wake up and...be covered with big ugly bumps," and that Nola has distorted the truth. Nola also accuses her father, Barton, of "pretending it wasn't happening." One is at first inclined to believe Nola and not Juliana. But given Nola's singular ability to embody her feelings (the brood), and given also her daughter Candice's bodily reaction to traumatic shock (she develops bumps on her arm), it is conceivable that Nola could have given herself those "big ugly bumps," and read her feelings literally in retrospect to remember psychological injuries as physical ones. The ambiguity of the situation is very appropriate to the tangled emotional underbrush of family relationships, and to the *Marienbad*-like memories of them. Similarly, the responsibility for the breakup of Nola and Frank's marriage (which occurred well before the beginning of the action) is first assumed to be Nola's. But after a while the distinct moral opposites of his sanity and her craziness become smudged as other elements come into play: Frank's unwillingness to face the seriousness of the situation and his unrealistic desire to avoid messy or unpleasant emotions, Nola's real suffering, her need for emotional support and her attempts to confront the experiences that have made her disturbed. The family histories of Juliana, Barton and baby Nola, and of Nola, Frank and little Candice are suggested by fragments of testimony and evidence rather than being presented in clear, factual terms, and in this way attain a rich, ambiguous complexity. The terrifying appearance of two wartlike excrescences on Candice's arm at the end of the film in the wake of her horrific experiences suggests the future in the same evocative manner. This expressive gesturing towards the unexplained — and probably unexplainable — past and future is accomplished structurally through a narrative that covers only a few days but crams into them events indicating a nexus of obscure necessity stretching backwards and forwards and determining the lives of those caught in its web.

Although considerable sympathy is extended to all the participants in this Atrean tragedy (*The Brood* gets closer to its characters in general than previous Cronenberg films), the most painful focus of involvement for the viewer is five-year-old Candice. Mute and defenceless, she is the purest victim because the most purely innocent. It is she who most clearly demonstrates the helplessness of the characters in a situation they cannot control or even understand. Candice suffers terribly at the hands of the brood (her siblings, as Raglan points out), being beaten by these strange little monsters, witnessing the death they wreak, being forced to live with them and finally almost being killed by them herself. Her response is silence and blankness of expression, a quiet but very deep traumatization, and finally the development of physical symptoms of mental stress in the form of "big ugly bumps" on her arm — an indication that the cycle of destructive parental behaviour and psychological damage in children will continue into the future. Candice's experience is a heart-breaking one for the viewer and one without hope or consolation. Unlike *Rabid*, *The Brood* contains no elegy or cathartic release at its finish — merely an image of Candice deeply bruised and shocked in spirit, staring straight ahead in huge closeup.

As Nola was mistreated by Juliana, so Candice is mistreated by Nola. Like her own mother, Nola refuses to acknowledge that she is doing anything wrong: "good mummies don't hurt their children," only "bad, fucked-up mummies" do, and the unwillingness of both Juliana and Nola to recognize their acts is a feature of their common neurosis — which is now being passed on to Candice. And just as Barton, whom his daughter Nola loved and trusted, did not protect her from her mother's attacks, "pretended it wasn't happening," so Frank, despite his efforts to shield Candice from her mother, wants to pretend nothing really awful is happening and in the end fails to protect his daughter from traumatic experience. Frank first fails to understand what has happened during Candice's weekend visit to Nola at the clinic (he knows she was beaten, but not that she was attacked by something monstrous); fails to encourage her to remember and speak about her experience when Juliana was murdered (he is clearly uncomfortable with the police psychiatrist's suggestion that he do this, and in effect avoids doing it); assures her that the thing she saw at Juliana's is dead and will never hurt her or him or anyone again (a pathetically false prophecy); and finally he is not there to save her from abduction from her school and imprisonment in the brood's dwelling place. For all his running around and deep concern (he is a bit like Hart in *Rabid* in this respect), Frank's sole effective act is to strangle his wife to death and thus to save Candice from being torn apart by the enraged brood...though not from later consequences. It is a rather extreme act, one in which he, too, at last gives concrete expression to his inner feelings.

But no one is really at fault here. Nola behaves as she does out of psychological necessity. She does not will the deaths of the brood's victims — indeed she doesn't even know about them. Nor can one say that Juliana should be held responsible for her actions. Barton and Frank are just ordinary men trying unsuccessfully to cope with situations they can't be expected to master. Even Dr. Raglan is motivated by a desire to help his patients. Once again, there is a bleak determinism operating here — almost a maleficent fate, which is all the more dispiriting for being the product of the contradictions inherent in human nature. And the poignancy of human suffering in such a context is all the more moving: one sees it clearly in Candice's mute sadness and in Barton's sorrowful caressing, just before his own death, of the outline of Juliana's body traced on her kitchen floor by the police. One sees it also in the desperation of Raglan's other patients, Mike and Jan, despite the black humour of their presentation; in the constant anxiety on Frank's face; and in the torrents of pain that emerge from Nola during her sessions with Raglan.

Raglan is an especially ambiguous figure in the film. Our impression of him throughout much of the action is that he is a sinister manipulator of other people's lives. The conspiratorial exchanges with his assistant Chris, his iron-hand-in-velvet-glove stonewalling of outsiders, his assumption of absolute authority in every situation all confirm this view. But he is clearly an extremely gifted therapist — the therapy sequences are splendidly convincing — and the last section of the film, in which he ventures into the brood's den to remove Candice, reveals both courage and conscience. His brainchild, psychoplasmics, is an attempt to liberate destructive subconscious feelings from the cage of the mind, where, cooped up, they do so much damage. The case of Jan Hartog is a spectacular example of experimental failure: the uncaged subconscious has wreaked havoc on its own body. Nola is Raglan's "star pupil," who was "born to prove that psychoplasmics is the ultimate therapeutic device" because she alone has succeeded in really exteriorizing her feelings, coaxing them entirely from their cage.

That Cronenberg connects the irrational with the body and the animal is evident in the scene near the end of the film where Nola actually gives birth to one of the creatures. Tearing with her teeth through the silver-green sac protruding from her abdomen, she removes a fleshy embryo, spilling placenta graphically onto her legs, and then proceeds to lick the blood from the newborn creature, finally caressing and cradling it gently to her bosom. It is a scene that invariably makes audiences gag in disgust (as indeed Frank does when he witnesses it). But viewed objectively it resembles a very natural moment in the animal world: birth is messy, visceral and, perhaps, to the cloistered civilized eye, disgusting, but it is absolutely essential to life. As usual, Cronenberg's feelings about the body are anything but simple. (As a sidelight, it is interesting to read this scene also as a kind of ironic view of what happens in psychotherapy: the patient discovers his buried feelings, carefully removes them from their organic context, and examines and caresses these messy organs of the personality with pride and loving fascination.)

The brood-children are, as befits creatures of pure angry emotion, mindless, genderless, inarticulate, seeing only in black and white, and very interestingly, short-lived (they have a camel's hump or gas tank of nutrient matter that keeps them alive for only a relatively brief time). The implication of the latter characteristic is that feelings of anger, when externalized, burn themselves out, and consequently Nola's destructive emotions can be truly purged in this way. But in the world of Cronenberg's films no method of liberating the irrational completely beneficially is possible. Nor can the irrational be ignored or suppressed. If it is loosed from its cage it runs

The *Brood* focuses on family relationships; here Frank says goodbye to his daughter, Candy, at school

amok despite the best efforts of reason to control it; and if it is ignored or denied it rises up and stages a jailbreak. The only course of action, apparently, is to keep a constant watch on the creature behind its bars, acknowledging its existence and its necessity as a dynamo of the personality, giving it sublimated expression, tolerating its destructiveness, never indulging in the folly of supposing that there is some way to render it harmless, and never embracing it as a saviour. A precarious balancing act, with the powers of the personality shared uneasily between reason and emotion (or, in other terms, between mind and body) is all that is possible — as Cronenberg himself says in the interview. Raglan thinks he has succeeded in defusing the id by liberating it, getting it out there where it can be seen and dealt with. But when given its head the id will always devour and destroy, for that is its nature, and it is a tragic mistake to assume that the brood can be controlled once it exists as a distinct entity freed from the watchful eye of reason. Of course the brood is not evil, it is merely pure subconscious feeling, capable of destructive acts when roused by anger, but impossible to judge morally. And even the brood is ambiguous at moments: its insane fury towards the objects of Nola's anger is combined with its authoritative, protective manner towards Candice when she is kidnapped, as if she is, as Raglan says, "in a way, one of them."

The purely human side of the film — the "realistic" context for the horror — is admirably complex. Not only are the major relationships provided with the kind of detail and suggestive elisions that characterize real experience, but the less central figures are also deftly drawn. Juliana's one scene is a brief but full portrait of a complicated, neurotic personality. Barton's death scene operates the same way, by giving depth to an important character who doesn't get much screen time. Ruth Mayer, Candice's schoolteacher, is the centre of an extremely subtle set of circumstances. Although there is nothing overt to indicate a romantic or sexual interest between her and Frank, the two of them are obviously checking each other out, and so Nola's jealousy is not totally unfounded. (The essence of her sickness is not total delusion, but radical overreaction.) Both Mike and Jan Hartog are given splendid tour-de-force scenes that carry on the Cronenberg tradition of combining genuine humour with genuine pain, and even such minor functionaries as the police sergeant and the coroner who examines the dead brood-child have their own personalities.

In this deeply felt and very personal project, it is not surprising to find some significant changes in Cronenberg's visual style and mise-en-scène. The look of *The Brood* is in many respects quite different from any of the previous films. The overall hue is darker and more organic. Browns, yellows, pale greens and blues replace the brighter side sharper colours of *Shivers* and *Rabid*. The lighting moves further towards chiaroscuro — though never at the expense of clarity. The decor and settings are markedly different. In place of the clean modern blankness of the buildings and rooms in the previous films, here there is an older, more obviously lived-in environment. Juliana's house, with its brocade furniture, wooden doorframes and pastel lime walls, is as coolly attractive as any of the locations in *Shivers* or *Rabid*, but it is older, more graciously refined and more human. Frank's house, although more modern, has a degree of clutter and natural energy. This choice of sets is also seen in such secondary locations as Jan Hartog's residence (old dark wood, leaded glass and dull plastered walls), and the office of Frank's lawyer (an old room modernized by furniture and the presence of huge potted plants). Although the main building of the Somafree Institute and Candice's school both show Cronenberg's earlier predilection for space-age-functional gothic, the interior of the school is not as sterile as its facade. Somafree also encompasses the primitive wooden sheds where Nola and the children stay. This shed is the setting for the climax of the film, and its unvarnished wooden walls, makeshift wooden beds and bare-bulb or candle lighting amidst natural darkness and forest surroundings create a strong sense of organic simplicity — it is by far the most different setting in all of Cronenberg's work to this point. This is the birthplace and home of the brood, and one is inclined to say that the primitiveness of the environment is as typical of body/ unconscious as the clean modern blankness of *Shivers* and *Rabid* is of mind/rationality.

In addition, the photography is somewhat different. There is the same — and perhaps even an augmented — sense of clarity and detachment in the sharply focused and often north-lit images, and as great a fondness as every for low-angle shots. But the film's deep-focus, slightly creepy emptiness is also combined with wintry lighting and the bleakness of the landscape to produce a feeling of coldness and hopelessness. In this film the sun never shines, and if it does (as in the scene where Frank is taking snapshots of Candice's bruised back as evidence that she's been beaten), it is used ironically rather than to express joy.

Nola gives birth to one of her "brood" in *The Brood*

The Brood is definitely Cronenberg's most pessimistic film so far, expressing a cold, sad helplessness that is more despairing than even the stoic resignation of *Rabid*. *Rabid* ends in the almost consoling finality of death, but *The Brood* ends with a powerful image of suffering and a promise of much more suffering to come. Even on a thematic level the film seems less hopeful about human nature than *Shivers* or *Rabid*. The manic outbreaks of appetite in the two previous films are in a sense provoked by scientists (i.e., men of reason) performing concrete alterations to the body — physical operations of implantation or transplantation. In *The Brood*, the demons are not even metaphorically imported, but are completely native to the individual human psyche: Raglan may be a catalyst, but Nola produces the brood all on her own. One's own physical nature can be altered by mere thought; one is capable of bearing monsters without outside help; one can devour others and be devoured oneself by an unstoppable force emanating from the self; and worst of all, the terrible process is passed on to others unconsciously, and they in turn pass it on themselves. One is thus doomed to destroy those whom one most loves and wishes to protect. Is it possible to imagine a more pessimistic creed? In *The Brood*, human nature itself is sick, and there is no cure. No wonder Cronenberg entitled both his monsters and his film "the brood": they are at once the products and the initiators of gloomy meditation, inner turmoil and confusion. And the film expresses a flatter, more defeated vision (lacking even the "savage joy" of *Shivers* and *Rabid*) than almost any work in the genre.

Scanners (1980)

For *Scanners* Cronenberg again enjoyed a quantum jump in budget (to $4.1 million). Partly because of better American distribution, and perhaps because of its increased emphasis on plot, the film had very good initial box-office in North America. Furthermore, it received favourable notices in the important American weeklies, especially *Time* and *Newsweek*, and considerable attention was drawn not only to *Scanners* but to Cronenberg's earlier films.

To say that *Scanners* is superficial relative to Cronenberg's other work is not to condemn it. Despite its many incidental similarities to his earlier films, it is a new kind of movie for Cronenberg — less obsessive, less regurgitative, finally less personal and more interested in straightforward excitement and conventional plot. Long admired by John Carpenter, the young American director of horror films, Cronenberg has made a very Carpenter-like film in *Scanners*: an effective story rendered distinctive by fine mise-en-scène, a flair for detail, and much evidence of a sophisticated, controlling intelligence. *Scanners* is closer to the common notion of good entertainment than anything of Cronenberg's so far, but to a large degree it lacks that dynamic core of compulsiveness and rich thematic ambiguity that fuels his earlier work and the subsequent *Videodrome*.

There are two basics to note about the plot of *Scanners*: its complexity and its strong forward drive. The film chronicles the adventures of thirty-five-year-old telepath (or "scanner") Cameron Vale. Beginning as a derelict confused by his own gift, he is rehabilitated by psychopharmacist Dr. Paul Ruth, and enlisted by him on behalf of the private security organization Consec, as an underground agent trying to penetrate a sinister rival scanner organization headed by the megalomaniac Darryl Revok. He stumbles into yet another group of scanners and teams up with nice lady scanner Kim Obrist; together they discover Revok's devilish scheme to create a new generation of scanners (using Dr. Ruth's drug Ephemerol, administered to pregnant women) and take over the world. Ultimately Vale confronts Revok and learns that Dr. Ruth is the father of them both. He also learns that the scanner phenomenon was initially the side effect of Ruth's pregnancy-period tranquillizer Ephemerol. In the last scene Vale and Revok fight a spectacular scanning duel, and Vale survives by destroying Revok's mind and inhabiting his body.

The extraordinary complications of the story (three scanner groups, two sinister organizations, two double agents, crucial information buried in the past and not revealed until late in the film, etc.) are not made easier to comprehend by Cronenberg's elliptical narrative style: action comes first and explanations are almost always deferred until later. Many things are comprehensible only after the film is over, some things not even then, and others remain obscure or seemingly contradictory even after multiple viewings. These holes in the plot are not the kind encountered in earlier Cronenberg films. Whereas in *The Brood* our incomplete knowledge of the past actually improves the film by suggesting that *any* of the possibilities might have produced the same result, in *Scanners* the lack of explanation is often simply puzzling. Whether Nola was physically beaten as a child becomes a fascinating uncertainty, whereas the questions one asks about Cameron Vale — where does a lifelong derelict get the knowledge to handle a computer-terminal keyboard, or why does Vale have no childhood memories — are merely irritating.

The abundance of obscurities in *Scanners* is only another indication of its action-oriented nature and of the filmmaker's desire to make the action effective. The convolutions of the plot are there to produce mystification, strong curiosity and a sense of menace; Vale knows how to punch in a question to a computer because he is the hero, and the story demands that he find a new clue at this stage; and likewise he has no childhood memories because Revok's revelations of their mutual genealogy would not produce the required jolt of surprise if he had. The plot is designed pragmatically, for maximum excitement, intrigue and surprise, rather than for consistency or thematic wholeness.

But *Scanners* also reaps the rewards of its "superficiality." None of Cronenberg's films is so fast-moving, so relentless. One feels the strong pull of conventional adventure-genre values: the protagonist rescued from the junk pile and reborn as hero; his mastery of his latent superpowers; his initiation into a complex and violent ongoing war between two rival powers; his discovery and penetration of treachery and false appearances; his maturation into an independent being after the death of his patron; his alliance with a worthy female companion; his final confrontation with his moral antithesis who is also his dark brother; and his ultimate victory. The innocence of the dramatic mode, with its lone unseasoned hero plunged into a maze of bewildering, premeditated evil and its clear moral opposites, gives it an affinity with fabular quest narratives stretching from the Arthurian tales to *Star Wars*, and, again, distinguishes it from all of Cronenberg's previous films. Furthermore, the nature of the action sequences is, at least for Cronenberg, surprisingly clean. The famous exploding head and the final duel are certainly visceral enough, and there is some bloody shooting, but there is no sex at all and little to compare with the messily explicit body horrors of the other features.

Thematically speaking, *Scanners* is full of recognizably Cronenbergian motifs. The premise of the story can be succinctly summarized by the phrase "if thoughts could kill," and that encapsulation is enough to identify the film with Cronenberg's established concerns. Telepathy is also the subject of *Stereo*, and a number of the details characterizing its presentation in *Scanners* are inherited from the earlier film. In *Stereo* the telepathic experience is "overwhelming, exhausting, akin to pain"; in *Scanners*, "the scanning experience is usually a painful one, sometimes resulting in nosebleeds, earaches, stomach cramps, nausea, sometimes other symptoms of a similar nature." In *Scanners*, as one might expect after Cronenberg's three previous features, there is an emphasis on the physical nature of telepathy, a phenomenon general thought of as purely mental. Telekinesis — the ability to create physical effects by mental means — which scanners possess, is only a step from the psychoplasmics of *The Brood*, and in particular from Nola's literal incarnation of psychic impulses.

As in *The Brood*, the strange mental-into-physical gift is inherited in a peculiar way, and in both cases the catalyst is created by a

medical scientist to relieve emotional pain (Ephemerol is a tranquillizer for pregnant women made uneasy by growths in their
bodies). Tranquillizers, like the plastic surgery of *Rabid* or the
cosmetics of *Crimes of the Future*, are a device to smooth over the
surface, to treat the symptoms rather than the disease. And in
Scanners, as in all of Cronenberg's earlier films, the attempt to
improve the human animal produces an unexpected, disconcerting
and potentially destructive side effect.

However, in *Scanners* there is a great difference. If the scanners
were true monsters like the sex maniacs in *Shivers*, the predators in
Rabid or the brood, then this would indeed be a thematic continuation of the earlier work. But they are not. Scanners may be insane
and destructive like Revok; but they may also be virtuous and
beneficent like Vale or Kim Obrist or most of the other scanners we
see. Scanners are in a sense victims of fate and science like the
monsters of *Shivers* and *Rabid*, but their condition is not at all
necessarily fatal or destructive to themselves and others — merely
freakish and interesting. Most of the "monsters" in the film lack that
deep division between rationality and instinct that has hitherto been
the trademark of Cronenberg's meaningfully bizarre mutants. The
hero, Vale, is a whole man — his reason and his instinct combine in a
positive quest, his "monstrous" difference is used for good. He
undergoes no tragic struggle as do the protagonists of *Rabid* and *The
Brood* or *Videodrome* but only an adventure. With the ultimate
wholesomeness of Vale and Obrist before us, it is hard to regard the
prospect of a new generation of scanners as a threat.

What genuine ambiguities do exist in the film are mostly contained
in the characters of Dr. Ruth and Darryl Revok. Here we have
Frankenstein and his monster (Ruth as father and as scientist creates
Revok), and in their context the disturbing questions raised by the
scanner phenomenon achieve real force. Is the ability to scan a gift or
a curse? Is it (as both Ruth and Revok assert) "brilliant and
glorious," or is it destructive and horrifying (as their actions would
seem to suggest)? Are Ruth's Faustian ambitions noble or merely
mad, and is Revok to be considered as a predator or as a victim? In
these characters (and in the more peripheral figure of the strange
scanner-sculptor, Benjamin Pierce) there is a fertile drama of
contradiction and conflicting motive, played out in the thematic and
philosophical terms of Cronenberg's earlier work. But it is a drama
sealed off into essentially secondary characters, and it withers away
with their deaths, leaving us with Vale's relatively two-dimensional
"goodness." The movie is forced back into the shallows of the
adventure film, with Ruth and Revok reduced essentially to colourful
glosses and the culminating struggle becomes a straightforward battle

Kim Obrist and Cameron Vale join forces in *Scanners*

between good and evil. Even the potentially resonant dualism of Vale and Revok as brothers (i.e., mirror images of each other), and of Ruth and Vale/Revok as father and sons, is damped by making the information a late, shock development, so that the ambiguities are no sooner uncovered than they are swept aside in the final battle. This makes for a splendidly effective final scene, but also for much more straightforward action than is usual with Cronenberg.

Perhaps this is to underemphasize the complexity of the film. For example, neither Vale nor Obrist is wholly good. When each of them is using the scanning gift there is inevitably a suggestion of great power and an insidious and disturbing suggestion of the pleasure each takes in wielding that power. Each of them has flickers of "savage joy," and this naturally complicates the moral picture. Also, the whole idea of a mind's ability to interfere telepathically with other minds and physical objects is disturbing in itself, as is the notion that for the scanner there is the danger of having no privacy and no self: both Vale and Revok are tormented by the trespass of other people's voices in their heads. In this sense, *Scanners* explores the fear of what would happen if the barriers of mental and corporeal self-contain-ment were broken down and the fear (experienced in different ways by both the scanner and the scannee) of being engulfed, taken over. One feels the fascination in *Scanners* with invading other people and with being invaded. Only very briefly is there an example (in the rather group therapylike communal scans of Kim Obrist's friends) of telepathy as a communicative or sharing activity. Instead one finds it being used as a weapon (even if in self-defence) and as a tool of espionage and subversion. Not for Cronenberg the cosy imaginings of a community of thought readers and senders: for him it is nausea and nosebleeds and mental rape. And it is interesting to recall Ruth's didactic affirmation that "telepathy is not mind reading, it is the direct linking of two nervous systems separated by space," implying a connection more biological than cerebral — once again familiar Cronenberg country. Scanning is as much a bodily function as a mental one.

This truly interesting notion is most strikingly embodied in the black-and-white archival footage of the twenty-two-year-old Revok as a mental patient that Dr. Ruth shows to Vale as part of his rehabilitation and indoctrination — one of the highlights of the film. Revok, an evidently deeply disturbed young man, alternately grinning and bleakly serious, has (like one of the characters in *Stereo*) drilled a hole in his head, "to let the people out...whole people — arms, legs, hands," and on the forehead bandage covering the wound he has painted a staring eye. His interlocutor asks him what he has put over the hole:

> A door. Put an eye on the door so they won't know it's a door, and they can't get back in 'cause they see the eye.

This idea of an almost physical invasion of the mind and of the seeing eye as a barrier to intrusion and the guardian of privacy and self is a nice symbol of the related ideas of control, awareness and aggression. The people in Revok's head are trampling him, stripping him of control. To keep them out he must establish an appearance of awareness and vigilance (the "eye"). Thus is established the notion of seeing as a weapon — awareness as an aggressive tool. Revok the monster scanner, using the "eye" in his head to control and destroy others, is born in this act of his younger self.

It is in the area of mise-en-scène that *Scanners* makes much of its impact. In his interviews Cronenberg has remarked on the difficulty of giving visual expression to a mental phenomenon like telepathy, and it is remarkable how vivid is the impression of a physical event during the scanning scenes, despite the relative absence of overt visual symptoms. Crosscutting, facial contortions, and, above all, a dazzling array of soundtrack effects are the principal means employed to dramatize the scanning scenes with success. A neat touch is seen in the nosebleeds suffered by the subjects of simple low-level scans — the single droplet of blood on the otherwise unblemished face suggestive of a greater turmoil, like the modest trickles of blood on white porcelain and fibreglass in *Shivers* and *The Brood*.

But the most memorable scanning effects are the biggest ones — Revok's explosion of the brain of an earnest Consec scanner near the beginning as a mere illustration of his powers; Vale's and Obrist's flinging of Revok assassins bodily across rooms, in the latter case causing them to burst violently into flame; the tour-de-force of Vale's computer scan, in which he blows up the terminal room by long distance and sets telephone circuits and wires sparking hotly, in a demonstration of a power so awesome that the telephone receiver he is holding actually melts and begins to burn; and of course the majestic final duel with Revok, with its Christ-like icons of power and transcendence (Vale's arms outstretched, his upturned palms cradling tongues of fire, his torso enveloped in flames, and his bloody face wearing an expression of godlike serenity).

As ever, Cronenberg enlivens his narrative with a penetrating use of setting and decor. The Consec and Biocarbon Amalgamate complexes are fine examples of clean but alienating and dehumanized architecture (once more associated with science and corporate society). The riotous red and chrome and lightbulbs of the opening scene in the shopping mall, the aluminum, glass and cement of the two subway sequences and the aggressively unadorned art gallery are variations of the same principle. Consec in particular, dominated by unpainted concrete, pearly greys and whites and very hard, clean textures, is a plain signpost. On the other side of the fence we have such locations as the old brick warehouse where Dr. Ruth runs his operation, Ben Pierce's farmyard-barn of a studio, and the house inhabited by Obrist's group. These settings, darker and more human if not always welcoming, repeat to a degree the *Brood* syndrome by looking older and more lived-in, relatively full of character and not so monolithically antiseptic.

Throughout, Cronenberg presses the narrative forward with tense editing and upsurges in tempo for the transitions from one phase of the plot to the next. The colour scheme is shifted over to blue, grey, silver and white, less dominated by primary colours than *Shivers* or *Rabid*. The lighting is sometimes darker and more shadowed than the norm, rather reminiscent in this respect of *The Brood*. (The presence on both films of cinematographer Mark Irwin and designer Carol Spier must of course be taken into account here — though Cronenberg has always been prepared to use a degree of chiaroscuro in his lighting.) One must also note the subdued, almost colourless costumes. Vale is often dressed in plain white, Ruth is invariably in black, and this visual antithesis is carried over into the white-clad chemical workers and the black-uniformed Consec guards, with a wealth of charcoal-grey suits and jackets in between. The general look of the film, then, is cool and sharp, with a discreet enrichment of shadows. Even the notably slow, hypnotically stretched dialogue delivery has the paradoxical effect of stripping the film for action.

And action is principally what we get in *Scanners*. In contrast to the earlier features, we see very little of the human suffering produced by explosively released inner forces. There are, certainly, a few moments in the film where this prospect is glimpsed: the 16mm medical footage of the young Revok, the mute despair of the security man who is telepathically forced to kill his colleagues and himself, the two guards whom Vale and Obrist disarm by an affliction of scan-induced traumatic guilt and remorse, and above all the character and especially the work of Ben Pierce. Pierce's sculptures are memorably introduced in the incongruously clean and hushed surroundings of the Crostic Art Gallery. They have a wrenching, violent power, expressing

Darryl Revok is the evil schemer in *Scanners*

the nightmarish chaos and horror the scanner can experience when the boundaries between inside and outside are demolished, and the self is cracked open like a nut. Eerily, tapping his head, Pierce says, "It's my art that keeps me sane": clearly, what the sculptures represent is madness. But despite their emotional power, all these things are peripheral to the main thrust of the film, and their status as detail is significant.

Flanked by *The Brood* and *Videodrome*, Cronenberg's deepest and most painful films, *Scanners* seems to be anomalous in its relative ease and optimism. Nevertheless, there are important respects in which it may be seen as a continuation of Cronenberg's developing attitudes. From *Shivers* to *Scanners* there is a relative movement away from the body side of his dualism and towards the mind side. Of the features, *Shivers* is the most physically messy, and *Scanners* the least, with *Rabid* and *The Brood* each marking a definite step along that path. In this progression, the horrors become less physical and more psychological. Whereas *Shivers* revels in visceral explicitness and the orgiastic excesses of the body, *Rabid* moves towards a more complex balance by endowing its "monstrous" heroine with humanizing doubts and fears. *The Brood*'s violence, less gaudy and socially apocalyptic and more personal, is exercised by literal projections of private psychological hostility, and in *Scanners* the process has become yet more mental, a dominance exerted telepathically by one mind over another. In *Videodrome* the body breaks forth again — but the development is continued, for everything is specifically located within the mental realm of private perception and imagination, and in a sense the horrors do not exist in the outside world at all.

In *Shivers* the thematic mechanism is a relatively simple one of collective social repression overthrown by rampaging animal instinct, and the question of personal responsibility never really arises — the parasite plague is initiated by a mad scientist who kills himself in the first scene, and one can hardly hold the parasites themselves morally accountable for the chaos they create. If anything is responsible for the explosion, it is society as a whole, whose immanent ordered sterility denies universal human needs. In *Rabid* the notion of individual responsibility is overtly introduced in the person of the Typhoid Mary heroine, whose predatory activities are motivated by an irresistible need that she struggles against and agonizes over. *The Brood* narrows and intensifies the moral question further yet: it is a Freudian drama of parent-child love and hate, and its subject is partly the relation of conscious and subconscious within the individual human being. From this point of view, the movement from *Shivers* to *The Brood* represents the gradually more specific application to individual cases of *Shivers*'s underlying assumptions about human nature. It is a

movement away from metaphor and towards analysis, away from the
social and towards the psychological. This development may be seen
as a progression from convulsive rebellion against "rational"
repression to a conscious understanding of the true complexities of
life and a resigned, even pessimistic, acceptance of them. *Shivers*
rejoices in its chaos of liberated energies; *The Brood* is much more
circumscribed, internalized, soberly thoughtful. *Scanners* suggests the
battle has been fought and won, as though the ultimate despair of *The
Brood* has opened the way for a brighter, more straightforward
understanding of the world. Indeed, in *Scanners* the fiercely contradictory dualism of Cronenberg's earlier features is almost entirely
allayed, and human nature is presented as — at least potentially —
whole and ordered, in control of its raging inner fires.

The notion of control is important in Cronenberg's films, as it is in
the genre as a whole. *Shivers* posits a society in the unhealthy grip of
Cartesian ideals of order — animality and spontaneity are under the
control of a sterile, repressive rationality. The tensions inherent in this
sort of control finally explode into a garish, violent repudiation of order,
and obsessive control is replaced by obsessive release: one extreme gives
way to the other. The same scenario is re-enacted in *Rabid*, but with
the difference that the drama of control/release is played out not only
in a social setting, but also in the more complex and specific terms of
the heroine's character. Whereas the characters in *Shivers* are
essentially pawns to be shifted this way and that by the forces of
repression and animality, Rose in *Rabid* is partly an agent, at the edge
of consciousness in the exercise of her aggressive appetite. We have
here a first step towards the conversion of idlike animality into
power, which in turn may be wielded by the will instead of merely
exploding chaotically at the dictates of instinct. The development is
carried further in *The Brood*, where the destructive forces of the
subconscious are actually directed at specific targets — Nola's brood,
the externalized hostile energies of her mind, is aimed at those
whom she feels to be tormenting her. Yet the process remains an
unconscious one, or at least only a byproduct of conscious will. Dr.
Raglan's therapy encourages Nola to feel her feelings "through to the
end" — he does not encourage her to *think* them through. But in *The
Brood* subconscious energies are presented more clearly than before as
potential tools of the will, as power.

In *Scanners* the transformation is almost complete. The forces of
the id are not presented as necessarily uncontrollable and therefore
destructive to what we value, but simply as power, to be used for
good or ill. The telepathic ability is by far the purest expression of
power in Cronenberg's work. If it is not controlled it creates misery
and destructiveness in the personality — unadept scanners complain of

being drowned by voices and engage in unfocused destruction. But if it can be mastered it becomes precisely a source of power, of control. In psychological terms, Cronenberg's work has completed the journey from unresolved schizophrenic conflict, through the initial discovery of the sources of conflict and the expression of pain and hostility, to a final ability to control and utilize inner energies in a conscious manner, as a direct extension of the will.

The gap between *The Brood* and *Scanners* in this progression is enormous — a leap from the blackest pessimism to amazing optimism. *The Brood* suggests that it is impossible to know one's own mind entirely; *Scanners* makes it possible actually to know another's. In *The Brood*, subconscious wishes, once liberated, kill and maim; in *Scanners* the instinctive telepathic power can be mastered and used positively. The outward direction of inner impulses in *The Brood* is useless to the subject as well as destructive to the object; in *Scanners* the subject is in a state of trauma until he can learn to direct his powers outward, and the object of his directed power often suffers no lasting harm.

From this standpoint *Scanners* is not so much positive as wildly idealistic. At the end, Vale, having overcome the dark, idlike Revok, inhabits his body, underlining the suggestion that the constructive part of the self can not only defeat the destructive part but also unite with it, co-opting and assuming the id's strength for good purposes. Telepathy in the film is practically synonymous with strong will, and the combination in Vale and Obrist of moral purity with superhuman will that can manipulate the world carries overtones of Fascist idealism — the most extreme form of romantic idealism yet devised. This is the complete opposite of *The Brood*'s gloomy, no-fault determinism.

Scanners also carries overtones of such simplistic adventure/science-fiction films as *Star Wars* (whose final scene has itself been connected with *Triumph of the Will*,) and this suggests another interpretation of its significance. The raging subconscious energies of the earlier works seem to have been brought under control and put to healthy use in *Scanners*; but perhaps what has happened instead is that the subconscious has been banished entirely from the film. Certainly the relative superficiality of the characters and the ease with which Cronenberg's habitual tragic dualism has been resolved would support this notion. *Scanners*, with its suggestion of the possibility of taming inner forces and achieving wholeness and integration with the world, is the "healthiest" of Cronenberg's features, but it is also the least powerful. This is surely because neurotic conflict, and even pessimism, are, at least within the horror genre, richer sources of artistic complexity than health can ever be. It may indeed be that the genre requires insanity as a major component. To present a complete and untarnished victory of repressed forces, in effect to deprive the monster of its essential monstrosity, would carry such a work right out of the category of the horror film, no matter how many other trademarks it possessed. Pushing the process to its logical extreme would make *Sisters* into *An Unmarried Woman* (or, as Cronenberg is fond of pointing out, would make *The Brood* into *Kramer vs. Kramer*). Certainly one is nervous about calling *Scanners* a horror film, without serious qualifications.

When many of the ideas raised by or developed in *Scanners* are re-examined in *Videodrome*, the probing is much deeper, the basic doubts and contradictions reappear, and the results are far more unsettling. It is a little depressing to find that, as Cronenberg's most aboveboard and in some ways least characteristic film, *Scanners* should also have been the most commercially successful. But of course that is also a tribute to its fine qualities as a science-fiction/action/adventure movie, and it can scarcely be criticized for them.

Videodrome (1982)

Videodrome is probably Cronenberg's finest film to date. Though it lacks the formal completeness and precisely delineated human structure of *The Brood*, it displays an intensity of self-examination and a richness of detail that go beyond anything in the filmmaker's earlier work. It is a flawed film; but when it succeeds, it is so impressive and resonantly affecting that one begins for the first time to think that perhaps Cronenberg has artistic greatness in him, as well as originality, intelligence and flair. Nevertheless, it is a difficult film, and to my way of thinking virtually unavailable on a single viewing. I confess to initially having thought it a failure. It seemed confused and undigested, and after many viewings I still feel that certain aspects are needlessly complex and obscure, and that it creates too many unfulfilled expectations. But its confusions are very much a part of its subject. Just as the events of the film are hard to untangle, so too, is it difficult to determine to what degree the contradictions and blind alleys are problems for the viewer that Cronenberg should have solved and to what degree they are the features of an essential experience of disorientation.

Cronenberg has said that *Videodrome* is "a first-person film," and this idea is the key to the film. The protagonist, Max Renn, is present in every scene of the movie, and again to quote Cronenberg, "We get no information that Max doesn't get himself." President and part owner of a Toronto independent television station (Civic-TV, Channel 83) specializing in sensational programming with heavy doses of sex and violence, Max encounters test transmissions of an experimental show called "Videodrome" consisting of nothing but sadistic torture and murder. Soon he is led into a realm of "Videodrome"-induced hallucinations, which intensify and proliferate until they dominate his life and cut him off from outward reality. There are other forces operating on him, too: radio pop-psychologist bombshell Nicki Brand, who introduces him to the forbidden joys of S-and-M sex; the video pronouncements of "media prophet" Professor Brian O'Blivion, who preaches that television has usurped reality, and, as inventor of the hallucination- and tumour-causing "Videodrome" signal, has fallen victim to its destructive effects; the current owners of "Videodrome," a conglomerate called Spectacular Optical, which wants to use the device for political ends and wishes to programme Max to give them his television station; and O'Blivion's daughter, Bianca, who is dedicated to spreading her father's gospel of trans-formation-through-television, and inculcates Max in the transcendent idea of "the New Flesh" as an apotheosis of the psychological changes occurring in him.

But although Max is manipulated by these exterior forces, he is not simply a victim, for what happens to him, and even the destructive acts he eventually performs, have an equal and perhaps even more authoritative source within his own personality. His fascination with the sadism of the "Videodrome" show, his reluctant but strong appetite for Nicki's explicit sexual masochism and his unresolved feelings about his own role as a purveyor of sensation (which are quite apparent through a layer of glib rationalization) are all clear indications of pre-existing instability and insufficient self-awareness. It is appropriate that Max is Cronenberg's first truly dominant protagonist because he fully encapsulates the Cronenbergian problem in himself: by denying the forbidden parts of his nature or assuming he can control them, and by experimenting with them without any thought of consequences, he ensures that they will rise up and assume command. Max is hubristic consciousness and raging unconscious locked in paradigmatic struggle within a single man, the culmination of Cronenberg's thematic movement from the social to the individual and his most complex and engaged statement on the problem of personal responsibility.

The precise characteristics of Max's hallucinations (the confusions of setting and of the identity of women, the organic television sets and cassettes and video images, the vaginal slit in his abdomen and the penile Flesh-gun with which he kills) are all embodiments of his inner personal conflicts. His destructive acts in the real world — four murders and a suicide — are inextricably bound with these conflicts, and he cannot wholly escape their moral taint no matter what the degree of his manipulation by outside forces. In *Videodrome* the balance between social and individual accountability is more complex and tangled than ever before in Cronenberg's work. The question of whether chaos is initiated by power-hungry institutions like Spectacular Optical, by crazed intellectual idealists like Brian O'Blivion, by an entire society whose basic reality is becoming vicarious or whether it springs from the swirling undertow within Max Renn is mirrored in the imperceptible shifts between hallucination and objective fact. (The question is epitomized in the mechanism by which the hallucinations are created: the "Videodrome" subsignal, transmittable under any picture, is one cause; but so is the presence of sadistic sexual fantasy in the viewer. Final responsibility is never clarified.) In the end, society and the individual, objective and subjective, become indistinguishable to almost the same degree for the spectator as for Max, and the point is made that for each of us the problem of life is unsolvable — even the dimensions of the problem unknowable — because none of the data coming in can be verified.

*

Before turning to Max himself and attempting to trace the lines of dreamlike projection emanating from him and colouring everything in the film, let us look a bit more closely at the outside forces acting upon him. Spectacular Optical is an extension and continuation of all the previous institutions in Cronenberg's films, from *Stereo*'s telepathic institute onwards, and has particular affinities with the menacing corporate anonymity of Consec in *Scanners*. Both Spec Op and Consec are powerful organizations engaged in military and scientific development with conspiratorial overtones, and both of them have co-opted the inventions of the films' idealistic scientists (O'Blivion and Paul Ruth respectively.) Spectacular Optical is particularly sinister in the wide reach of its influence ("We make inexpensive glasses for the Third World and missile-guidance systems for NATO," says Barry Convex, Spec Op's Chief of Special Programmes and the suave, flinty-eyed personification of its power.) The extent of Spec Op's manipulation of Max is extreme: in order to ensure his exposure to the "Videodrome" signal the organization has actually gone so far as previously to plant an employee in Max's business — his favourite technician and trusted right-hand man, Harlan. Having deliberately messed up his nervous system with the

"Videodrome" signal the organization goes on to record the exact pattern of his hallucinations with a special helmet as a key to manipulating him more precisely — to murder his two partners at Channel 83 and to attempt the murder of their enemy Bianca O'Blivion.

The role of Brian O'Blivion is even more clearly a continuation of those earlier mad scientists. Like his immediate predecessors Hal Raglan and Paul Ruth, he is the spokesman for the particular facet of the mind-body connection going haywire in the film. O'Blivion's primary idea is that television images are so widespread and penetrating that they have become indistinguishable from reality and indeed have begun to replace it. What takes O'Blivion out of the McLuhanite realm and into the Cronenbergian one is the alarming literalness with which he presses the notion of the physical effects of television and the "substitutableness" of video existence for real existence:

> The television screen is the retina of the mind's eye. Therefore the television screen is part of the physical structure of the brain. Therefore whatever appears on the television screen emerges as raw experience for those who watch it. Therefore television is reality, and reality is less than television.

O'Blivion is quite enthusiastic at this prospect, and his religious fervour to advance the process is evident in his establishment of the Cathode Ray Mission, a Salvation Army-like video soup-kitchen where derelicts are parked in front of televisions to "help patch them back into the world's mixing board." Nor does he seem particularly disturbed by his status as "Videodrome's first victim." He describes the growth of his hallucination-causing "Videodrome" brain tumour with something approaching zest, speculates that it is not a tumour but a "new organ of the brain" (a direct echo of one side effect of Rouge's Malady in *Crimes of the Future*) and exclaims:

> I think that massive doses of the "Videodrome" signal will ultimately create a new outgrowth of the human brain, which will produce and control hallucination to the point that it will change human reality.

This "next phase in the development of man as a technological animal" reaches its final stage as the spirit is translated entirely into the video world — O'Blivion is in fact physically dead and exists only in video form. "At the end," says Bianca, "he was convinced that public life on television was more real than private life in the flesh. He wasn't afraid to let his body die." This passing-over of boundaries, the transformation into something else, is what Bianca is referring to later in the film when she reprogrammes Max as "the video word made flesh" and dubs him a knight errant of "the New Flesh."

If Max is a victim of Barry Convex, Harlan, and Spectacular Optical, he is also a manipulee of Brian O'Blivion, or at least of Bianca, who blithely reinfects him with "Videodrome" signals by giving him encoded tapes on two separate occasions, and later quite calmly turns him from a Spec Op robot of destruction into a "New Flesh" robot of destruction, showing no more concern for him as a person than Convex does. Spec Op's brutal manipulation is motivated by cold expediency and power hunger, and Bianca's by missionary zeal in the service of (bizarre) spiritual ideals, but neither party is, or wants to be, in touch with the volcanic upheaval of sexual and moral feeling going on inside Max, which they simply tap in order to manipulate him.

*

But nothing in the film can be understood fully without reference to Max himself, and the Spectacular Optical conspiracy and the gospel of the O'Blivions are no exceptions. Max is not only overwhelmingly the centre of *Videodrome*, he is Cronenberg's first really three-dimensional character. Earlier characters — Rose in *Rabid*, Nola in *The Brood* — were complex by implication; Max is complex in fact and in detail. The intense interest hitherto displayed by Cronenberg in important secondary characters (e.g., Raglan's patients in *The Brood*; Paul Ruth, Darryl Revok and Ben Pierce in *Scanners*) is here invested in the protagonist, and furthermore a protagonist who is the absolute focus of interest throughout the film. In this respect *Videodrome* represents an advance for Cronenberg and a commitment to the notion of *character* rather than *idea* as a structuring principal. Max is endowed not just with a job and ambitions and specific relationships with people and a daily routine and a whole set of moods and behavioural niceties, he is also given a complex, multilayered inner personality, complete with contradictory motives (conscious and unconscious) and an extremely detailed range of perceptions, which work their way into every corner of the film. Indeed, if the film as a whole cannot be understood without reference to the exact nature of Max's character, Max cannot be understood without reference to every other aspect of the film, including those that at first sight appear to have nothing specifically to do with him. It is an entirely symbiotic relationship.

The cool, confident Max Renn runs a television station that panders to sex in *Videodrome*

What kind of a man is Max? On the surface he is cool, confident and energetic, an entrepreneur in life as in business. Independence and control are important to him. He is proud of his status as a maverick, thriving in his small and unrespectable way on the edges of an industry dominated by vast corporate forces — he likes to think of himself as a likable but cunning pirate, swooping down from nowhere and cutting out a prize, surviving by his wits and having room left over to show some style doing it. He dresses unobtrusively — perhaps in a manner that encourages people to underestimate him — in neutral colours and casual, functional styles that nevertheless express his sense of independence and his belief that he can impose his will on situations from behind a cleverly unimposing facade (they are in a way part of his pirate's false colours). He tries to charm everyone with his boyish arrogance, cheerful irreverence and conventional good manners; and he succeeds to a degree. His secretary, Bridey, is plainly attracted to him and wants to mother him in his bachelor disorder, Harlan is devoted to him (or so it appears), and sales agent Masha Borowski shows many signs of liking him and considering him special.

Everything in Max's world revolves around Max: he is a doer, not a sufferer; one who acts on other people, not one who is acted upon. He is constantly asking people for things — he asks Nicki for a date (very cheekily on live TV), he asks Masha and Bianca for information (and presses them aggressively when they are reluctant to give it), he asks Harlan for favours above and beyond the call of duty. He is constantly trying to get something from people, and he is confident that he will be able to get it. The film confounds this expectation of Max's that he can do and not be done by. He really gives very little in return. Bridey has to be content with occasional flashes of charm thrown her way; Harlan, too, is mostly taken for granted; and Masha is callously wooed by Max in his lust to find out more about "Videodrome." Both of the latter are quite hurt when Max does not recognize them as friends but only as people he wants something from. In more overtly competitive situations the aggressiveness underlying all of Max's behaviour comes out in small bursts. He often wears a slight smirk or utters a tiny snort of contempt or displays a sneaky grin of anticipated victory: he has the mien of a winner who knows he's a winner.

If this paints a harsh picture of Max, it is by no means the whole story. Max behaves as he does not only because he wants to, but because he needs to. He has a closed personality, distrusting softer feelings, unconsciously wary of becoming vulnerable, not knowing how to open up — even supposing he should want to. His strategy for dealing with threatening emotions is to pretend they do not exist. Emotionally, he avoids; intellectually, he rationalizes. It is not that he lacks feelings — either moral or compassionate or of raw appetite — he just doesn't know how to deal with them. What the film demonstrates is that this kind of closure and insufficient awareness is dangerous. Thinking that he controls his feelings, Max can only watch as his circumscribed emotions well up and overwhelm everything. He is opened up literally — and with a vengeance.

Max's chosen profession of sensation-panderer seems like an attempt to demonstrate his control over deep and dangerous instincts by showing that he can arouse them in others (with Channel 83's programmes) and yet not be touched himself, and furthermore that this pandering has no harmful moral consequences. Interviewed on the "Rena King Show" on the subject of Channel 83's offerings ("everything from soft-core pornography to hard-core violence"), Max is glib:

RENA
But don't you feel such shows contribute to a climate of violence and sexual malaise? And do you care?

MAX

Certainly I *care*. I care enough, in fact to give my viewers a
harmless outlet for their fantasies and their frustrations. And
as far as I'm concerned that's a socially positive act.

Throughout the film Max is unwilling to admit that his secretly
motivated, automatically rationalized acts have consequences, or
indeed even that they exist. His unconscious attraction to basic and
extreme forms of sex and violence is indicated even before he sees his
first "Videodrome" show, when he and his partners discuss the slick
and arty "Samurai Dreams" series submitted to them by the
Hiroshima Video (!) company. Max says:

I don't know. Soft — something too...soft about it. I'm
looking for something that will break through — something...*tough*.

In this respect the "Videodrome" show is certainly the answer to
Max's prayers, and yet during the first two pirated viewings arranged
for him by Harlan he refuses to acknowledge the electric surge of
response he feels towards its explicit sadism and simply ignores
Harlan's moral judgements. And, in a later scene, when Masha
expresses a similar disgust at the idea of the "Videodrome" show,
Max comes back with the easy remark "better on TV than on the
streets." (This is also the scene in which Max refuses to become a
producer of sensational films, and in which Masha describes him as
lacking "a philosophy." Max wants to fantasize and to play with
feelings, but he doesn't want to expose himself or to take
responsibility.)

*

   The "Videodrome" show begins the process whereby Max's latent
desires come to the surface, and immediately a second catalyst is
added: Nicki Brand. Unlike Max, Nicki does not deny her involvement in the chaotic liberation of unconscious forces. On the "Rena
King Show" she condemns the excessive craving for stimulation
characterizing present-day society, but when Max calls attention to
her stimulating red dress (the pirate strikes again!), she replies, "I
admit it — I live in a highly excited state of overstimulation." At
Max's apartment she goes straight for the sexual jugular, pushing
right past Max's tentativeness and layer of guilt when she finds the
"Videodrome" tape. Of course it turns Max on, too, though he will

not admit it. He is also reluctant to follow Nicki into whole-hearted enjoyment of these impulses. But he does follow her and discovers a whole realm of feeling buried within him; its depth and intensity are signalled by the appearance of the first of his hallucinations. As he sensuously pierces her earlobe with a pin, and they make love, we see them locked in sexual embrace within the reddish-orange-and-black "Videodrome" torture chamber.

As Max's hallucinations increase in number and power, the image of Nicki continually reappears to lead him past each new frontier (the "real" Nicki vanishes from the film, ostensibly on a trip to Pittsburgh in search of active involvement in the "Videodrome" show and perhaps murdered there by its controllers). The idea of her becomes for him a token of seductive warmth, of approval for the part of him that is restrained by fear and denial, of courage and strength and finally of feeling itself and even love. She represents insight into and understanding of him that he doesn't even have. (When Max comes to meet her at the radio station for their first date, she is talking to a distressed caller whom she accuses of lacking self-knowledge: "It's not your sister, it's *you*, lover — can't you tell? Isn't that why you called me?...You want help, you need help...I've got your number, haven't I?" These words might be addressed to Max.) Towards the end of the film particularly, amidst all the horrors and confusions of Max's life Nicki seems to him like an anchor, a haven. At key moments, his surrender to the hallucinated experience comes in response to a huge video closeup of Nicki's lips, hypnotically incanting, "Come to me Max...come to Nicki...don't make me wait" in a pouting, childlike, sexy voice that at the same time has the authority to command Max irresistibly. In the final scene it is this image of Nicki, this command, that lures him to suicide. In this guise Nicki stands for the happiness and the relief of giving way at last to feelings long kept in the closet. This reward for surrender is by no means the only consequence of Max's journey beyond the pale, perhaps not even the most important, but it is there.

Nicki is the embodiment, so to speak, of what Max desires in a woman, and it is interesting to note how she contradicts and connects with the other women in his life. Both Bridey and Masha have a sexual quality he is reluctant to recognize. The opening shot of the film shows Bridey on Max's wake-up videocassette easing him into consciousness with modest flirtation ("I have been called a vision of loveliness"), and thereafter she repeatedly expresses concern for his welfare. Like a good secretary she tries to keep him informed and oriented, to anticipate and fight off disorder in his life, but her ministrations extend far enough to suggest that the qualities that make her a devoted and loyal secretary might also make her a devoted and loyal wife. She tries to take care of Max, to mother him. Max's response is to take her for granted, but it is evident that he attaches a moral value to her in the scene where she comes to his apartment to deliver a Brian O'Blivion cassette. Her arrival interrupts Max's first contemplation of his handgun — the same gun whose phallic aggression is to be so powerfully symbolized later on — and he covers it up guiltily when he hears her at the door. When she starts poking around near his "Videodrome" cassettes he suddenly screams, "Don't touch that!" and hallucinates slapping her brutally across the face — except that in mid-slap she turns into Nicki. He is quite appalled at what he thinks he has done — because the surging impulse to hurt has come crashing from Nicki's world into Bridey's where it shouldn't be at all. Max fears that his secret desires will be discovered by decent Bridey, and he is shocked to find that he is unable to keep the two categories of desire and decency separate.

This point is made equally graphically in connection with Masha. Masha is an older woman who remains sexually alive, but though he likes her she is very much out of date in every respect in Max's eyes. The soft-porn show she is peddling, "Apollo and Dionysus," is absurdly veiled in the cultural respectabilities of its classical setting, while her garishly ornate clothing and jewelry are likewise meant to attract but seem outdated. The film cuts from the second of Max's torrid sex scenes with Nicki to the preposterous shakings and clankings of a belly dancer in the Turkish restaurant where Max meets Masha — a setting that seems to reflect Masha's style — and the jolting contrast emphasizes the distance for Max between her and Nicki. Yet a connection is made almost instantly as Max lights Masha's Turkish cigarette and a closeup signals his memory of the cigarette with which Nicki had burned her breast the night before. Max flirts easily with her ("We can take a shower together any time you say") in a way that shows his confidence in controlling the situation. But when he is hallucinating a whipping session with Nicki while wearing the Spec Op helmet, Nicki is unaccountably replaced as his victim by Masha; and upon awakening in the next scene, he finds Masha's dead body — bound, gagged, and bloody from his whip — in the bed next to him. He is devastated and saddened. Masha, like Bridey, is substituted for Nicki in a moment of sexual anger/aggression, and the substitution is unwilled in both cases, showing that the separate compartments in which Max keeps his feelings have broken down, and the contents are running uncontrollably together. He doesn't want to consider either Bridey or Masha as sexual, and in particular he wants to keep them clear of the deep, kinky side of his sexuality, since they are "good" women; but they get confused with it on an unconscious level anyway, and Max feels shock and guilt.

Max's attempt to keep the sexual feelings he likes while discarding the others is doomed to failure once his sexuality is truly liberated.

Another relationship that provides insight into Max's situation is the one with Harlan. Harlan is perhaps the only person in the film with whom Max seems to have real two-way communication based on mutual affection and respect, although even here the relationship exists within a boss/employee structure with Max holding the ultimate power, and of course later Harlan turns out to have been manipulating Max. Max likes Harlan's solitariness (he always seems to be tinkering around in the lab by himself); his unkempt appearance; his general air of being a stray-dog engineer good at his work and at not much else; his sly-pirate instincts; and his quirky sense of artistry and pride. In all these respects Max sees Harlan as a crude prototype of himself, and he responds not only to Harlan's loyalty and admiration, but to the sense that what Harlan is drawn to in him is just what Max most wants to be. He thinks of Harlan as a fraternal kindred spirit, and he particularly identifies with his zestful sneakiness ("You cannot fool de Prince of Pirates"). Max even responds to Harlan's awkward tentativeness, and the little half-defensive half-affectionate protective habits he has adopted, such as calling him *patron*.

Even more than Max, Harlan refuses to grow up emotionally. He cannot deal with strong, messy feelings, preferring to play at pirates in his lab (and elsewhere) and to sublimate emotional attachment. The phallic satellite-dish rooftop aerial connected to Harlan's lab and the screwdriver he is always toying with express a sublimation of sexual impulses into mechanical vicariousness. Cronenberg describes Harlan as "deliberately seductive in his cute little way," and when he comes to Max's apartment to corroborate Max's Masha hallucination he is nervously flirtatious: "Well, here I am, *patron*...camera, flashgun. What's up — you wanna be a centrefold?" But when Max explodes at him, he seems genuinely upset by the display of open anger to the point where he lashes awkwardly back. As soon as Max withdraws, so does Harlan, apologizing:

MAX

I'm not just fucking around here, do you hear me?

HARLAN

(*with a force he can't quite sustain*): Well, fuck you! I'm not just a servo-mechanism you can turn on and off when you want to. You want me to fall out of bed at 7 a.m. and act like an asshole, you tell me what I'm doing it for. Otherwise, I'll see you during office hours, *patron*.

> MAX
>
> You're right. I'm running like an express train here, I don't know how to stop. Meet me at the lab in an hour...I'll tell you everything, I promise.

> HARLAN
>
> (*tentatively*): I'm sorry if I freaked out, *patron*. (*he puts his hands on Max's sides*) I don't work with you just for the money you know.

> MAX
>
> I know that. Piracy is never just for the money, is it?

The final display of affection is the closest the two characters come to expressing their mutual attachment directly. What is underlined is how much *in*direct emotion is present in the relationship.

Max has some unperceived doubts about his own sexual desires, but Harlan carries this all the way to a total hatred of sex. He plainly disapproves of Max's enthusiasm for the "Videodrome" show, but it is not until the scene where his treachery is disclosed that that hatred is fully expressed. His speech here is full of profound sexual disgust. The feelings he has are categorized in terms of mess versus order in a kind of Fascist sublimation of aggressive (i.e., sexual) unconscious impulse into idealistic terms:

> North America's getting soft, *patron* — and the rest of the world is getting tough, very very tough. We're entering savage new times, and we're going to have to be pure and direct and strong if we're going to survive them. Now you, and this... cesspool...you call a television station, and your people who...wallow around in it, and your viewers, who...watch you do it — you're rotting us away from the inside. We intend to stop that rot.

This Draconian prescription for unruly sexual instinct may seem very far from Max's experiments in pandering to sadomasochism, but in fact Max's lack of sexual awareness and Harlan's sexual repression find an echo in each other. Certainly Harlan's adoption of Max's soft/tough vocabulary in the speech just quoted is startling, and his bitter, nauseous condemnation of Max's sexual indulgence is a dramatic reflection of Max's own resolved feelings of guilt.

This brings us to another crucial point: the fact that Harlan's betrayal of Max seems very much like a projection of Max's inner fears rather than a simple case of treachery. In a film where the objective veracity of everything is ultimately questioned, this line of inquiry is surely legitimate and indeed necessary. It can scarcely be accidental that the relevation of betrayal comes immediately after the scene at Max's apartment, with its edgy disclosures of friendship and esteem. Max is certainly subconsciously aware of and sensitive to Harlan's remarks about the sick nature of the "Videodrome" show ("for perverts only"); and the moral part of him — the part that wants to stop Nicki from burning herself with the cigarette and that is horrified at the involvement of "innocent bystanders" like Bridey and Masha — agrees with Harlan and convicts his other half of sin. Hence the peculiar force of the scene of Harlan's betrayal, where the alternating voices of Harlan and Barry Convex bore into Max with the impact of a dreaded reckoning or come-uppance. Max is not merely confounded in this scene, he is humiliated, as his secret desires are paraded, his rationalizations stripped bare, his hubris exposed, his precious "smartness" and control blown to the winds. It is a very dreamlike — or rather nightmarelike — moment, with Harlan and Convex harshly embodying Max's own conscience and sitting inexorably in judgement. It is as though *Max* is creating the moment, as though he is graphically imagining what Harlan really thinks of

Max and his video pirate henchman, Harlan, try to pick up the video signal in *Videodrome*

him. And following as it does on the friendship scene, it is as though
Max is reacting to the closeness by making Harlan into a traitor —
though this is not at all what the film is proposing literally. Harlan
accuses Max of using him like a servomechanism: now the tables are
turned, and it is Max who has been used by Harlan. "Good pirate,
that Harlan," Max says to himself at one point with real appreciation
and affection: now Harlan turns out to be more of a pirate than Max
ever bargained for. Harlan's treachery seems strangely related to
Max's unresolved feelings towards him: fear of judgement, fear of
emotional seduction, fear of closeness and of losing control. It might
be argued that on a literal level Max's paranoia turns out to be
justified — his buddy does betray him — but that is to ignore all the
other strands in the film dealing with the same question of Max's
detachment from his own feelings and unwillingness to open up.

What happens to Max in the "judgement scene," is that he is
forced to open up — or rather he is opened up like a tin can by
Convex, with ghastly literalness. "I want you to open up, Max —
open up to me," says Convex; and Max's slit opens, to allow Convex
to ram in a videocassette to programme him. What gives Convex this
power is his knowledge of Max's fantasies as recorded earlier on the
hallucination helmet; but in a more general sense it is his insight into
Max's "dirty secrets." To an even greater degree than Harlan did,
Convex in this scene seems a projection of Max's fears. His soothing,
lilting voice and his constant use of Max's name seem dreamlike, a
voice projected from Max's own mind (like Nicki's "Come to me
Max" and O'Blivion's "Max — I'm so glad you came to me"). In a
way, Max gives Convex the power to judge and control him, through
his rationalizations, his lack of self-knowledge and his guilt. All of
Max's weapons — his sarcasm, his counterattacks, his sneer of
contempt — are quite powerless to affect this man who controls him
through knowledge of his weaknesses.

Convex is a man who does for real what Max only plays at. He is
Max's corporate opposite: Max is a small-time capitalist, a pirate who
is in business for the fun of it; Convex is the smooth face of the large,
awesomely powerful conglomerate. Max plays with soft-porn "breakthroughs" and gets pulled in over his head; Convex actually produces
"Videodrome" — "real" torture, murder, mutilation. Max congra-
tulates himself on his boldness, but Convex is the really bold one.
Convex can handle the whole subject, manipulate it, without being
affected ("I just can't cope with the freaky stuff"). Max, (though he
assures Masha that "I stay away from the scary stuff") makes the
error of thinking he can sample and not be burned, only to be hooked
and overwhelmed. And finally, Convex is like a father — adult,
mysterious, powerful — and Max is like a child, who thinks he knows

what's going on but really knows nothing, and who thinks he is strong but is in fact only immature. It makes perfect sense that Convex should exert such power over Max: he is the one who finally calls Max's bluff.

Cronenberg has said that many of his characters have some of the qualities of medieval allegorical figures. Certainly a number of *Videodrome*'s characters seem to have quasi-allegorical functions. In particular, Brian O'Blivion, Convex, Nicki and Bianca form a quartet (two pairs) of almost totemic status who at various points act as guides to Max in his Pilgrim's Progress to hell. Convex and O'Blivion are competing father figures — the former calculating, realist, power hungry, antisexual, the latter passionate, idealistic, mystical, asexual. Convex is a castrating Freudian father, punishing sexual fantasy; O'Blivion educates Max about what is happening to him and emphasizes that Max must follow in his path. A state of war exists between the two (as between their two opposite related concepts "Videodrome" and the "New Flesh"): Convex has killed O'Blivion, and only his ideas and his image remain; in turn, his daughter Bianca kills Convex (through Max) — and Max is crushed in the conflict. Furthermore, both Convex and O'Blivion are hung with the trappings of historical culture: Spec Op's trade show is presented in the secular terms of the Renaissance, and O'Blivion's study is heavy with the decor of the religious Middle Ages.

By the same token, Nicki and Bianca are contrasting women figures. Nicki is erotic Aphrodite, steamy and languorous and direct; Bianca is chaste Artemis (the huntress), cool and remote, even her name signifying a kind of purity. In thematic terms, Nicki leads Max towards a full exploration of his suppressed sexual desires and a discovery of his body, and Bianca leads him first to an understanding of at least the context of what's happening to him, and then into a leap of faith that turns the forces of aggressive sexuality (the Flesh-gun) against the hated enemy and finally transcends (and also kills) the body. Nicki encourages Max's sexuality, exciting the wrath of the punishing father Convex and the disapproval of the male-bonding Harlan; Bianca, a Vestal icon of filial devotion (and herself a calm and wise sibling), encourages his spiritual idealism and allows him to conquer his sexuality.

And yet Nicki and Bianca are also connected. Nicki's radio station is called C-RAM, and Bianca runs the Cathode Ray Mission (C.R.M.) Both of them extend aid to people in distress — Nicki to neurotics suffering from excruciating family conflicts on her "Emotional Rescue Show," Bianca to derelicts adrift in a hostile society. Nicki simply overwhelms Max's doubts and fears and pulls him across a frontier into sexual experience; Bianca's "reprogramming" of Max —

itself like a sexual act, with its agonizing Flesh-gun erection, ejaculation and exhausted subsidence — is in effect a traumatic relieving of inner tensions and draws Max across another frontier, allowing him to kill his doubts and fears (Harlan and Convex) and find a "new flesh." In the reprogramming scene, furthermore, the image on the TV screen that begins the process is that of Nicki being killed on "Videodrome." (It is fascinating to note that in an earlier version it is Bianca who appears on the screen here, dressed as Nicki and with Nicki's three cuts on the neck.) And, most tellingly, the Nicki idea and the Bianca idea are finally unified at the end in the scene of Max's suicide: Nicki beckons Max across the last frontier into Bianca's world of the New Flesh where all confusions and conflicts are resolved.

This unification of opposites (a reworking on a higher level of the earlier confusion involving Bridey and Masha) is nothing less than a resolution of the primary mind/body dichotomy in all of Cronenberg's work, as the body (Nicki) and the spirit (Bianca) are made whole in a new state of existence — which may, however, only be death. The flames that leap up as Max raises the gun to his head are not only those of the sexual body consuming itself in conflagration, but also those of the purifying fire of spiritual faith. "The Eternal Feminine leads us onwards," says Goethe in *Faust*. This final moment is a culmination of all Max has done as Nicki and Bianca lead him onwards. One by one, each of his walls and partitions has been broken down, and after the horrors unleashed in that process Max wearily contemplates the haven of rest and wholeness at the end of the line — even if this may simply be extinction — and then, with solemn gravity, he goes to it.

*

It is time to speak a little more specifically of the horrors that propel Max to this end. As ever in Cronenberg's films, they provide the most vivid and striking moments in the film. *Videodrome* is in fact Cronenberg's most visceral film since *Shivers*: Max's abdominal slit is as graphically startling as anything in his work; and the Flesh-gun, emerging from his body covered with protoplasmic jelly and boring its way into his arm, and the grotesquely corrosive cancer death of Convex should be explicit enough for anyone. This is not to mention the Flesh TV and cassettes, the whippings and strangulations in the "Videodrome" torture chamber or the simple murders. Except for the latter, however, all of these occur, at least to some degree, inside Max's head as hallucinations. As an explosion of *body* into the outside world, *Videodrome* is even more restrained than *Scanners*; but on the inner stage of the mind (which is also the stage of the film to a great extent) it is amongst Cronenberg's most ravaging works; and the combination of subjectivity and graphic horror gives the film its special intensity. Max's hallucinations are introduced in stages and connected carefully with each of the several elements triggering them: the "Videodrome" show, Nicki, Brian O'Blivion and so on. The moment the film bursts past the boundaries of similar narratives is the moment Max's slit appears — *now* it is a Cronenberg movie, and there is no going back. The slit appears while Max is watching one of O'Blivion's tapes, just as O'Blivion is saying that hallucinations will "control human reality":

> After all, there is nothing real outside our perception of reality, is there? (*he laughs harshly*) You can see that, can't you?

At that point Max looks down and sees the slit, in stark reality.

The precise symbolic significance of Max's various specific hallucinations is difficult, perhaps impossible, to pinpoint, but there is no doubt that they are the physical expressions of his moral, and especially sexual, malaise. Sexual categories are overturned and conflicting inner urges act themselves separately out as Max develops a gaping vagina into which he thrusts a phallic pistol in a self-contained enactment of intercourse (or perhaps "self-abuse" would be more accurate). This slit is raped with programming video-cassettes, and he later gives birth to the transformed Flesh-gun from it — a surrogate penis and the instrument of murderous (sublimated sexual) aggression. These manifestations are the objectification of forces already seen earlier in less extreme form: the confusion of place and person, the "breathing" cassettes and TV sets, the bulging screen with Nicki's mouth on it into which Max thrusts his head. His visions become more visceral as the liberated energies escalate. Max's vagina is like a wound, and it is also the embodiment of his most sensitive inner feelings. After he kills his partners he holds the gun under his jacket next to his stomach, and Bridey thinks he is wounded there (she tries to examine the damage, but naturally Max will not allow her to). When he is reprogrammed by Bianca an image of the Flesh-gun extends from the television screen, turning skinlike and finely veined in the most explicit penile representation in the film, and shoots him in the abdomen; he collapses, and the screen now shows his abdomen pierced by bullets. (One is reminded of Amfortas's sexual torso wound in Wagner's *Parsifal*, cured at last by the Holy Spear.) And when Convex exerts the power gained by his knowledge of Max's secret urges, the slit opens to allow Convex to programme him.

All of these things signal Max's loss of control, a development that is accompanied by a confusion of categories on all sides. Image and reality, animate and inanimate, male and female, moral and sexual, internal and external, good and bad are all smeared together in a nightmare of disorientation wherein Max, battered and enslaved by one force after another, feels himself quite lost. This inability to distinguish self from the outside world and fantasy from fact is the ultimate punishment for Max, who has had so much invested in maintaining control and keeping categories separate. His unwillingness to understand his own makeup, his wariness of allowing other people to come too close, his need to feel himself the master of every situation (and every relationship) are in fact what set him up for the horrors that overtake him. There is a terrible justice in what happens to Max — and *Videodrome*, is thus like *Shivers*, *Rabid* and *The Brood*, another grim cautionary tale from Cronenberg.

And yet Max is not a particularly awful person. He has ethical principles and compassion, and his little self-deceptions are not much — if at all — worse than the norm. Max's condition is in fact the human condition, and like other Cronenberg films, *Videodrome* is making a philosophical point. But it is distinctive in the intensity of its commitment to a private point of view and also in its despairing wish for some miracle to bring wholeness at last. Before *Scanners*, Cronenberg was content to accept the dichotomy in human nature as unalterable fact — it might have given him pain, but there was nothing he could do about it. But in the high-spirited fabular contest of *Scanners* there emerges the idea that perhaps the warring oppositions in human nature may be somehow united. At the end of *Scanners* Vale and Revok meet head-on (!), there is a violent combustion and what comes out is a fusion of the two. The ending of *Videodrome* and the concepts of the New Flesh and transformation must be understood in this light if they are to make any sense at all. The hellish confusions of Max's situation are quite unresolvable on their own terms; only through a leap of faith to some other dimension can they be escaped. Let us hope (the film says) that the New Flesh, whatever it is, will bring wholeness, because the old flesh certainly isn't going to. The change in Cronenberg's view is quite apparent when we remember the catastrophes that arise in *The Brood* from Raglan's advice to his patients to "go all the way through" their feelings: at the end of *Videodrome* it is Nicki who is telling Max "you have to go all the way — total transformation," and in this equally extreme advice there is plainly at least the wish to believe that such a process may result in salvation rather than destruction.

The transformation in *Scanners* can be accepted without problem because of the wonder-filled science-fiction nature of the story; but *Videodrome* is a more sober case altogether. Although Cronenberg has said that for him the ending of the film is a happy one (he at once time contemplated a final shot of the TV screen after Max's suicide, showing Max together with Nicki, pleasantly nuzzling), he is careful to preserve a deep ambivalence in the film itself. Max's dereliction, his confusion and helplessness and the strong pathos of his plight are all plainly rendered; and if there is a threshold to be crossed, and not just a suicide to put an end to everything, then any joy and strength Max may feel in crossing it is counterbalanced by the fact that he has been programmed to believe in the New Flesh, is acting like an automaton and has to project an image of Nicki to lead him over the edge. The explosion of the television set, which disgorges viscera all over the floor, may signal an end to all the horrors, but it is also a powerful image of disgust and final regurgitation. Max blowing his brains out in the derelict ship is a conclusion at least superficially not so different from that of *Rabid* (Cronenberg's most protagonist-centred film before *Videodrome*), where Rose's body is dumped into the garbage in an expression of profound waste. The ending of *Videodrome* certainly has grandeur; but I am not sure how much real hope one can take from it.

*

The deep subjectivity of the film is achieved not just by passing on to the viewer Max's inability to tell hallucination from fact, and not just by the uncanny way in which the other characters seem like projections of aspects of Max's mind. The subjectivity is also, in a subtle way, greatly strengthened by the whole mise-en-scène. The colour scheme and the photography have a subdued richness unique in Cronenberg's work. The dominant hue is a kind of earthy, dried-blood orange-red — a visceral colour that invades the outer world as a fine counterpoint to the way Max's feelings take on physical shape. It is, primarily, the colour of the "Videodrome" show, with its clay wall and naked victims; and it is found in a multitude of other places, from the pizza stain smeared over a black-and-white photograph of a naked woman, to the rusted hulk of the condemned ship. Red and yellow suffuse the scenes in Max's apartment, especially when Nicki is present; and it is associated with her later in the film (she wears a red dress, and her hair is orange-red when she appears as a video image). The hallucination helmet pulsates in "Videodrome" orange; Max sports an orange-brown cowhide jacket in the later scenes. Reds are combined with black in the torture chamber, and that combination also appears in the most surprising places: in the red-lined black briefcase belonging to the Hiroshima Video salesman, for example; in the medieval furnishings of Brian O'Blivion's study; and in Max's black gun in its red case. Max's apartment throbs with organic shadows and coloured lights, creating an atmosphere of Sternbergian sensuality unprecedented in Cronenberg's work, while the pervasive camera movement evokes a sense of immanent and emerging feeling.

There is an opposite set of colours, too — though by comparison they are almost noncolours — representing the superficial order that is to be overwhelmed. The charcoals and greys of Max's costume, particularly in the first part of the film, signify his repressed and self-deceiving conscious self (but note his black dressing gown with red pinstripes expressing his private "secret" life). The spiritual O'Blivions also lack strong colour. Bianca dresses in neutral shades, and O'Blivion's television image is washed out. The "Rena King Show" and the C-RAM studios are presented in dull blues, pale greens and greys, and there is even a tiny motif of pastel stripes linking the TV talk show decor and Nicki's costume at C-RAM. The Spectacular Optical logo is in cool, bright yellow-greens, and there is much pale green and off-white to be seen in corridors and on walls in public places throughout the film. Finally, of course, all these colours give way to the "Videodrome" pigment in the last scene.

The movement in Cronenberg's films from a clean modernism of setting to an older, duller, more disordered environment is carried another step further in *Videodrome*. Indeed, there are only a few scenes (notably the "Rena King Show," the C-RAM studios and the Spec Op trade show) that are not characterized by age or mess or decay. The peeling walls of the Civic-TV lab, the rooftops and back alleys walled with dirty brick, the accumulation of junk in Max's apartment and in the Civic-TV offices, the heavy clutter of O'Blivion's study, the down-at-the-heels location and decor of the Cathode Ray Mission and the Spectacular Optical shop and, most powerfully of all, the condemned ship all darken and depress the film with their weight and intimations of chaos. The motif of dereliction, first peeping out perhaps in the garbage-truck conclusion of *Rabid* and in the brood shack in *The Brood*, and then articulated much more fully in the Cameron Vale and Ben Pierce characters in *Scanners*, is here elevated to the status of a major element. Not only are both of the organized forces pulling at Max (the O'Blivions and Spectacular Optical) housed in seedy surroundings, with the Cathode Ray Mission actually catering to derelicts, but Max himself is identified as one by Bianca ("You look like one of father's derelicts"), and he comes to a derelict's end amidst refuse and decay. It would seem that for

Cronenberg exterior disorder — the slow death inflicted by time and the real world — is a representation of inner confusion and uncertainty, and that dereliction in particular is a symbol for personal isolation and the inability to feel a part of the social world. Certainly this is the plight, in differing ways, of Rose in *Rabid*, of Vale at the beginning of *Scanners* and of Max at the end of *Videodrome*.

Another important motif that is largely conveyed by mise-en-scène is that of seeing. The idea of the video image is of course central to the film. The first thing we see is a TV picture; Bridey and Nicki are first introduced on television screens, and Brian O'Blivion exists solely as an image, as does Nicki later in the film. Video images are transmuted from passive to active things and change their viewers from active watchers to passive victims (one might paraphrase Nietzsche: "Look not too deeply into the television screen, lest it begin to look into you"); and finally video and actuality become impossible to tell apart. In fact most of the "video" hallucinations have no perceptible connection with video images: they are simply seen, by Max and by us. The seeing motif is echoed in the name and activities of Spectacular Optical (and Barry *Convex*), whose misattributed trade slogans — "Love comes in at the eye" and "The eye is the window of the soul" — are both literally applicable to Max's situation. The Spec Op shop sells eyeglasses, which Max tries on ("You're playing with dynamite," Convex tells him ironically), and the hallucination helmet records what is seen by the (mind's) eye.

Glasses are important and so is glass. Max's apartment has a series of thick, ridged, pebble-glass windows around its door (signifying Max's myopia?). The windows of both the Spec Op shop and the Cathode Ray Mission are smeared with grime (Max smashes the latter brutally on his way to kill Bianca and later in the scene rips down a *pane* of brown paper to find the Nicki-image being strangled). The door to Max's bedroom is made of clear glass — decorated with red paint.

Glass and doors are in fact associated throughout the film, and doors themselves constitute a motif. Metaphorically, Max passes through one door after another into new realms of experience — a voyage of discovery and revelation, though by no means a pleasant one. The door imagery begins when Max visits the second-rate hotel where the Hiroshima Video delegation is staying: down the hall, a man is pounding on a door and shouting "Open the door! You know I love ya! Open the door for fuck's sake!"; Max knocks at the door in front of him, and when it is opened the chain lock breaks off (obviously there is going to be trouble going through doors in this film — first they won't open, and when they do they can't be locked again). After he has killed his partners, Max ducks out the back door into an alley where, very strangely, some workmen are transporting a number of glass-windowed doors from one place to another (the doors, like Max's whole experience, are unhinged). In the scene of Harlan's death the explosion of his "hand grenade" blows a hole in the wall — a new door — through which Max leaves. The last door, on the ship, has Condemned written on it.

It is the multitude of cross-references of this kind that sets the final stamp on *Videodrome* as a dreamlike subjective experience. Max's first word to Nicki is "Cigarette?"; later she burns herself with a cigarette and offers it to him to burn her again. The cigarette in the next scene links Masha with Nicki. And the motif resurfaces in the final scene. The chain-link fence, which Max lingers by outside the Cathode Ray Mission on the night he goes to kill Bianca and is reprogrammed, is echoed in the chain-link fence guarding the waterfront where Max goes at the end of the film (he has to squeeze through its Keep Out labelled gate — another door). Max is fenced in, and the links recall the chains in the torture chamber and on the ship. Even microscopic details like the bag of orange Cheesies and the

The magnificent last scene in *Videodrome*: Max alone in the condemned boat just before his suicide

green bottle on the table in the Hiroshima Video room have associative connotations. The patterns are so dense and so subliminally presented (this is by no means an exhaustive list) that the entire film seems to float in them, taking on a somnambulistic air that calls the reality of everything into question. At the beginning of the wake-up cassette (which itself utters the first words of the film) Bridey says, "No, I am not a dream" — suggesting the possibility that she is a dream and so is the whole film.

The culmination of this imagistic atmosphere comes in the superb final scene — the finest single thing Cronenberg has done. As Max, weary beyond measure, the perpetrator of four murders whose significance for him would in a court of law be interpreted as clear insanity, arrives at the waterfront in his cowhide jacket, the dawn is breaking with a cold, grey beauty, He makes his way to the rusting ship's hulk; it is utterly dead and old and forgotten. He pulls open the iron door reading Condemned and goes inside. The colours are those of the "Videodrome" torture chamber — orange rust-red and excremental-brown — absolutely visceral but translated now into the deathlike dull brutishness of ancient cast iron. It is a place of ultimate desolation and death — the death of everything that had once been alive and throbbing — Max's death. Inside the compartment is the recapitulation of the whole film in terms of dereliction and uselessness and final decay. The gargantuan hanging chain and coiled ship's rope recall the chains and ropes of the torture chamber; an old iron-banded frame bedspring recalls the rectangular grate on the chamber floor. Max walks past these things and flops down on a wretched, stained mattress: the mattress in his apartment on which he and Nicki made love. His hands encounter an empty cigarette package (his brand, Nicki's "brand"), and a green bottle like the one on the table in the Hiroshima Video hotel room (the most amazing stroke of all, this, because of its marvellous trivality — *everything* is coming back). His life is finished. Max Renn, the confident, dynamic entrepreneur with everything under control and the world on a string, is a derelict and a murderer and an outcast — and shortly to be a suicide in this deserted garbage bin. The whole scene, with its perfect balancing of objective tragedy and subjective release, its majestic marshalling of so many of the film's reverberating ideas and motifs and its expressive flowering into the flames of both funeral pyre and phoenix is an overwhelming conclusion to the film, and as great an individual piece of cinema as I know.

*

There is one final aspect of *Videodrome* — another part of its "first-personness" — that I feel deserves a comment: the range of similarities between Max Renn and David Cronenberg the filmmaker. To begin with, there is a physical resemblance between the actor James Woods and Cronenberg (he even tries on glasses in the first Spec Op scene). Furthermore, like Cronenberg, Max is a purveyor of visual images. And the content of Channel 83's programming is sensational, like the content of Cronenberg's movies. Max has to endure a degree of public censure for this, as Cronenberg has had to (especially in his native Canada). From this perspective, the "Rena King Show" cross-examination is an ironic reworking of a specific situation Cronenberg has no doubt found himself in more than a few times. Max's glib comebacks about violence, sex, and imagination are later pinpointed as such by Bianca. Cronenberg has talked on occasion about catharsis and vicarious outlets for dangerous aggression; and it is a joke at his own expense to have Max say that his programmes are harmless or beneficial and then have him, in effect, eaten by his own television set. Max is "playing with dynamite" from the beginning, and he gets blown up. Far from being a "harmless outlet," the "Videodrome" show (which Max wants for Channel 83) encourages the impulses it is supposed to ground, to the point that they completely unseat volition and obliterate all moral control. This is made especially clear when Max visits Bianca towards the end of the film to kill her, and he numbly repeats his self-introduction almost word for word:

> MAX
> I run Civic-TV. I was on a talkshow with your father.

> BIANCA
> So it was to be you after all. You've come to kill me.

> MAX
> No. I'm Max Renn. I run Civic-TV. I don't — I don't kill people.

> BIANCA
> Oh, but you do.

Of course Max's remarks on the panel show don't really represent what Cronenberg thinks, since the whole movie is a conscious demonstration of the dangers of that attitude. But one must assume that to a degree *Videodrome* expresses Cronenberg's ambivalence about the material he is handling or at least his consideration of the hypothesis that, yes, perhaps he is playing with dynamite. To be sure, no Cronenberg film merely plays irresponsibly with potentially explosive forces. All of them contain a strong sense of the catastrophe involved in releasing the id's powers. I think it is true to say that for all the visceral energy in his work, it finally bespeaks a cautious and even a conservative philosophical temperament. Nevertheless, *Videodrome* remains a self-questioning film, and the intensity of its "first-personness" is an eloquent testimony to Cronenberg's painful involvement with his subject matter. In that respect it is a courageous work, and even its confusions make it more touching and honest. As I have indicated, many of the contradictions and false leads and smearing of categories are incorporated right into the structure of the film. But to the extent that this is not so and the film is simply confused itself, it feels like a result of the filmmaker's unwillingness to step back from his material lest it lose its hot immediacy and personal truth. To a degree *Videodrome* is a relatively unconsidered work. But what it gains in return for its relinquishment of clear thinking is a passionate directness unprecedented in the earlier films. The air of lucid observation and unflinching clinical detachment characteristic of Cronenberg's previous work is nowhere to be found here. *Videodrome* is a wholly engaged film, far more than anything preceding it, and it bears every mark of personal commitment, even down to Cronenberg's insistence (through his resemblance to Max) on his own subjectivity. Within the context of Cronenberg's development as an artist, it is a bold step forward.

Conclusion

Cronenberg's films contain a deeply buried knot of struggle at their heart. It is, of course, the conflict between emotional repression and emotional release (though these terms are somewhat too loaded in favour of release to describe Cronenberg's viewpoint truly). This basic theme is one that characterizes the horror genre as a whole — though it is hardly peculiar to that genre and indeed has an impressive artistic pedigree. Cronenberg's movies, in their distinctive insistence on body and in their lurid employment of sex and violence, are definitely a part of the horror genre. But as we have seen, the horror film as a form is a symbolic treatment of ordinary human conflicts, and the horrific aspects of them are specifically symbolic of the psychological violence of the struggle. In Cronenberg's work the particular ordinary human conflict is the central question of emotional involvement as such: whether it is desirable, how it relates to instinct, what its consequences are and what are the consequences of its lack. The question forms a kind of substructure underlying the horror dialectic in Cronenberg's films.

The topic may be divided into two aspects: what the films say about sex, and what they say about relationships. In the first instance, sex is associated with the raging body, with sickness and death, with emotional mania and chaos and also, on the positive side, with a volcanic liberation of inner tensions. The other pole is represented by social and personal order, by ethics and morality, and also, on the negative side, by an unrealistic and often smug denial of the power and vitality of sexual feelings. There is an intense counterpoint of the fear of losing control and the equal desire to lose control. Relationships, meanwhile, constitute a slightly different problem, though an overlapping one. Here the difficulty arises from the failure to communicate, which in turn arises (usually subtextually) from a fear of emotional risk and a consequent closed and self-centred personality. Once more there is an unwillingness to give up control, lest strength and all defence go with it, only here it is counter-balanced by a guilty sense of failed responsibility to other people (again often expressed subtextually).

It is notable that none of Cronenberg's male protagonists before *Videodrome* is at all sexual. There is not so much as a real kiss to be seen (except, significantly, in the case of St. Luc in *Shivers*, where the hero first refuses to kiss his girlfriend on the mouth and in the end has a kiss forced on him that changes his nature). To be sure, a couple of the heroes are provided with good alibis: Hart keeps trying to go to Rose in *Rabid* but is prevented by outside circumstances, and in *The Brood* Frank's wife is in a psychiatric clinic. But the pattern is there whatever the characters' alibis. One might also note in these three films the heroes' inability to accomplish anything positive. Indeed despite their good intentions they can only destroy: St. Luc kills three men, Hart manages one anguished and ambivalent embrace and in the end can only break the telephone in impotent despairing rage, and of course Frank's only effective act is to kill Nola.

Sex in these films is in fact vested in the female for the most part. The overtly sexy Forsythe finally wins St. Luc to her cause in *Shivers*, as Betts wins Janine to hers. Despite all the men on the make in *Rabid* it is Rose whose attacks most powerfully represent the sexual instinct, while Nola's raging emotional fires have a component of strong sexual possessiveness towards Frank. There is perhaps a connection between the relative exclusion of sexuality from central male characters, its ambiguous embodiment in central female characters, and its reification into a violence force that overwhelms from without (the parasites, the rabies plague, the brood). Even though it exists within the self, it is Other; and these films' attitude towards it is ambivalent. (Incidentally, it is this ambivalence that I would suggest Robin Wood is misreading as sheer sexual disgust and hatred of female sexuality in his critique of Cronenberg's films. Forsythe in *Shivers* and Rose in *Rabid* are both clearly attractive as well as threatening, while Nola's rage in *The Brood* is, if in no way attractive, at least depicted as springing partly from the ineffectuality of her father and her husband, and also partly from the irresponsible effectuality of her male doctor.) The struggle here, powerful but relatively unarticulated, is to express the conflicting feelings aroused by sexuality.

Scanners, entirely sexless, offers a respite from the struggle. But *Videodrome* returns to it in the most direct and responsible way yet. For in this film not only is the hero sexual and his sexuality very much part of the subject of the movie, but the attractive/destructive sexual woman (Nicki) is represented more and more as a projection of the *hero's* feelings. At the same time his sexual vulnerability (the slit) and aggressiveness (the Flesh-gun) are depicted not just as aspects of his own body but also as hallucinations — that is, as psychological problems within Max. Here, despite the sexual violence inflicted on women, there is clearly no animus towards them as a gender — indeed, Nicki and Bianca become the vessels of Max's deepest aspirations and tenderness. And insofar as there is any agent outside Max that can be held responsible for the destruction caused by loosed sexuality, it is either society in general or the patriarchal male (O'Blivion and Convex).

Relationships also describe an interesting arc in the features. There are essentially two male-female relationships in *Shivers*: St. Luc and Forsythe, and Nicholas and Janine Tudor. In both, the "triers" are the women, while the men are self-absorbed and more or less oblivious to their partners. St. Luc doesn't know what to do with feelings and simply ignores them; Tudor is so onanistically obsessed with his own feelings (the parasites in his belly) that he ignores other people. Janine's desperate attempts to reach her husband emotionally are fruitless (only Betts, another woman, pays any attention to her). And St. Luc finally has to be dragged kicking and screaming into sexual involvement. In short, male-female relationships in *Shivers* don't work.

They don't work in *Rabid* either, though it is not through any fault of the parties concerned. Rose's motorcycle accident is an accident, but two males (Hart and a camper-driving paterfamilias) are at the controls when it happens. She is operated on by a man (against his wife's advice), and when she wakes up Hart is not there to help her (again, only another woman, her friend Mindy, does anything for her). Hart feels anxiety for Rose, and also guilt about what has happened to her. It is almost as though Rose's destructive needs are released because Hart is not there to help her; in any case, they are released entirely without her volition. Long-distance communication, by telephone, is all that can be managed, and Hart finally smashes the useless instrument. What is ultimately expressed is hopelessness, and particularly a sense of powerlessness on the part of the male to affect the situation in any way.

In *The Brood* the central relationship has gone from one of male self-absorption (*Shivers*) or failure to help (*Rabid*) to one of mutual destructiveness. Rose's feelings of isolation have mutated into Nola's feelings of hatred at having been abandoned to her mother's aggressive feelings by her father's passivity. Nola's father is nice, but he isn't there when he's needed. The same may be said in a more circumspect way of Frank, for although we see nothing of what went on in their relationship before the present state of hostilities, he clearly tries to avoid the messy feelings getting thrown around and fails, also, to protect his daughter from trauma. No wonder Nola turns to a strong man — Raglan — for help. One cannot exactly blame Frank for his actions (or inactions), but the destruction that takes place is at least in part traceable to his unwillingness to confront the situation squarely, to a kind of emotional avoidance that strangely echoes the emotional encapsulation of St. Luc and Tudor and the practical impotence of Hart. But whatever the cause, the relationship has broken down teminally. It is a disastrous failure, but *whose* it is not easy to determine.

Scanners at last offers a male-female relationship that works — but at the extreme price of excising all sexuality from it. Vale and Kim Obrist are mutually supportive, they respect each other, they work as a team. But it is a friendship and an alliance of two innocents, kept artificially uncomplicated by the adolescent-mythic nature of the narrative. Only between men (Vale/Ruth, Vale/Revok briefly) is there a spark of deep feeling.

In *Videodrome* Max has no real relationships to speak of (his closest perhaps is with Harlan, a traitor). But in contrast to *Scanners*, this absence is part of what the movie is about. Once again Max is the avoiding Cronenberg hero, but here he bears the responsibility for his avoidance. His closed personality collapses in on him, a process depicted with far greater emphasis and detail than in St. Luc or Tudor in *Shivers*. He does, however, have yearnings for contact, seen in his behaviour late in the film towards Bianca and Nicki. But in neither case can the contact be described as a relationship, for Bianca inspires him quite impersonally (and he responds quite impersonally), while Nicki isn't even there except in his own mind. By the end of the film Max fervently does want to understand himself and come to terms with his feelings (a first for a Cronenberg hero), but he will be able to do so only by becoming an entirely different animal. Either a

miracle happens, or Max simply kills himself — these are the only
ways that his emotional inability to get out of his own head can be
ended. There are indeed no relationships in *Videodrome*; but while
that may seem like a step backward in comparison to the earlier films,
it may in fact paradoxically be a step forward, because it actually
confronts the problem directly, begins an analysis and, not least,
looks the feeling of despair and emotional failure underlying all the
other films in the face. Certainly it is a long way from *Shivers*, and
even further from the alienated emotional coldness of *Stereo* and
Crimes of the Future.

From this general standpoint, Cronenberg's work represents a
search for wholeness, first by articulating the absence of wholeness,
and then by beginning a process of restitution, or reconstitution. (The
"transformational" endings of *Scanners* and *Videodrome* are leaps,
still faltering in their different ways, in this direction.) The problem of
coming to terms with sexuality and with the difficulties of emotional
involvement in general is not by any means the only one explored in
Cronenberg's films. Even when it is present it is usually complicated
by, amongst other things, the equal and different problem of the
influence of society and environment on individuals, and· by an
intermittent philosophical pessimism — not to mention by the
symbolic exaggerations inherent in the genre itself. But it does seem to
me to lie very close to many of the energies that fuel his work and that
burst forth into such spectacular flame.

*

Cronenberg's stimulating career is of course far from finished. As
this is written, *The Dead Zone* is in postproduction, and it will be
succeeded no doubt by many other films, for Cronenberg is an active
and young filmmaker. If his career to this point is anything to judge
by, he is an artist to whom development and new means of expression
are essential. Thus, this commentary can hardly hope to be anything
other than a progress report. Each new Cronenberg film has cast much
light on the ones preceding it, and that process will doubtless continue
(perhaps we will only *really* understand *Stereo* or *Shivers* thirty years
from now). And it is quite likely that in 1993 Cronenberg will not
only be making very different films from the ones he makes now but
will also appear to be a different filmmaker in retrospect. I feel
particularly that *Videodrome* has opened up strikingly new areas for
exploration — but of course only time will tell about that. What does
seem certain from this perspective is that Cronenberg's originality and

expressive gifts must at the very least result in films that are full of interest, that challenge and that wholly repay our attention. He is a filmmaker with a rare vision of his own, and he has always followed that vision faithfully. From the earliest films onwards Cronenberg has struck a measure of artistic gold wherever he has looked. Surely we can expect a continuation of riches.

The Comedy
of Cronenberg

Maurice Yacowar

Canada's "Baron of Blood" is also our crown prince of comedy. David Cronenberg's films are as distinguished for their wit and humour as for their gore. Apart from the cerebral ironies of Michael Snow, he is our funniest filmmaker. Who but a comic would ever postulate a Canadian Academy for Erotic Enquiry? Cronenberg did, in *Stereo*. The idea of such an institute, of course, is comic only in Canada (pity).

As Alfred Hitchcock pointed out, comedy and horror are Siamese twin genres, joined at the nervous laugh. Infants laugh at what is intended to be a frightening "boo". Both genres trigger laughter. Horror may actually need a comic element to palliate the dreads against which it innoculates us. Moreover, both genres relish the overthrow of the forces or order, the freeing of chaos and misrule. The comic chaos of comedy is the white-magic version of the horror film's unleashing of the forces of night. Cronenberg could have been speaking for either genre, horror, or comedy, when he observed that "We all need periodic releases from the tyranny of 'good taste.' " In any case, Cronenberg's horrors include both the formal effects and the essential spirit of comedy.

There is a basic delight in seeing the fragile illusion of order exposed — in art. It's funny when a doctor in *Rabid* leans across the operating table to deliberately snip off the tip of a nurse's finger. It's hilarious to see the variety of ways those *Shivers* critters contrive to invade and conquer. And it is a comic energy that unleashes the demons of the id upon sleek, sterilized settings such as the Starliner Towers in *Shivers* or the futuristic landscapes of *Stereo* and *Crimes of the Future*.

Sometimes the characters articulate the humour themselves, even at its blackest. For example, the doctor in *Shivers*: "Look here. What have you got? A diseased kidney. But introduce a parasite to the body and what have you got? A perfectly healthy parasite." More often, Cronenberg's comedy comes from beyond the character's perspective. It expresses The Maker's view. So, a sweet little old lady will faint as the little critter climbs up her cane and burrows into her arm. We laugh. When Pierce in *Scanners* says, "It's my art that keeps me sane," *that's* when we know he's nuts. But that's where we can also hear Cronenberg's point of view — sincere, sane and straight.

This perspective provides an element of satire in Cronenberg's work, of criticism by ridicule. The army dumping bodies into garbage bags in Montreal at the end of *Rabid* strikes a political note. But the implication of the thalidomide and DES scandals behind *Shivers*, *Rabid* and *Scanners* makes more immediate points. Antoine Rouge's disease, "possibly a form of creative cancer," is the affliction diagnosed in all Cronenberg's horrors, the unforseen side effects of power, progress and our new liberties. We don't laugh at Cronenberg's targets here, as in traditional satire. But we sense a warning finger behind his laughing nightmares.

Foremost among Cronenberg's comic effects are his wordplay and witty neologisms. The puns betray a playful, literate intelligence (even though he did his English Literature degree at the University of Toronto). There is a real wit in the paradox of "underground airwaves" in *Videodrome*. Its literal impossibility points to the alternatives of political subversion and the subconscious. That hero's utterly irresponsible cable TV company is called Civic TV ("The television you take to bed with you"; First Choice?). The villain, Barry Convex (a barefaced, vexatious con) sells eyeglasses and missile-sighting systems. This combination of fronts merges the personal and the public, the social and the political forms of voyeurism. The company's slogan, "Keeping an Eye on the World," assumes an ominous range of reference in the film. The "Emotional Rescue" promised by the C-RAM (!) radio show is undercut by the sado-masochist implications of the heroine's name (and nature), Nicki Brand (played by the equally well-named Deborah Harry).

In *Videodrome* Jack Creley plays a Marshall McLuhanatic named Brian O'Blivion, who no longer exists except on television cassettes. The ultimate example of a person becoming a media personality or

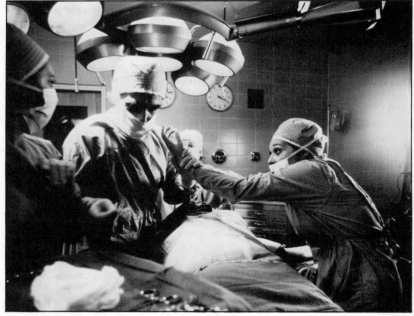

The fragile illusion of order is exposed — Dr. Keloid cuts off a nurse's finger in *Rabid*

image, he is sunk in the oblivion of the medium. Whether this fate is a tragedy or a glory remains the central ambiguity at the end of the film. Cronenberg finds more hope than I do in the call, "The flesh is dead; long live the New Flesh." This question of salvation is posed in the comic scene of the Cathode Ray Mission (successor to our Salvation Army hostels), to which the derelicts of the future repair for a spiritual recharge in private TV cubicles. (The reruns could give new meaning to the term "flophouse." The afternoon programmes would make it a soaps kitchen. I digress.) The hero's right-hand man is named Harlan, presumably in homage to Harlan Ellison, the sci-fi author also known for trenchant warnings about TV. Knowing Toronto audiences (not always a contradiction in terms) especially enjoy the scene in which the hero murders his TV partner, Moses (a Znaimer by any other name).

Such parody is common in the names of Cronenberg's characters. Dr. Emil Hobbes, the scientist who in *Shivers* liberates the flesh by combining an aphrodisiac with a strain of venereal disease, evokes Thomas Hobbes, whose materialist philosophy was used to rationalize

Restoration libertinism. His assistant, Rollo Linsky (comic actor Joe Silver), who complains that modern man's excessive rationality has cost him his sense of his own body, suggests Rollo May. The doctor in *The Brood* is named Raglan, appropriate for the notion of people wearing their feelings on the outside (like seamless, continuous overcoats, their hearts literally on their sleeves). Raglan's art is Cronenberg's: making mental things physical.

In Cronenberg's mirror, we can sometimes understand the character better by reading the name backwards. In *The Brood* Nola is really alone (as Cronenberg pointedly was at the time, in the smoking ruins of a marriage). In *Scanners* Revok is really a cover, while the hero is the vulnerable, transparent Vale. The villain, Dr. Paul Ruth, is not just ruthless but a dominant parent, assuming both paternal and maternal responsibilities, with none of the leavening sentiments of the feminine nature. A reversed Welcome mat and the motif of turning heads inside out invites this backwards reading in *Scanners*.

In a broader vein, the hero of *Crimes of the Future* is Adrian Tripod, a follower of the mad dermatologist Antoine Rouge, whose cosmetics cause post-pubertal girls to ooze a fatal fluid, strangely attractive but fatal. Rouge's Malady is not just cosmetic but the essence of sexual appeal, a metaphor that also pertains to the heroic Tripod. A mounted rifle echoes his name.

Cronenberg's extravagant imagery often takes the form of a bawdy joke. We warmly recall the blood-coloured phallic little critters of *Shivers*, the vampiric phallus that shoots out of Marilyn Chamber's armpit in *Rabid* and the vaginal stomach wound (which one friend in a burst of questionable taste has named "beaver belly") in *Videodrome*. In *Shivers*, when the hero talks to the little parasite bopping around under his skin, the joke expresses a chilling intimacy that the image straight could not convey. In *The Brood* Cronenberg takes a comic delight in having the elegant Samantha Eggar bite her mutant baby out of its sac and lick off its blood. This grandest guignol has a comic extravagance. In such cases — to paraphrase Lord Byron — we laugh that we may not barf. After all, there are two kinds of gag.

But let's go back to beaver belly. The image is so outrageous that we laugh at it. But as it is the film's most shocking and funniest image, its prominence compels analysis. When the hero begins to lose his ability to distinguish between the real and the TV worlds, a scar appears on his stomach. This is immediately an image of his vulnerability due to his living by "gut reactions." He is told that he is helpless before villains who have "a philosophy." The wound is also an image of the way man is physically altered by his mental experiences (as in *The Brood* and *Scanners*) and by new technologies (as in all the Cronenbergers). In addition, the wound's similarity to a vagina (any vagina) emphasizes the hero's ambiguous state. He has transcended the limitations of his old flesh in developing this female component. However, the wound makes him passive, abused, a receptacle, indeed turning him into the very thing he was guilty of exploiting before. When his wound bites off a programmer's hand, the image draws upon the archetypal fear of the vagina dentata. This vagina is not the bed of fertility but of death; hence the fetal dripping when a gun is drawn out of his womb. Its comic and shocking aspects make this not just the most striking image in the film but the core of its meaning.

Often the puns are a matter of just such physical imagery. In *Scanners* the sculptor Pierce literally "lives in his head": we see him inside a giant skull he has sculpted (so to speak). Of course, this image is central to a fiction about telepathy and mind control. So, too, the spectacle when the characters literally blow each other's minds.

Verbal puns become physical imagery — the sculptor, Pierce, "lives in his head" in *Scanners*

In one particular kind of wordplay, Cronenberg's neologisms project an identifiable future on the premise of the present. In his Somafree Institute of Psychoplasmics in *The Brood*, the "Somafree" combines the implications of the real Summerhill, Huxley's projection of a pacifying drug (soma) in *Brave New World* and the eternal illusion that "some are free." The "psychoplasmics" concentrates Cronenberg's basic premise in the film: that one's feelings can be made physically real. The union of such remote aspects in one word affirms the continuity between mind and body. Like the puns, too, the neologisms express his essentially playful spirit. They show an intelligence constantly reaching beyond the thing itself to metaphor. Cronenberg probably had to switch from biochemistry to English because the world of mere things was not as enchanting to him as the world of flex, of metaphor.

Beyond these specific gags, Cronenberg's comedy is often a matter of tone. In his first two features, *Stereo* and *Crimes of the Future*, a comic effect derives from the effete, detached narrators. In *Rabid* there is a delightful irony in the scene where Rose (Marilyn Chambers) tries to slake her thirst on cow's blood instead of human. Cronenberg gives the shot a painterly composition. The stuffed baskets of vegetables and the rustic, pastoral air are quite at odds with the action but indicate the heroine's traditional virtue.

As in any comedy, there are unintended gags. In *Crimes of the Future*, for example, Brian Linehan makes a prophetic/ironic appearance being interviewed by Adrian Tripod; the no-name Linehan character packages someone else's underwear in a transparent bag. *Plus ça change....* Then there is the immortal presskit background to *Shivers*: its special effects man, Joe Blasco, also did makeup for "The Lawrence Welk Show"! But in the final analysis, what really distinguishes Cronenberg among horror filmmakers who have made us laugh is that his jokes are intended. They bring us to the heart of his spirit and meaning.

Cronenberg's films are dominated by his spirit of play. He may quote the Latin *Timor mortis conturbat mea* (The fear of death disturbs me) as the creed of his films, but he approaches his dread subject with the playfulness of a drunk whistling past the cemetery. He's drunk on the elasticity of language, on the power of the medium to flesh out our most horrifying phantoms and on the thrill of being able to treat such heavies lightly. Just because you deal with death doesn't mean you have to be grave about it.

In this profound respect Cronenberg is the comic philosopher. Cronenberg takes the basically bifocal vision of man and of life. He can hold contrary perspectives at once. He can see the serious and the trivial in the same moment of the human condition, death as at once the most important and the silliest fact of life, man with his dream in the ether and his hangnail in the slime, man at once the magnificence and the speck. This is the philosophy of the comic.

Cronenberg's work lies within the forms of classic comedy. As one wag has shrewdly observed, comedy ends in marriage, and tragedy starts with marriage. The point is that comedy celebrates our sense of community and our confidence of rebirth. Of these marriage is a primary emblem. Conversely, tragedy deals with the disintegration of illusions of community and solace. Its focus is the doom of the individual. This is also the logic behind Charlie Chaplin's observation that comedy is long-shot, tragedy closeup. Cronenberg's horrors deal with this old form of comedy when he anatomizes our age of new freedoms, especially sexual. But Cronenberg strips sexuality of its traditional meaning of fertility. He strips the community of its familiar associations of warmth and reasonableness. Cronenberg pulls the comic narrative around to a vision of a maddened mob and a sexuality that is a terrible, compulsive disease. Fertility patterns have turned to sterility. In Cronenberg the classic comic structure leads to nightmare and despair. If we recall the good doctor from *Shivers*: health is the parasite. But the form is still that of classic comedy.

The genre also allows him the comic's assault upon his audience's complacency. Cronenberg's crowning joke involves the television metaphor and format of *Videodrome*. The film abounds with full-screen shots of a threatening, surreal, even animated TV screen. In addition, the film's most upsetting shocks involve the insertion of a TV videocassette into the hero's stomach. This sets up the film for a glorious afterlife as a videocassette. That's when this film will most directly upset the viewer. He will feel an itch in his stomach, his own gut reaction, when he inserts his cassette. Then its relationship will not be the detachment of flat image from film viewer, but something rather more sculptural, in which the imagery will work on the physical space it shares with the viewer and his own real involvement with setting loose the imagery. This chilling joy will provide Cronenberg's most profound laugh. It will be in us.

The Word, The Flesh and David Cronenberg

John Harkness

Let's talk about evil. In the horror film, there are basically two kinds of evil, with characters and actions falling on a continuum between interior and exterior evil. Interior evil is that created within characters (Norman Bates in *Psycho*, Michael Myers in *Halloween*) through an interaction between a warp in the characters' own psychological makeup and their relationship with the world. Exterior evil is an outside force that attacks what Robin Wood would no doubt refer to as the bourgeois patriarchal norms of our society — the devil invading Regan in *The Exorcist* is a good example, as are the vampires in *Dracula* or the shark in *Jaws*.

When the films of David Cronenberg are dealt with by critics, however, there is generally a basic methodological error made since critics tend to confine his films to the realm of the horror film. This limits the range of treatment because it ignores the fact that they are much more science-fiction films than horror, based on a speculative approach to events and scientific advances within the real world.

It is an easy mistake to make, because the pure science-fiction film has become increasingly rare in the past two decades (*The Andromeda Strain*, *THX-1138*, *Silent Running* and *The Forbin Project* are the only examples that spring to mind) and the boundaries between horror and science fiction have never been quite entirely clear.

Indeed, it is significant that of the major horror-story archetypes, Cronenberg's are the closest to *Frankenstein*, which has the strongest links to the speculative world of science fiction.

The important difference between horror and science fiction is that they operate on different continuities of evil. Science fiction's evil is not interior and exterior, but rather on a scale of accidental to intentional. Did the mad scientist create a monster or a human being, and which did he mean to create? When horror and science fiction intersect, one can almost graph the relationship of the two forms of evil. In *Alien*, the evil is quite intentional (the monster was what the Nostromo was really looking for) and socially interior (the structure of capitalism is using the workers on the ship to bring the monster, a biological ultimate weapon, back so they can exploit its power). In *Them* (the best of a series of nuclear big-bug movies from the 1950s), the monsters (giant ants) are created accidentally through nuclear mutation, so the evil is accidental and socially interior, as the bomb is an expression of the power of capitalism.

Thus Robin Wood's assignment of Cronenberg's films to the category of "reactionary" horror films (see page 24 of *The American Nightmare*) and his discussion of them as based in "sexual disgust" and "the projection of horror and evil onto women and their sexuality" misses the point because he is dealing with Cronenberg in the same terms as Wes Craven and George Romero, as a horror director who attempts to examine the nature of society's structure and its dehumanization of the individual.

If I take issue with Robin Wood, it is less out of dislike (Wood, with a group of like-minded fellows — Andrew Britton, Richard Lippe, and Tony Williams, most of whom studied with Wood at some point — is one of the few major critics to examine the subterranean side of the American cinema represented by exploitation filmmakers like Romero and Craven) than resentment of the way his quintessentially ideological approach to the contemporary cinema acts as a straitjacket on the films he examines. Politically correct filmmakers who attack the notions of bourgeois normality (Craven, Romero, Tobe Hooper, Stephanie Rothman) are by definition better than conservative directors like Brian De Palma and David Cronenberg, who by almost any critical standard are better filmmakers than the aforementioned directors.

Wood and company operate within a critical system that acts to limit their viewpoint to issues that deal with repression of alternative forms of sexual and moral expression in the structure of contemporary capitalist society.

It is significant that these concerns emerged in Wood's criticism after he came out of the closet (in the London Times Educational

Supplement in 1974) with his own gayness, for it is possible to argue seriously that Wood was a better critic when he was repressing his homosexuality. His books on Hawks, Bergman and Hitchcock are classics of bourgeois humanist criticism (using neither of these terms pejoratively), whereas the tone of his more recent work suggests that we should ignore that earlier phase of his criticism because it was presented to us under false pretences.

The critical limitations of the system come from the premise that the horror film is saying "Because of this, that happened." Cronenberg, a speculative director, is saying "What if...?"

The ideological tunnel vision of Wood's group ignores the component of science in Cronenberg's work, and that is the very element that lifts it out of the category of the exploitation horror film. It would be interesting to see what Wood now has to say about *Shivers* — "a film singlemindedly about sexual liberation, a prospect it views with unmitigated horror.... The release of sexuality is linked inseparably with the spreading of venereal disease" — now that the most explosive liberation of sexual energy, in the gay world, has been linked with the spread of AIDS and Kaposi's Sarcoma (which has become known as "gay cancer").

What I hope to do is examine the way in which science and scientists in the cinema of David Cronenberg create the possibilities of new worlds; the narrative function of his victims; the way that science and its relationship to its victims create an ambivalently disturbing alternative vision to contemporary life; and the way that Cronenberg's thematic concerns have evolved in terms of the intentionality from experimentation to accident, from specific to general malaises in the films themselves and within the oeuvre. What happens when the director asks, "What if...?"

I. The Road to Hell Is Paved with Good Intentions

It is worth noting that there are very few outright villains in the cinema of David Cronenberg. Dr. Emil Hobbes, who creates the parasites in *Shivers*, is attempting to break down the barriers in man, "an over-intellectual creature who has lost touch with his body." When he realizes what he has done, he commits suicide. Dr. Dan Keloid, who performs the skin grafts that become much, much more in *Rabid*, is attempting to save the life and beauty of that film's heroine, who has been horribly burned in a motorcycle accident. *The Brood*'s psychotherapist, Dr. Hal Raglan, is attempting to get his patients to bring their repressions and terrors into a physical manifestation that can be cured, removing their neuroses. Dr. Paul

The Brood concentrates on the problems of the family — Dr. Raglan gives psychiatric advice to Nola

Ruth had no idea he would be creating a generation of scanners when he invented his tranquilizer Ephemerol.

With the exception of *Videodrome*, which we will deal with later, the villains in Cronenberg's films are not his scientists, but outsiders to the central worlds of the characters — *Scanners*' Keller, who is collaborating with the scanner underground for his own power; *Fast Company*'s corporate manager, who fails to understand the obsession with speed that powers his drivers; the collector in the short film *The Italian Machine*, who buys a phenomenal motorcycle and puts it in his living room as an objet d'art. The crime in all these films is not ambition as much as it is stupidity.

The problem with intelligence, of course, is that it is human and thus limited. The failure of the majority of Cronenberg's scientists is that the implications of everything they do is never quite apparent. Unlike, say, a computer with a chess programme, they cannot work out all the implications of each move.

Cronenberg has said "I make no attempt to say that scientists go too far. I'm very ambivalent about the ecology movement, for instance. It's not at all clear to me that the natural environment for man is the woods — for all we know, it could be downtown Chicago. The thing about man, the unique thing, is that he creates his own environment. It's in his nature to try to take control of it away from chance. So in a sense my doctors and scientists are all heroes. Essentially, they're symbolic of what every human tries to do when he brushes his teeth.''

The irony, of course, is that chance cannot be controlled, and it is the accident that defeats human intelligence in every one of his films. The distance between what Cronenberg says his films are about (the intentional fallacy), and what people perceive them to be is immense. Were the people in the Starliner apartments of *Shivers* better off as repressed zombies living in a sterile planned environment, or are they better off as crazed sexual zombies in the throes of orgiastic hunger? Cronenberg views the spread of the parasites in that film as liberating. Yet the predatory sexuality of the various victims is presented in terms of the classic horror film, as if proving the dictim found on the wall of the doctor who is one of the film's centres of sanity: ''Sex is the invention of a clever venereal disease.''

Rose in *Rabid* is a zombie in a different sense, for she has almost literally been resurrected from the dead by a team of dedicated surgeons. The scientific explanation of the strange new organ she develops — a syringe in the armpit that draws blood from her victims and leaves them carrying a virulent form of rabies — is one of Cronenberg's great coups in scientific terms. When Rose receives skin grafts, the graft tissue is rendered morphogenetically neutral (all tissue is the same tissue), assuming that body will absorb the tissue, ignoring the fact that in intensive care the body is operating under a different system (being fed on plasma) and that the grafts may absorb the body into a new ecology.

In *Shivers* and *Rabid*, both the ''villains'' and the ''victims'' (both terms are to be used with extreme care) assume their positions unwittingly. The scientific intervention is a physical invasion that affects the brain. When Dr. Hobbes in *Shivers* and Rose in *Rabid* realize the nature of their actions the result is death because both commit suicide. The message is quite plain — knowledge kills.

This is reflected very clearly in the straightforward style of the two films. These are not horror films that delight in dark corners concealing lurking menace. Instead they are composed around rigidly controlled visual frames and taut Apollonian environments — sterile modern apartment buildings and hospitals, clean Canadian shopping centres and subways. In the American horror film, it is not at all surprising to find deranged slashers stalking 42nd Street or wolves in the South Bronx, for these are deranged environments, decaying and corrupt. Cronenberg's environments with their high-tech beauty are logical monuments to clarity and order, and the eruptions of madness and disease are consequently much more shocking. Even his casting of Marilyn Chambers in *Rabid* reflects this, for Chambers, all muscle and sinew, is the most high-tech of all the porn queens, a product of self-design (this is clearly a lady who spends a lot of time in the gym). The film would have been very different had he been allowed to follow his original casting of Sissy Spacek in the lead.

II. Children of Rage

The relationships in *Scanners, The Brood* and *Stereo* reverse the terms of *Shivers* and *Rabid* in two major ways.

First, the films move from the relative freedom of the rootless characters of *Shivers* and *Rabid* into the heart of the basic unit of our society — the family. Second, the emphasis shifts from the effects of the body on the mind to the effects of the mind on the body.

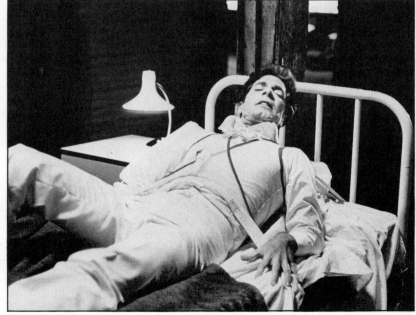

One of Cronenberg's children of rage — Cameron Vale in *Scanners*

Almost as importantly, there is a difference in the type of science involved. Dr. Raglan in *The Brood* and Dr. Ruth in *Scanners* do not intervene nearly as radically in the biology of the human body as did their predecessors (*Stereo*, Cronenberg's first, experimental, feature film, is somewhat different, and is included in this discussion because it stands as a rough draft for *Scanners*). There is no surgery in *The Brood* or *Scanners*. Both films deal with a sort of telepathic murder.

The Brood is Cronenberg's version of the white-bread melodrama (he himself has described it as his own version of *Kramer vs. Kramer*), and the genre is concerned with the violation of privileged middle-class territory by unbearable emotions, usually centred on the loss and recovery of a child. (cf. *Ordinary People*, *Without a Trace*, *Kramer vs. Kramer*, *Table for Five*).

As a psychiatrist, Dr. Hal Raglan is doing exactly what he is supposed to do — help people bring out their repressed emotions and conflicting desires. His tragedy is that he succeeds all too well, and being one of the few characters in Cronenberg's work to suffer from hubris he has no idea when to stop. Confronted with mad Nola Carveth, whose husband has institutionalized her because he fears for the safety of their daughter, he uncovers the bruised, violent soul of a child abused by her mother and ignored by a weak, ineffectual father. While his other patients remain attached to their violent neuroses — one develops a series of welts on his body, another a set of lymphatic enlargements that dangle from his neck like the wattles of a turkey — Nola is his prize patient because she produces actual children, monstrous simulacra without retinas, teeth, speech, sexuality or navels. They are, quite literally, manifestations of her rage (they are short-lived) who are connected to her not by an umbilical cord but by a mental link that directs them against those she sees threatening her — her mother and father, a pretty schoolteacher her husband finds attractive and ultimately her doctor.

There has been much research on the effects of emotion on our physical beings — calmness and tranquillity seem to be related to longevity almost as surely as natural foods and physical exercise — in which case *The Brood* has a beautiful perverse logic. If a healthy mind can help the maintenance of a healthy body, cannot the forcing of sick emotions to the surface cause physical changes?

Yet Dr. Raglan is not the villain of the piece. The villain is Nola's own family and the uncomprehending decency of her husband, whose job is restoring old homes (a nicely pointed bit of symbolism). In *The Brood*, science is only able to discover and awaken monsters; the seeds are planted deep withing the characters themselves, and Nola contains so many seeds that only death can cure her. *The Brood* demonstrates the way that the family can serve as a source of evil and delusion. As Nola's mother remarks, "Thirty seconds after you're born you have a past; sixty seconds after, you start lying to yourself about it."

Like most of the characters in *The Brood*, *Scanners*' Dr. Paul Ruth is a master of self-deception, believing that the generation of superhuman telepaths created by his sedative Ephemerol (designed for pregnant women) are capable of creating an era of a new renaissance in human society.

He simultaneously gathers unto himself the guilt of having created them, clutching it to himself like a treasure. He seems to ignore the strong possibility that the scanners may not have been created by Ephemerol but, like Nola Carveth's monsters, may have been released by his action. It is no accident that the beginning of the "scan tone" heard on the soundtrack when one of the scanners unleashes his power sounds uncannily like the creaking open of a huge iron door, suggesting that when the scanners were created it was not a deformation of the brain that produced their power but the "unlocking" of a part of that organ not normally used by human beings.

In a very real sense, both Cameron Vale and Darryl Revok in *Scanners* and Nola's brood are children of rage, one set released chemically and the other through pure mental energy. This is quite different from the artificial telepaths in *Stereo*, who are created surgically and locked into symbiotic and intense telepathic relationships during their stay at the Canadian Academy for Erotic Enquiry, where Luther Stringfellow's motto is, "If there can be no love between the researcher and the subject, there can be no experiment."

Intriguingly, the created telepaths in both films develop pathological symptoms — an inability to deal with the flood of information received by their minds and a tendency towards self-destruction. Both Darryl Revok and one of the telepaths in *Stereo* have drilled holes in their foreheads to relieve the pressure of having all those voices in their heads.

Of course, Dr. Ruth is not merely a metaphoric father to Vale and Revok but their literal father. That there is no mother physically present and his oddly androgynous name — masculine forename, feminine surname — suggest that his sons were not mothered at all, the same way that Nola Carveth's brood has no literal father. Consequently Vale and Revok's competition is not merely between the dream and the nightmare of a scanner society but is shot through with sibling rivalry and an increasingly Oedipal relationship with the father. In addition, Ruth as head of the scanner programme at Consec suggests a domineering father unwilling to admit to the adulthood of his children; thus, Revok's rebellion is as Oedipal an action as Nola Carveth's responsibility for the death of her own mother and father (who are responsible for Nola's rage — an endless circle of guilt).

The sleep of reason breeds monsters, and in *Shivers*, *Rabid*, *The Brood* and *Scanners* the monsters function in a world of appetite, desire and murder that is the absolute reverse of the rationality that led to their creation.

Yet from these films, it is difficult to understand precisely in what direction Cronenberg is moving. His overtly Cartesian concerns and his fascinated horror at the spectacle of physical decay are quite evident. While the technological aspect of scientific intervention is present, it is not nearly as evident as in his most recent film, *Videodrome*, which finally comes face to face with the concern that is at the heart of Cronenberg's world — the interface between the human and the inhuman, between biology and the other sciences.

III. The Evolution of Man as a Technological Animal: Videodrome

If *Videodrome* is David Cronenberg's masterpiece, it is because its narrative confusion and profusion conceals a driven, inexorable logic. Max Renn, a Toronto television entrepreneur with a taste for the bizarre (mostly prime-time sex and violence), discovers a strange television programme featuring nothing but torture and murder, emanating from a satellite signal. He assigns his in-house video pirate, Harlan, to discover the location of the signal and a sales agent to buy it.

What he does not realize is that implanted in this "Videodrome" signal is an encoded message that works directly on his brain, leading to massive, hyperrealistic hallucinations and eventually to physical mutation.

Investigating, he discovers a set of interlocking conspiracies involving "Videodrome," which is attempting to reorder the morality of society, and a counter-conspiracy led by Bianca O'Blivion, daughter of Brian O'Blivion, who created "Videodrome," attempting to liberate society and move man to a higher state of evolution through integration with the machinery and content of television.

Locked inside what Cronenberg has called the "paranoid inventiveness" of Max Renn, we watch as he may or may not commit murder, may or may not commit suicide, may or may not have a video programme inserted into a strange, vaginalike organ that develops in his stomach.

The inexorable logic of *Videodrome* is that the illusion is the reality, and when dealing with a medium as insidious as television, it doesn't make any difference which is which. One can interpret the narrative in any way and find no textual clues to deny any possible reading. Is Nicki Brand, the radio personality that Renn falls in love with, an agent or a victim of "Videodrome"? Is Bianca O'Blivion an enemy of "Videodrome" or part of a struggle for power within the conspiracy that is using Max Renn to eliminate her rivals?

Max Renn's suicide — the final scene of the film — is equally ambiguous. What leads him to suicide is the promise of rebirth into a more highly evolved state — the next stage in the evolution of man as a technological animal — but there is no guarantee of this rebirth, which suggests that Renn, whose dying words are "Long live the New Flesh," may be the first martyr of a new religion.

One of the most interesting elements of *Videodrome* is the fact that while there is overtly evil scientific activity for the first time (Barry Convex and Harlan are explicitly turning Max into a monster that they can direct), the film also presents the first victim who is a witting accomplice to his own destruction. Were Max Renn not interested in the pornographic violence that his television station peddles to the public, he would not be hooked into the "Videodrome" signal. Were he not fascinated by the changes happening in his own body, he would not continue to view the signal. While his first murders, those of his partners, are done under the compulsion of "Videodrome," his second murders, those of Harlan and Convex, are committed as acts of vengeance: while the actions are programmed by Bianca, Max clearly enjoys these murders as he does not enjoy those of his partners.

Despite its narrative and moral confusion, *Videodrome* serves to clarify the relationships of science to man, destruction to creation and man to society in the works of Cronenberg. There is little of good and evil in the world. There is accident and evolution, whereby creation can become destruction, villains become victims (often the first victims), and victims can turn the tables with frightening suddenness.

The connection between science and evil is a perverse one, almost entirely separate from intention, and society is less important by far than individual morality. What anti-Cronenbergians who attack his films on social grounds fail to see is that his work is not so much about present society and its discontents but about alternative social structures based on our world.

It is an essentially visionary world that would be capable of arising from our own, and while Cronenberg publicly expresses his belief in man as a technological animal, the bloody fear and mutant desires of the films are deeply ambivalent towards these changes. Science can create (or unleash) a new race of beings without knowing what those beings are capable of — and unaware of the potential of that race for self-destruction. It is a world fully cognizant that every human endeavour, every human institution and every human relationship is a two-edged sword and that good turns to destruction in a blink of the eye. It a world that reflects the incoherence of reality (explain, if you disagree, the logic to be found in mass murder, nuclear weapons, starvation, television and bureaucracy) and thus strikes at the heart of the way our world works.

This article first appeared in *Cinema Canada* No. 97, June 1983.

A Canadian Cronenberg

Piers Handling

David Cronenberg's films are looked upon as aberrations in the cinematic landscape of this country: stylistically and imaginatively the films apparently do not belong. Formally, Cronenberg finds himself working within genres — horror and science fiction — that are totally alien to our artistic tradition. Beneath the obvious excesses inherent in these genres it has been difficult to discern Cronenberg's thematic concerns; most critical reaction has been so obsessed with the blood and gore of parasites or exploding heads as to be heedless of what the films are saying to us. This has been unfortunate; the tone of critical response has been set by Marshall Delaney's (alias Robert Fulford) vituperative review of *The Parasite Murders* in *Saturday Night*. Critically, Cronenberg has never really recovered from this article in Canada. His reputation in Europe, England and the United States is established, and a devoted coterie of admirers write about his work with great admiration. This article does not pretend to be an apology for the films. Instead, it will attempt to situate Cronenberg as a Canadian filmmaker, touching on a number of points to try to clarify some of the imaginative bases of his cinema.

The overwhelming artistic tradition within which the Canadian artist functions is realist. Realism has informed our literature, our painting, our theatre, our television and our filmmaking. Cinema in this country is virtually synonymous in many people's minds with the documentary film. Even our fictive creations are born out of this soil. It is a heritage that has an extensive history, and it stretches back through most of our filmmaking endeavours, from Richard Benner's *Outrageous!*, to Michel Brault's *Les ordres*, Don Shebib's *Goin' Down the Road*, Don Owen's *Nobody Waved Good-bye* and further back into the early part of the century — *Back to God's Country*, *The Viking* and *The Silent Enemy*. With their particular form of narrative construction, rejection of studio shooting and use of actual events (historic and personal) they are thinly veiled documentaries, portraits of real people living in a recognizable world, as remote from the celluloid fantasies of Hollywood's Luke Skywalkers and Supermans as can be imagined. We have become highly adept at making docu-dramas, fictional works based on real events. Peter Pearson's CBC film *The Tar Sands* was so successful in its representation that Alberta Premier Lougheed sued the corporation for damages and won his case! The realist or documentary tradition is central to our imagination as Bruce Elder notes:

> According to one of the most widespread convictions concerning Canadian art, the quintessential feature of our cultural tradition is the activity of documenting the landscape. Canadians, it is said, have found themselves in an alien — indeed a hostile and somewhat frightening — landscape; consequently Canadian artists have assumed the task of presenting us with an image of the landscape so that its otherness might, if not be overcome, at least be understood. For this reason, the documentary image — an undistorted image that is faithful to the object it represents — has a place of great importance in Canadian art. [1]

The documentary tradition in Canadian film was not totally due to John Grierson's influence and his creation, the National Film Board, but it was certainly consolidated by him. Robert Fulford in a recent article [2] traced the tradition back to the nineteenth century, to Methodism and Egerton Ryerson, the great preacher, by way of the educational system, the United Church, and the CCF and NDP parties, who carried this thinking into the political arena. Grierson's philosophy was essentially educative and informative in nature. It proposed that the cinema could be used as a teaching device in the broadest sense, giving people an enlarged understanding of the world that they inhabited. All this was of course totally antithetical to the

---

1. Bruce Elder. "The Canadian Avant-Garde." Canadian Images Programme Book, Peterborough, 1983, p. 27.
2. Robert Fulford. "We need to liberate ourselves from chains of puritan conscience." *Toronto Star*, 2 April 1983. p. C5.

escapist, entertainment cinema emanating from Hollywood, especially at the time that Grierson was writing, the thirties.

The realist tradition deserves a great deal of attention when one approaches Canadian cinema. It both provides the basis for the documentary film and the inspiration for our fictional cinema. While the tradition has been predominant, it could be argued that it has also been stifling. Fulford quotes a sentence from Robertson Davies that helps situate Cronenberg in all this:

> We live in a country where the depths of the spirit are too often sealed wells, and where the human psyche which is the womb and matrix of all great art, including poetry and great fable, is regarded with mistrust.

While the realist heritage allows work to be rooted in an identifiable social context, it also has its disadvantages. In its faithful adherence to reality it can lapse into positions that verge on determinism. In other words it depicts social and political relationships as they are, not as they can be, and there is often something immutable about this reality. Change, or the possibility of change, is significantly not felt within the majority of these films. Reality seems fixed within patterns that are beyond the power of the individual to influence. Powerlessness is often the feeling that we take away from these films.

Few have challenged the realist tradition. Who even remembers films like René Bonnière's *Amanita pestilens* or Morley Markson's *The Tragic Diary of Zero, the Fool* and *Monkeys in the Attic*. Those who have worked against the dominant practice have suffered the ignominy of total rejection. It seems that fantasy and dream, often with a strong desire for change attached to these visions, has no place in our films. Most recently, women's cinema has gravitated in this direction, perhaps in reaction to the essentially patriarchal nature of the realist tradition. Dream and fantasy, which implicitly challenge the underlying ideology of realism, can allow for the potential of change and rebellion. Mireille Dansereau explores this tension brilliantly in *La vie rêvée*, while other filmmakers like Patricia Gruben (*Sifted Evidence* and *The Central Character*), Joyce Wieland (*The Far Shore*) and Anne Claire Poirier (*Les filles du Roy* and *Mourir à tue-tête*) have also incorporated this dialectic into their films.

Cronenberg would seem to stand outside the realist tradition. His interest in the subconscious and its hidden depths has led him away from a strict observation of, and adherence to, surface reality. When the unconscious is given a form, it is as a grisly parasite in *Shivers*, a proboscis growing out of a woman's armpit in *Rabid*, a family of genderless, angry children in *The Brood*, telepathic power that can explode heads in *Scanners*, or the subjective hallucinations in which a gun merges into the hand that holds it in *Videodrome*. Reality for Cronenberg is immediately divisible into two, subjective and objective or internal and external, perceptions of it. While this schism is evident in almost all his work, it forms the central questions of his first two features, *Stereo* and *Crimes of the Future*. *Stereo* in particular posits a world where the gap between objective and subjective reality, what we see and what we hear, image-track and soundtrack, is irreconcilable. Knowledge is completely undermined. The world remains unknowable and mysterious. When Antoine Rouge reincarnates himself as a little girl at the end of *Crimes of the Future*, his disciple Adrian Tripod can only marvel at this magical moment. It cannot be accounted for. Almost all of *Videodrome* is structured around this principle of epistemological uncertainty. Reality and illusion become indistinguishable from each other.

But if Cronenberg stands apart from this pervasive tradition of realism because of his fascination with the subconscious, has he also managed to break away from the central concerns and characteristics that have developed out of this tradition? If he has resisted the dominant aesthetic (partially through his interest in excess and release), has he also broken away from the imaginative continuum that one can trace in Canadian cinema?

Much of Cronenberg's work reveals a consciousness alienated from the world. In many of the films, architecture becomes the landscape that in so much Canadian art is seen as hostile and threatening. *Stereo* and *Crimes of the Future* use the sterile concrete constructions of modern architecture to suggest a world that has lost touch with itself. The same can be said of the Starliner Towers in *Shivers*, the Keloid Clinic in *Rabid*, the Somafree Institute of Psychoplasmics in *The Brood*, the Consec complex in *Scanners*, and even the concept of Spectacular Optical in *Videodrome*. All of these environments are dehumanizing and alienating. They do not bring people together. They also presume order and control, yet nothing could be further from the truth. Beneath the appearance of order, repressed forces of sexuality, passion and desire are lurking, waiting to be released on an unsuspecting society. It is at this moment that Cronenberg moves furthest away from the realist tradition. When the forces of the unconscious, the Freudian id, are unleashed, it is to ravage the world of apparent order. This impulse ranges from the telepathic experiments in *Stereo*, which end in suicide, physical violence and self-mutilation, through the infected multitudes of *Shivers* and *Rabid*, who wreak havoc upon the world, to Nola's brood who also kill and destroy, Darryl Revok in *Scanners*, who engages in a form of telepathic warfare, until we arrive at the destructive hallucinatory

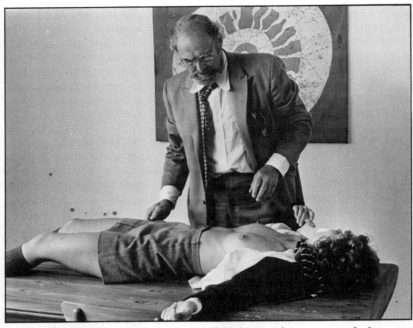

One of Cronenberg's scientists, Dr. Emil Hobbes, releases a sexual plague on the world in *Shivers* by experimenting on a woman

world of Max Renn's fantasies in *Videodrome*.

Cronenberg's world is full of this continual dialectic tension, incorporating the dualities of good and evil, the mind and body, the rational and the irrational, the id and the superego, liberation and repression. This tension is translated structurally into themes that are commonplace in a great deal of Canadian cinema. In some, the dialectic translates into the struggle between the individual and the community (Luther Stringfellow versus the telepathic patients who form themselves into a community to exclude him in *Stereo*; Max Renn wandering between the conflicting powers of Spectacular Optical and Brian O'Blivion's Cathode Ray Mission in *Videodrome*; or Frank Carveth taking on society in his struggle to wrest control of his daughter away from his wife in *The Brood*). In *Scanners*, *Rabid* and *Shivers* we are shown couples who confront communities (Cameron Vale and Kim Obrist versus Consec and Revok's gang, Hart and Rose wandering through a society gone mad, and finally the two couples of *Shivers*: Nick and Janine, and Dr. Roger St. Luc and nurse Forsythe confronting the infected apartment dwellers). Our cinema is full of these imaginative structures. Claude and Barbara of *Le chat dans le sac* and Peter and Julie of *Nobody Waved Goodbye* sired a generation of similar characters whose struggle with their society provided the thematic groundwork to express a number of Canadian concerns. More often than not the independence of the individual is destroyed (*Paperback Hero, Réjeanne Padovani, Red*), or the fusion that the couple represents, often between contradictory forces, is not allowed to take place or is ruptured (*The Apprenticeship of Duddy Kravitz, Goin' Down the Road, A Married Couple, The Act of the Heart*). Cronenberg's couples find themselves in a similar predicament. Holism is denied. Fragmentation and disintegration predominate. Whether we see Stringfellow, Max Renn or the aforementioned couples, the exterior world denies them access to each other or to the community.

The *Brood* is the most pessimistic of them all, being predicated on the abolition of the couple before a form of normality and health can be restored. *Rabid* is scarcely less bleak; the struggle that Rose and Hart undergo to preserve their relationship is as deeply felt as that of Joey and Betts in *Goin' Down the Road*. The most optimistic vision is the potential coupling of Cameron Vale and Kim Obrist in *Scanners*, but the ambiguity of the final shot, with Vale's voice coming from the evil Revok's body after the scanning battle, points towards an uncertain future.

Over all these painful struggles stands the Cronenberg father figure, more often than not a benign but misguided scientist, who wants to better the world but ends up releasing nightmarish forces that he cannot control. Luther Stringfellow (*Stereo*), Antoine Rouge (*Crimes of the Future*), Dr. Emil Hobbes (*Shivers*), Dr. Dan Keloid (*Rabid*), Dr. Hal Raglan (*The Brood*), Dr. Paul Ruth (*Scanners*) and Brian O'Blivion (*Videodrome*) preside over a variety of experiments that at some point go completely awry. None of them are immorally fiendish. When they realize their mistakes, they invariably recoil in horror from what they have done. Often there is the implication that they represent the patriarchal order. Most of them experiment on women, with horrifying results. Antoine Rouge started a clinic for skin conditions induced by contemporary cosmetics in *Crimes of the Future*, and the disease that bears his name has resulted in the deaths of hundreds of thousands of women. Hobbes invents an aphrodisiac with a venereal disease component in *Shivers*, experiments with it on a female student, and her subsequent licentiousness assures the spread of the disease. Keloid operates on Rose after a serious motorcycle accident, and the skin grafts produce an appetite that can only be satiated by human blood. Raglan's experiments in externalizing rage end in Nola's brood, the purest form of that process, killing everyone who stands in her way. Dr. Ruth, who has invented the drug that creates scanners, presides over an all-male family where no mother is apparent. He, like O'Blivion in *Videodrome*, is linked to a preponderantly male corporate world that perverts his invention.

If "society" destroys either the individual or the couple, then it is unwittingly abetted by these mad scientists. This sense of an external force beyond our control is another recurring pattern in our cinema. It suggests a power that manipulates us all, and we find ourselves helpless when we confront it. Throughout Cronenberg's films there is the implication that the various contaminations can affect or infect any of us. The parasite (*Shivers*) and the rabies (*Rabid*) are epidemic. A new generation of unborn scanners is envisioned beyond the end of that film, and we feel helpless to alter this fact. The universal implications in *Videodrome* for anyone who owns a television set are inescapable. We have lost control and, more insidiously, don't even know where control lies anymore. For if the scientists display a certain kind of control, they are also ineffective and ultimately weak. Rouge has been exterminated, Hobbes commits suicide, Keloid is infected by the rabies he has unleashed, Raglan is killed by the brood, Ruth is shot during a moment of intense self-questioning and O'Blivion, also dead, only exists through the videocassettes that his daughter assembles.

Father figures in Canadian cinema are similarly inconsequential when visible. Some are callous and remote (Peter's father in *Nobody Waved Good-Bye*), others spiritually dead (*Don't Let the Angels Fall*) or crippled and consequently impotent (*Paperback Hero*). Often they are drunken louts (*Le vieux pays ou Rimbaud est mort*) or born losers (*Between Friends*). *Le temps d'une chasse* gives us a portrait of three fathers on a weekend hunting trip: one is a drunk, another a sexual lout, and the third is killed. The assassination of the father is plotted in *Kill*. In *Les beaux souvenirs*, he is mad. Quebec cinema is littered with absent fathers: in *Il ne faut pas mourir pour ça* he lives in Brazil, in *La mort d'un bûcheron* he is presumed dead, and in *Mon oncle Antoine* he leaves home for the bush.

If the older generation is bankrupt, its sins are certainly passed on to its children. Yet Cronenberg's attitude to his scientist/father figures is not quite this neat. All of them are visionaries, and some are philosophers. Within a sterile world they are trying to recreate human contact. Hobbes in *Shivers* feels that the human race has lost touch with its body and its instincts. Stringfellow in *Stereo* experiments with aphrodisiacs in an attempt to prove that the sexual norm is omni- or bisexuality. Raglan's psychiatric experiments are an attempt to release repressed anger, and O'Blivion envisions a new form of person in *Videodrome*. Ironically, within many of the father figures, the tension between good and evil and the rational and the irrational is held in a fine balance.

At the same time, Cronenberg's male protagonists fall into a time-honoured tradition of Canadian men. Most are uninteresting, particularly when contrasted with the scientists, have a certain flatness as characters and find themselves consigned to the periphery of much of the action. Stringfellow (*Stereo*) and Tripod (*Crimes of the Future*) drift through life without energy or force. They are laconic and ironic in their distance from reality. Tripod takes pride in the anonymity that he has achieved, and at one point decides against a dangerous course of events for fear that "my hard-won equilibrium may become a morbid stasis." At first serenely confident, Roger St. Luc in *Shivers* can do nothing to staunch the spread of the parasite. Throughout *Rabid*, Hart is continually shown on the margins of the action. In his attempt to find Rose he is always in the wrong place at the wrong time. When he finally joins her, he is powerless to prevent the outcome of the film. He falls down some stairs to knock himself out while Rose escapes to her death. The robotlike Cameron Vale pales beside the malicious energy of his brother, Darryl Revok, although he gradually asserts more control over his life. The husband in *The Brood* is apparently the most dynamic male in all of Cronenberg's cinema, but he is as colourless and characterless as Vale (neither of these characters are helped by the performances of Stephen Lack and Art Hindle). Like Vale, he supposedly eventually triumphs, but the ambiguity of the endings of both these films suggest Pyrrhic victories. Max Renn in *Videodrome* has a real energy that so many of his counterparts lack, but he soon becomes embroiled in a web of intrigue that results in his death/suicide. Finally he, too, is as powerless as the others.

The emasculated Canadian male has been noted by many of our critics. John Hofsess has asked the question why our cinema does not deal with "stronger egos and more confident people, people who can because they think they can."[3] Robert Fothergill devoted an entire article[4] to the question. He concluded that the Canadian condition reflected "the depiction, through many different scenarios, of the radical inadequacy of the male protagonist — his moral failure, especially, and most visibly in his relationships with women." Fothergill goes a step further. The American male fought the Oedipal

3. John Hofsess. *Inner Views*. McGraw-Hill Ryerson Limited, Toronto, 1975. p. 79.
4. Robert Fothergill. "Coward, Bully, or Clown: The Dream-Life of a Younger Brother." *Take One* IV/3, September 1973. (Also reprinted in *Canadian Film Reader*, edited by Seth Feldman and Joyce Nelson. Peter Martin Associates, Toronto, 1977. p. 234-250.)

battle in 1776 to assert his autonomy, while his Canadian brother refused the combat and stayed dutifully at his father's side. Could this also account for the ambivalence directed towards the scientists in Cronenberg's cinema?

For someone as interested in the repressed consciousness, there is a surprising lack, or failure, of rebellion in Cronenberg's work. If the order of society is sterile and controlled, the forces of chaos, when they are released, never result in apocalypse or the complete destruction that we find in a *Texas Chainsaw Massacre*. He has yet to take this step. Both *Stereo* and *Crimes of the Future* view their subjects from a perspective of extreme detachment; and any hint at rebellion (the man drilling a hole in his head in the first film and the group of conspirators in the second) is either not seen or is held at such a distance that resistance is the last response we take away from these moments. *Shivers* and *Fast Company* are the closest that Cronenberg has come to endorsing a revolutionary position. In the latter work, Lonnie Johnson openly rebels against his corporate sponsor and its representative, a man who manages the racing team and coldly manipulates the people who work for him. When the parasite is

The final shot of *The Brood* — what kind of future lies ahead?

released in *Shivers* there is a relief that the sanitized order of the apartment complex has been disturbed. With its final shot of all the infected inhabitants serenely driving out of the building, apparently to infect the rest of the world, Cronenberg seems to approve of the release of this sexual energy. It is certainly preferable to the stifling deadness of the ''normal'' people who live in the tower, and it is the furthest Cronenberg has gone in sympathizing with the id. But even *Shivers* is coloured by a sense of loss. The humanism of a Janine Tudor has been destroyed, and there is implicit in the last shot a feeling of a new conformity that will replace the old.

In *Rabid, The Brood, Scanners* and even *Videodrome*, the unconscious forces of the irrational must all be destroyed. The plague in *Rabid* is not seen as the joyous liberation of *Shivers*. Nola and her brood share a similar fate. Darryl Revok in *Scanners*, with his plans to rule the world, has to be confronted and fought. Max Renn's sado-masochistic hallucinations finally lead him towards his suicide.

Yet the films are more ambiguous than this, and this has led to a great deal of confusion, a confusion that may lie at the heart of what Cronenberg is saying. The ambiguity is present *within* each film, and *from* film to film as well. *Shivers* will serve as a paradigm although much of what I will find here is applicable to the other films. Cronenberg establishes two conflicting realities in *Shivers*: the ''normal'' life led by average people in the Starliner Towers, and the libidinous, frenetic delirium of those infected by the parasites. The stifling decorum of the first has to be undermined because it is so repressive and antihuman. Yet the ''liberation'' of these people also carries with it a sense of horror and loss. This dialectic extends most importantly to the two central relationships in the film — Nick and Janine Tudor, and Dr. Roger St. Luc and nurse Forsythe, relationships that are mirror images of each other, although at times reverse images. Janine and St. Luc are both rational, normal, considerate people who have learned to keep their emotions in check. On the other hand, their mates, Nick and Forsythe, are more sexual, disturbing and threatening. We are also given variations on what constitutes normality and what constitutes the libido. St. Luc is a plastic, cardboard hero, while Janine is loving and caring. Forsythe is viewed as sexual but controlled, whereas her mirror image in the other relationship, Nick, is almost ''out of control.'' These two couples embody in an extremely sophisticated fashion all the warring forces in the film. Even our response to the infection of St. Luc and of Janine is very different. When Janine eventually succumbs to the lesbian kiss, we feel a sense of loss; her care of and love for Nick has ended in defeat. When St. Luc, however, is finally trapped in the swimming pool, the response is different; at last he has been ''humanized.''

Even one's sense of what constitutes humanness continually shifts throughout. The parasite itself incorporates so many of these opposites. It is both aphrodisiac and venereal disease, shaped like a phallus yet with excremental overtones and is the object of horror and humour.

Similar examples could be drawn from all the films — the notion of Rose in *Rabid* as both evil (she carries the plague) and human (her struggle with the knowledge that she is tainted, "out of control"). Rose's embrace is similarly equivocal, for it signifies both attack and affection in a tension that Cronenberg consciously explores. *The Brood* poses the question of exactly who has won the fight for the child. Frank drives off with her after having killed Nola, but the welts that rise up on Candy's arm are an ominous omen. Will she turn out to be just like her mother? The morality of *The Brood* seems more clear-cut; Nola is evil and Frank is good, but Nola's childhood background — she had been beaten as a child — and Frank's blandness combined with the fact that he has turned into a murderer muddies these distinctions. *Scanners* seems similar to *The Brood*: Vale is the hero and Revok the villain. But reality is not that simple. Revok's energy is contrasted to the colourless Vale, and, once we learn he had a confused childhood, he becomes more sympathetic. By the end of the film we still don't have a clear indication of who has won the moral struggle. *Videodrome* is perhaps the most complex of all, yet initially the distinction between right and wrong appears to be fairly clear-cut. Brian O'Blivion and his daughter, Bianca, are contrasted to the ruthless Barry Convex and his sidekick, Harlan. But by the end of the film even these distinctions become blurred. Bianca seemingly is responsible for Max's death, and there is the implication that he may have become just a tool in her revenge on Convex, the man who killed her father. Nicki Brand, the temptress, remains an enigma. Has she led Max to his death, or is she a saviour in disguise?

While the moral dilemmas are contained within each film, they are also visible from film to film. *Shivers* and *Rabid* take radically different looks at the notion of the epidemic. In the former, the release of sexuality is seen as a liberation from sterility. In the latter, the release of the disease is only viewed with horror. It must be exterminated because it serves no social function. The couple is central to *The Brood* and *Scanners*; in one it must be destroyed, in the other recreated. *Scanners* and *Videodrome* both entertain questions concerning the manipulation of the mind. In *Scanners* this allows for the potential of a harmonious scanning community, whereas in *Videodrome* we only confront the confused individual isolated from society.

The ambiguity of the films has been noted by many critics.

The enigmatic Nicki Brand in *Videodrome* — temptress or saviour?

Cronenberg has been accused of being incoherent and confused. But the films trace the path of human struggle to find within life a reason and a self-justification for all actions. This attitude has echoes in Hamlet's "there is nothing either good or bad but thinking makes it so." [5] Wagner's titanic *Der Ring des Nibelungen* poses a similar question. Where do good and evil lie and what motivates people to do either? This is not to imply that Cronenberg is a Shakespeare or Wagner of the cinema, it is only to suggest that he is traversing similar terrain. (The analogy to Wagner is not lightly made — the ambiguity of motivation and the continual blurring of moral evaluation that mark the *Ring* are shared by many of Cronenberg's films, and *Tristan and Isolde*, with its lovers yearning for the rapturous night and a common death that will unite them, has eerie echoes in Max and Nicki's rendezvous with extinction in *Videodrome*. Wagner, too, has been prone to misinterpretation at every level, a fate that has also been Cronenberg's).

5. *Hamlet*, Act II, Scene 2.

What seems to be incontrovertible, though, is the fact that everyone is a victim of one sort or another in the Cronenberg world. Vicious circles of victimization recur. Rose in *Rabid* succumbs to an experimental skin graft, and the doctor who invented the process is stricken by his own creation. This model is uniform throughout, from Hobbes and the apartment dwellers in *Shivers* to literally every major character in all the films. Finally no one is in control, no one is master or mistress of individual destiny. *Videodrome* is perhaps the most convoluted of all, with everyone manipulating everybody else. It is impossible to identify who is in control, and the film explores this ambivalence in a fashion reminiscent of the complexity of Wagner's *Ring*.

As Margaret Atwood has pointed out in *Survival*, her study of our literature, all this is archetypically Canadian. I have already noted the absence or failure of rebellion within the films, and the feeling of powerlessness that is so pervasive. A paragraph in Atwood's book carries a number of connotations for Cronenberg's films:

> A preoccupation with one's survival is necessarily also a preoccupation with the obstacles to that survival. In earlier writers these obstacles are external — the land, the climate, and so forth. In later writers the obstacles tend to become both harder to identify and more internal; they are no longer obstacles to physical survival but obstacles to what we may call spiritual survival, to life as anything more than a minimally human being. Sometimes fear of these obstacles becomes itself the obstacle, and a character is paralyzed by terror (either of what he thinks is threatening him from outside, or of elements in his own nature that threaten him from within). It may even be life itself that he fears; and when life becomes a threat to life, you have a moderately vicious circle.[6]

Atwood's thinking here is particularly applicable, for the external fear of the first films has been replaced by an internal fear in all the films subsequent to *The Brood*. The internalization of this dread achieves its apotheosis in *Videodrome*.

This sense of victimization is pervasive in our cinema. Some have argued that it expresses a colonized mentality. The land has been exploited but not for the profit of the people who live there. In other words we see ourselves as the exploited — historically and culturally. A feeling of entrapment contributes to this idea of victimization. This is a recurring feature in Cronenberg's cinema, whether it is Roger St. Luc surrounded in the swimming pool at the end of *Shivers*, Rose alone in a room with an infected man at the end of *Rabid* or Max Renn stumbling onto an abandoned tugboat, a "condemned vessel,"

6. Margaret Atwood. *Survival*. Anansi, Toronto, 1972, p. 33.

at the end of *Videodrome* to live out his last moments in confusion. One of Cronenberg's television dramas deals even more precisely with this imagery. Even its title, *The Victim*, embraces this notion, and it deals with an obscene phone-caller who strikes up a friendship with a woman he calls one day. He is in apparent control throughout, until he breaks into her apartment, only to hallucinate that he has become trapped in a cage while the woman whips him as a form of punishment. Again, control has proven to be illusory.

What also becomes fascinating is the way Cronenberg examines sexual entrapment by reversing the sex roles in *Rabid* and *Videodrome*. Rose is given a penislike proboscis, and Max a vaginal slit in his stomach. Rose metaphorically "rapes" her victims, while Max is continually violated — the pushing of a videocassette into his gaping slit is a graphic image of penetration. No freedom or "liberation" is achieved through these transsexual mutations. They are both tormented by their newfound organs, victims of them in the true sense of the word.

In the final analysis the individual is powerless to change anything. All fail to a greater or lesser extent. If the films are not determinist, there is nevertheless a grim overtone of fatalism that is difficult to ignore. Society, in all its guises, conspires against the individual or the couple. Nowhere is this more tragically stated than in the final shot of *Rabid*, where Rose, now dead, is picked up and tossed into a garbage truck, a shot that communicates such tragedy and waste and synthesizes individual and collective loss. As Wagner and Brünnhilde discover in *Götterdammerung*, love is not always enough.

Perhaps the next question then becomes: to what extent is a subversion of society depicted in the films? If the individual cannot really change the course of events, does Cronenberg imply that society needs to be changed? Some critics have noted a political subtext in Cronenberg's work; European writers in particular pointed this out in their reviews of *Shivers* and *Rabid*. Certainly in both worlds the bourgeois world is completely undermined. Incest, lesbianism and homosexuality all appear in *Shivers*, and "normalcy" in all its forms is almost universally ridiculed. The apparent, assuring calm of the opening sequence, a promotional slide show for the Starliner Towers, with its promise that "the noise and traffic disappear here" is gleefully ridiculed by what transpires. Traditional bourgeois patriarchal morality is consistently subverted in *Rabid*: a Santa Claus is machine-gunned in a shopping plaza, a woman goes berserk in a subway and attacks a man, policemen have to shoot other policemen, and a group of workers take their jack-hammers to a government minister's car. Even the traditional bastion of the family is swept away when a man returns home to find that his wife has killed their child. He then becomes her next victim. [7] In a nice parody of the imposition of the War Measures Act of 1970 (and *Rabid* was shot in Montreal!), martial law is proclaimed as society moves to restore "law and order." Rose's attacks can also be read as being directed against the traditional male predator — the truck driver, the doctor. But this point is given real resonance when the drunken farmer who tries to rape her is stabbed in the eye — a symbolic attack on the male "look" or "gaze"; and a man on the make in a pornographic cinema is stung on the hand as he tries to reach into Rose's blouse — an equivalent metaphor for the unsolicited male "touch."

This undermining of traditional morality is visible in all the other films. The nuclear family of *The Brood* (in fact there are two in the film: Frank, Nola and child, Candy; and Nola and her mother and father) is systematically destroyed. It is seen as the root of all evil. In *Scanners, Fast Company* and *Videodrome* the collective villain has a corporate face: Consec, Fastco and Spectacular Optical. Consec, an international security organization, deals in weaponry and private armies. Fastco manufactures gasoline additives for cars, but more pertinently treats its racing drivers as mere commodities. The ideological inconsistency and immorality of Spectacular Optical are made clear when we discover that it makes inexpensive glasses for the Third World and missile-guidance systems for NATO. All of these organizations are dangerously out of control and have to be stopped. Everywhere bourgeois society is shown to be bankrupt and in retreat, using the army, the police or its technology in attempts to restore order when it can within the hypocrisy and sterility of this society, is it any wonder that the couple, an image of fusion and completion, cannot survive?

Not only is society morally bankrupt, but its technology is dangerous, and antihuman. A cosmetics disease has killed every woman in *Crimes of the Future*. The apartment tower in *Shivers* is viewed with disdain. In *Rabid*, Hart and Rose are seen continually trying to make contact with each other by telephone. Hart is on the phone to Rose when she is attacked, and his hysteria ends in his brutally smashing the receiver. Communication in *The Victim* is done almost entirely by telephone. Cars and machines are often more important than the people who drive them in *Fast Company*. In *Scanners*, the computer is finally seen as the enemy. When Vale destroys it in the famous scanning battle, the scene ends with a telephone receiver melting in his hands. *Videodrome* is constructed to an enormous degree around fear of the machine. Here guns, videocassettes, even television sets come alive before our eyes. They

7. See Robin Wood's chapters in *The American Nightmare* for the significance of cannibalism and the family in the horror film.

seem to have their own autonomy. The power of television is awesome, apparently infinite and capable of great destruction. More insidiously, there is also a fear of the world as we know it in *Videodrome*. Technology becomes an extension of a treacherous and mendacious universe.

Finally, there is one more point I would like to make about Cronenberg's films. Most commercial cinema, and in particular the American entertainment film, is based on the concept of narrative closure. These films follow the traditional patterns of storytelling. Problems are stated, dramatic conflict is asserted, and a resolution is achieved. The concept of narrative closure has come under scrutiny recently because it is suggestive of a number of unspoken ideological implications (i.e., the world can be reduced to identifiable problems that are resolvable, the resolution of these problems reassures the audience and reaffirms its belief in societal standards — good always wins out over bad, etc.). Yet a great deal of Canadian cinema has resisted this notion. By the end of many of our films little has been resolved, and often we are left with more questions than answers. What does Peter's future hold for him at the end of *Nobody Waved Good-bye*; what is the meaning of the skater gliding in circles at the conclusion of *Le chat dans le sac*? There is certainly a sense that life has not come to an end when the credits come up.

Endings without resolution — the open text — are obviously diametrically opposed to the strategy of narrative closure. The open text suggests that the world cannot be reduced to simple schematic equations. This is particularly relevant to Cronenberg. He finds himself functioning within the entertainment mainstream, and in genres (horror and science-fiction) that essentially demand narrative closure, yet every one of his films denies this principle, with the possible exception of *Rabid* and *Fast Company*. The final shots of *Stereo* and *Crimes of the Future* are enigmatic and diffuse. All the other films end on questions. Is the plague going to conquer the world (*Shivers*)? Will Candy turn out to be like her mother (*The Brood*)? Has good or evil triumphed (*Scanners*)? Is death the end or the beginning of a new life (*Videodrome*)? This adherence to the open text is a radical structuring principle for a commercial director, but not for a Canadian filmmaker.

Where does all this leave us with Cronenberg? I began by situating him outside the dominant aesthetic tradition in Canadian art, only to recuperate him thematically into an imaginative continuum that marks much of our best cinema. Formally, he has resisted the Canadian mainstream at two points in his career. Both *Stereo* and *Crimes of the Future* fall well within the experimental tradition of filmmaking in Canada. They are innovative, personal and minimalist, which leaves them largely inaccessible to the average audience. Nevertheless, they speak to an indigenous aesthetic. The break, when it came, was absolute. With *Shivers* he moved into the mainstream of the commercial cinema. He also moved into forms of genre filmmaking that came with their own set of codes and conventions. The absence of Canadian genres would need another article in itself, but with this lack Cronenberg found creative domicile in a cinematic form totally alien to this country. That he did so without compromising his national roots attests to his integrity.

Cronenberg: A Dissenting View

Robin Wood

There can be no doubt that, after many years of critical neglect and disfavour, David Cronenberg is now "in": the film retrospectives, the growing number of adulatory articles, the high seriousness increasingly attributed to the Cronenberg "vision" all attest to it. Certainly, Cronenberg deserves recognition: he is perhaps the one authentic auteur of English-speaking Canadian cinema; he has several of the distinguishing marks of the authentic artist — thematic obsessiveness, combined with a remarkable tenacity that has enabled him to develop his career in the teeth of general critical reaction and without any substantial box-office endorsement (if his films have not on the whole been commercial failures, they have not been huge successes either).

When I attacked Cronenberg's films five years ago in *The American Nightmare* (also published in relation to a Toronto Festival of Festivals retrospective) I had no sense that I was doing anything outrageous, or even particularly controversial: the controversy, in fact, has largely developed since, with the steadily growing claims made for Cronenberg's work. I accepted the present editor's invitation to reiterate the attack initially with great reluctance. The original attack has been the object of numerous counter-attacks, but as far as I am aware it has not been effectively *answered*: no one, that is, has been able to demonstrate that Cronenberg's films do something substantially different from what I said they do. True, at that time I had seen only three of Cronenberg's eight feature films (two had not yet been made), but (I had better make clear at once, to avoid any false expectations) my position has not basically changed, and I shall not be offering any fresh revelations. On a cruder level, I was also deterred by the daunting prospect of sitting through at least some of the films again in order to re-assess them. Two considerations overcame this reluctance. I agreed with the editor that at least one dissenting voice should be heard within the book, and (such is the degree of Cronenberg's present "in"-ness) mine was apparently the only one that could be found. More important, however, was the realization that far more is at stake than the evaluation of a specific group of films: that the real issue is one of critical position. The counter-attacks I spoke of (by Cronenberg himself in the interview in this book, and by John Harkness in a recent issue of *Cinema Canada* also reprinted here) don't content themselves with disagreeing with me about the value of the films: they question my right to attack them from the position I hold. The basis of this is not entirely clear to me: at times the implication appears to be that my own political position is rigid and dogmatic, at times that it is radical positions generally that are unacceptable, at times that you shouldn't mix aesthetics with politics at all. What I wish to defend is the legitimacy of a politicized criticism.

First, however, I should point out that the distaste I feel for Cronenberg's films is *not* the product of my current political position. I was introduced to his work in the early seventies when I saw *Shivers* at the Edinburgh Film Festival and discussed it briefly in a festival report for *Film Comment*. That still belongs to the period when I was producing what Mr. Harkness is kind enough to call my "classics of bourgeois humanist criticism": indeed, throughout that period I was set up as the "enemy" (by *Screen* and its followers) and was writing explicitly anti-Marxist articles. (At that time, in my naiveté, I continued to swallow most of the bourgeois capitalist myths about Marxism, and assumed that the only possible form of Marxist criticism was hard-line semiotics.) Further, my reaction to the film would have been the same ten years earlier. It is a fallacy to assume that a change in one's political position automatically necessitates a change in one's whole system and habit of evaluation (the relationship between aesthetics and politics, though very intimate, is not a simple one). The films that I took, in my "bourgeois humanist" period, to represent the peak of cinematic achievement — for example, *Vertigo*, *Rio Bravo*, *Ugetsu Monogatari*, *Tokyo Story*, *Letter from an Unknown Woman*, *La règle du jeu* — still seem to me to do so, though I am now able to understand them much better, perceiving in them whole dimensions to which the blinkers of "bourgeois humanism" rendered me completely blind.

On these grounds I must take strenuous exception to Harkness's remark about the "ideological tunnel vision" of my present position in contrast to (apparently) the wider vision of my early work. Precisely the opposite seems to me to be the case. Since my work became politicized I have, as a direct consequence, enormously extended both my areas of interest and my sympathies. My sections of *The American Nightmare* would have been unthinkable to me prior to this: I had no tools with which to grapple with such material, and in general adopted an attitude of elitist intellectual superiority to it. Harkness continues to do this now when he tells us that "the science element" in Cronenberg's work lifts it "above the realm of exploitation horror films" — as neat as example of "ideological tunnel vision" as you could wish for, occurring, ironically enough, in the very sentence in which he uses the phrase of me. Similar examples proliferate throughout Harkness's mini-diatribe, alongside gross distortions and simplifications of my position. Consider the following set of notions attributed to me (the final clause presumably gives us Harkness's view): "Politically correct filmmakers who attack the notions of bourgeois normality (Craven, Romero, Tobe Hooper, Stephanie Rothman) are by definition better than conservative directors like Brian De Palma and David Cronenberg, who by almost any critical standard are better filmmakers than the aforementioned directors."

First, I have no idea what Harkness means by lumping together Craven, Romero, Hooper and Rothman as "politically correct." I have written about all four with varying degrees of appreciation, and I think have made some careful discriminations between them (and within their respective bodies of work). I am not at all sure what, in terms of aesthetics, *is* "politically correct," but I would not use the term of any of these directors. Second, the categorization of De Palma as a "conservative" director (although apparently attributed to me) is entirely Harkness's, and I wish to dissociate myself from it totally. In fact, I devoted one of the essays in *The American Nightmare* to defending the proposition that *Sisters* is one of the most authentically radical horror films ever to come out of Hollywood. I'm not sure whether Harkness has forgotten this, didn't read that far, or simply failed to follow the argument (his grasp of the book's general thesis is decidedly shaky). As for Harkness's last clause, the only "critical standard" according to which the superiority of De Palma's and Cronenberg's films to, say, *Last House on the Left*, *Terminal Island*, *The Texas Chainsaw Massacre* and *Night of The Living Dead*

Shivers is Cronenberg's response to the notion of sexual liberation — Betts and Janine Tudor

is obvious would appear to be the long-discredited bourgeois criterion of the "well-made film": it amounts to little more than the fact that De Palma and Cronenberg have had (since quite an early stage in their careers) much higher budgets to work with.

Cronenberg's own comments on my recent work are equally full of distortions — not to mention downright misrepresentations. One remark that Cronenberg appears to be attributing to me is "Unfortunately this is reactionary and should be suppressed." I have never suggested anywhere that any film should be suppressed; on the contrary, for the past five years I have been (intermittently — I don't see it as my life's work) at the forefront of the campaign to abolish film censorship in Ontario, and I think Cronenberg must be aware of this. During the horror-film retrospective that *The American Nightmare* accompanied, we screened two of Cronenberg's films and invited him to discuss them: a curious form of suppression. In fact, I believe that *any* film is potentially useful as a means to understanding our culture. I cannot, however, see that "understanding" in academic or neutral terms: to try to "understand" our culture is to attempt to sort out, evaluatively, what is progressive from what is reactionary. Cronenberg's work has value, for me, precisely in that it crystallizes some of our society's most negative attitudes — to physicality, to sexuality, to women, to all ideas of progress. The existence of the films helps make such traits accessible to examination.

I am also credited with the opinion that "despite the fact that this piece of film of Larry Cohen's is awful, it is admirable and should be seen because it proposes what I think is right for human beings to do in society." I had better say at once that I can think of no film of Cohen's that "proposes what I think is right for human beings to do in society": leaving aside that I have no dogmatic views of "what I think is right for human beings to do," I have certainly never discussed Cohen's work in such simplistic terms. Neither have I made, anywhere in my work, any such separation between the aesthetic and ideological aspects of films. I am puzzled by the view apparently attributed to me here that Cohen's films are "awful" (one or two of them are certainly not very good). I suspect that Cronenberg thinks they are awful; that this then becomes a "fact"; that since it is a "fact" then I must think so, too. If I continue to prefer *It's Alive* to *The Brood* it is because it seems to me so much more complex: so many more things are going on in it, so that it becomes the site of a genuinely rich and disturbing intersection of ideological conflicts.

Cronenberg goes on to imply that what I want is some form of propaganda; worse, he implies that this is what is demanded by *any* critics "interested in exploring the underlying ideology and patterns that are at work in the cinema." Films I have written on positively in the last few years include *The Deer Hunter*, *Taxi Driver* and *Cruising*. I don't really see that any of these can reduced to "propaganda," and certainly not to the kind of propaganda Cronenberg assumes I would be interested in promoting. But Cronenberg seems anxious, every- where, to reduce the complex issue of the role of ideology in art to something that could be isolated as "propaganda" in order to be rejected. Hence he can produce the astonishing observation that he doesn't "base [his] life's value or [his] work's value in any ideology": surely the statement is a logical impossibility for anyone who knows what the term really *means*.

In Defence of Political Criticism

In a sense, all criticism is political: every piece of critical writing, like every work of art, is rooted in a particular ideological position, is *implicated in* the dominant ideology of our culture. The position may be heavily disguised and the writer (or artist) may be entirely unaware of its existence; but it is always, inevitably, there, and susceptible to analysis. (My early remarks, sketchy as they were, will have sufficiently indicated the ideological position underlying the writings of John Harkness.) The difference with which we are concerned, then, is not so much between "political" and "non-political" criticism, but between criticism that *knows* it is political and criticism that doesn't.

This corresponds, broadly, to a distinction between conservative and radical criticism. I am using the term "conservative" here very loosely: not with reference to party politics (from this standpoint, *all* the parties that offer themselves for our votes are conservative), but to make a brutal and basic distinction between those who are committed to the continuance of the present economic/social/sexual organization (improved by whatever "reforms") and those who are not. Roland Barthes in *Mythologies* discusses bourgeois ideology's resistance to being "named," and my own experience has amply confirmed this perception. If one uses terms like "patriarchal," "bourgeois" and "capitalist" one is usually greeted (if that is the word) with uneasy and embarrassed laughter: to use such words is either absurd or reprehensible. Yet how else (without resorting to cumbersome periphrases) can one describe the dominant ideology under which we all live? The words are there, they exist, they have meaning, they correspond to verifiable material phenomena. Yet patriarchal bourgeois capitalist critics resolutely refuse to use them (unless to ridicule an alternative critical practice their readers will automatically recognize — alerted by a certain tone of voice — as beyond serious consideration: a strategy of which I have been the frequent victim in recent years). "Patriarchal bourgeois capitalist ideology" — ha-ha! Of course it doesn't exist, the *words* sound so silly. (They "sound so silly" because that is how patriarchal bourgeois capitalism makes them sound: of course no one is *really* patriarchal, bourgeois or capitalist, that is just a Marxist myth: we are all simply *people*).

It would be extremely interesting to find a patriarchal bourgeois capitalist critic who was willing to "come out" (I have not found one yet who is). The implicit assumption runs something like: "*They* have an ideology; *we* have truth" (or "common sense," which is patriarchal bourgeois capitalist ideology's favourite masquerade). Bourgeois criticism rests upon shared ideological assumptions that neither writer nor reader is encouraged to examine or challenge. Radical criticism, of course, has its ideological assumptions also (no thought, no mental activity of any kind, can exist outside of ideology), but they are of a different order: because they are oppositional to the status quo the kind of inertia that characterizes most bourgeois criticism becomes impossible, and the "assumptions" become consciously held beliefs that must be argued. Where bourgeois criticism masks its assumptions (and is frequently unaware of them), the assumptions of radical criticism are of necessity defined and foregrounded.

Before attempting to define the assumptions that underlie my current work (which necessarily influence, but do not determine, my attitude to the films of Cronenberg), I am forced to take a detour into areas of my personal life. What makes the detour obligatory is that both Cronenberg and Harkness raise the issue, and raise it in order to invalidate my work. According to Cronenberg, the purpose of my criticism is that of "justifying [my] own sexuality": "I think that's exactly what he's doing. When your work becomes an apology for an event or turn in your life, then I think you have invalidated yourself as a serious critic." According to Harkness, "...it is possible to argue seriously that Wood was a better critic when he was repressing his homosexuality." (In fact, I never "repressed" it: I simply didn't act on it, which is not at all the same thing.)

Of course, like anyone else, I cannot vouch for what goes on on unconscious levels of my psychic life; consciously, I am certainly not aware that my sexuality needs "justifying." I am, as the phrase has it, "glad to be gay" — not because I consider homosexuality intrinsically superior to heterosexuality, but simply because it is a relief to be outside the appalling strains, tensions, power struggles, mutual oppressions that appear to characterize most heterosexual relations in the present phase of social evolution. It is certainly true that coming out as gay had a decisive influence on my development as a critic; though equally decisive was the introduction into critical theory about the same time of concepts of ideology (I shall always be very grateful for the challenge and indirect support represented by the work of *Screen*). To identify oneself as gay is openly to acknowledge one's membership of an oppressed minority group. This consciousness of oppression is unlikely to stop there: it leads logically to an awareness of oppression as a central and characterizing fact of our culture, and ultimately to a view of our culture as a system of interlocking structures of oppression/domination (class, wealth, gender, race, sexual orientation...) that bourgeois ideology strives to conceal or disguise. It would be accurate, then, to see my "coming out" as the starting point for the development of a political position; what Harkness and Cronenberg make of that, however, strikes me as somewhat unscrupulous. Harkness adds a further distortion when he writes that the tone of my recent work "suggests that we should ignore that earlier phase of his criticism" (i.e., the phase of "bourgeois humanist classics"). Naturally, I have to view it with ambivalence and suspicion. Certainly, for example, I would want readers to be aware of the strain of unconscious sexism that runs throughout *Hitchcock's Films* — a striking example of the "ideological tunnel vision" of that earlier phase, when I had no awareness whatsoever of the ways in which women are oppressed within our culture.

Against the bourgeois critic's (usually automatic) commitment to established "norms," "common sense," etc., I would therefore set an overt commitment to the various radical movements that have sought to draw attention to the oppressiveness of our culture, the deceptions of its dominant ideology, and hence to increase the possibility of change: especially radical feminism, Marxist theory, and the political use of psychoanalytical theory. This last has been of immense importance in recent years in tying everything together: it offers a convincing explanation of how the human being is constructed as a subject within ideology, of the construction of those clear-cut gender roles that serves the interests of patriarchal capitalism, through (especially) the repression of constitutional bisexuality (which Freud showed to be our "natural" heritage).

The Brood deals with the oppression of women — Frank strangles his wife

Politics and Aesthetics

The relation of the political position I have defined to the criticism of specific films is not simple, though it is often made to appear so: the parodic version (with which I am repeatedly confronted) reduces it to something like: "Any film that does not perfectly correspond to these ideological presuppositions (i.e., is not 'politically correct') should be rejected and if possible suppressed." The function of this kind of parody is obvious: it reduces a disturbing and complex issue to something so simple, so silly, and so monstrous, that it needn't trouble us any further. The whole business of evaluation strikes me, frankly, as quite bewilderingly complex: every new work of art of any real significance or force demands a reconsideration of one's premises. I can, however, offer a few basic principles:

1. A total and uncompromising opposition to censorship. In view of the current escalation of increasingly violent pornography, this is becoming an increasingly difficult and beleaguered position. But it seems to me that the healthy and profitable response to what offends us is not suppression but active engagement and protest. Pornography/violence/degradation are not the sickness but the symptoms: we can't diagnose the social disease if the symptoms are obliterated.

2. The refusal to *pro*scribe has as complement the refusal to *pre*scribe. The routes of art are devious and unpredictable. Any reader who takes the trouble to peruse my work will not, I believe, find anywhere in it statements to the effect that, "Such films *should* be made." It is certainly one of my ambitions to help create a social climate in which certain kinds of art are encouraged above others: if I can do anything to affect the present desperate situation in which a *Heaven's Gate* becomes a "débâcle" and a *Return of the Jedi* a "triumph," I would like to do it.

3. Evaluation. The critic's job is to examine and discuss what is produced; s/he cannot do that without evaluating, and evaluation depends upon criteria that in turn are developed out of his/her position within, and in relation to, culture. All critics, like all artists, are engaged (whether they know it or not) in ideological struggle. It is quite impossible that there should be a single set of criteria that all critics could apply; when Cronenberg tells us it is a "fact" that Larry Cohen's films are "awful," he is, quite simply, talking nonsense. Certain criteria *appear* to be universally sharable: significantly, they can only be defined by abstract terms such as "intelligence," "sensitivity," "creativity," detached from any precise relationship to social/historical realities. As soon as they attempt to give such abstractions a concrete and specific application, conservative and radical critics will immediately part company. What, after all, is

"intelligence" in relationship to cultural product? Certainly not something you can measure in terms of I.Q. I am sure, for instance, that Steven Spielberg's I.Q. is extremely high, but I would never dream of describing his films as "intelligent." *It's Alive* seems to me a far more intelligent film than *E.T.*; to most bourgeois reviewers it is a senseless piece of crap. "Intelligence" can only be discussed in terms of the artists's engagement with the social/political realities of his culture, and conservative and radical critics will probably be unable to agree as to what those realities *are*, let alone agree on an attitude toward them.

For me, the major criterion (it encompasses all the others) is *usefulness*; and again, inevitably, one's view of what is useful will depend upon one's position. Films can be useful in a number of ways, which I shall now attempt to indicate:

1. *Pleasure.* One of the basic and dominant purposes of art has always been to give pleasure. "Pleasure" is, of course, another deeply problematic concept: as subjects constructed within ideology, we cannot simply take our pleasure for granted. I recently found myself "enjoying" *Return of the Jedi*: I was excited, I laughed, I cried, all right on cue. The experience did not, however, lead me to think very highly of the film: I am all too aware of the nature of my pleasure (pleasure can be reactionary, too) as arising out of a specific social conditioning. "Pleasure" in our culture is all too often assumed to be passive, even infantile (the baby's mouth finds the lost breast once again). There are other, finer forms of pleasure, in which intellectual activity and an active and critical emotional engagement play a part.

2. *Understanding.* This is by no means separable from the foregoing: understanding is one of the finest forms of pleasure. What I have in mind here is specifically understanding the culture in which we live and our positions within it. From this viewpoint, all films, all artifacts, are potentially useful. To take again *Return of the Jedi* as a convenient example: a critical examination of the film will reveal something of the fundamental Oedipal/imperialist structures on which patriarchal culture is based (precisely *why* we are excited, laugh and cry), something of the contemporary need for reassurance, in the form of fantasy in which we can simultaneously (on different levels) believe and disbelieve, and something of the bankruptcy (both economic and spiritual) of contemporary capitalism, which has endlessly to dazzle us with spectacle and "special effects" to keep us happily bemused. This is not, obviously, to attribute any very high value to the film: precisely the same information can be gleaned from hundreds of others. As with "pleasure," however, higher levels are possible. I think particularly of films that (without necessarily having any overtly "progressive" viewpoint) dramatize and foreground the

strains, tensions and contradictions that our culture produces. In this category, the work of Scorsese seems to me exemplary and outstanding. It is also from this viewpoint that a left-wing case might perhaps be argued for Cronenberg. I don't wish to undertake this myself, but I would be very interested in reading it.

3. *Progressiveness*. One thing (not the *only* thing) the radical critic will look for in films is the way in which they dramatize the major conflicts within our culture (especially those centred on class/wealth and gender). On certain levels, every work produced within our culture must necessarily be "about" these conflicts, whatever the particularities of the individual subject. If one believes in the possibility of a liberated society (as the only viable alternative to universal annihilation), then one will necessarily be drawn towards elements, signs, pointers in films that hint (perhaps quite inadvertently) at a progressive tendency, that engage with those major conflicts in a progressive way. It should be clear, on the one hand, that this has nothing to do with a demand for "propaganda," and, on the other, that it is not cleanly separable from the type discussed above, of which Scorsese was suggested as a salient example.

I shall close this introduction by saying that the North American film of the past few years that seems to me uniquely to fulfil this whole complex of the "useful" is *Heaven's Gate*; and that my problem with Cronenberg's films is that the use I have been able to make of them has been minimal.

In Defence of Cronenberg

Before reiterating my attack on Cronenberg (and I'm afraid I can promise little more than reiteration), it seems worth attempting to define his distinction: what it is that makes his work not negligible. Confronted with, say, the *Friday the 13th* movies, the critic need really do no more than try to define their function within contemporary culture; Cronenberg's work, on the contrary, demands careful attention and even, in a certain limited sense, respect.

I suggested the major concession at the opening of this article: that Cronenberg's work has artistic authenticity, guaranteed by thematic and stylistic consistency, the creation on film of a personal "world." It also has integrity. In recent years, Scorsese with *Raging Bull* and *The King of Comedy*, Ridley Scott with *Blade Runner*, Cimino with *Heaven's Gate*, have earned respect for their stubbornly oppositional stance in relation to the mainstream of cultural and cinematic development; I think that Cronenberg should be added to this list, without at all committing myself to any proposition that his achievement is qualitatively comparable. To offer *Videodrome* to a public that appears to want nothing but more Lucas and Spielberg is an action that commands a certain admiration. The last thing Cronenberg could be accused of offering is mindless reassurance.

Intimately bound up with this is the films' evident neuroticism: the obsessive repetition of themes and imagery, the pervasive fascination with forms of perverse sexuality. To offer this as a (potential) positive feature may seem at best a back-handed compliment, but it's not meant to be: some of the most distinguished bodies of work in the cinema are centred on a similarly obtrusive neuroticism: Hitchcock, von Sternberg and Scorsese come immediately to mind. Neurotic symptoms (like the monster of the traditional horror movie) can be read as at once the product of repression and a protest against it; they may therefore, in the context of a "normality" built on a system of interlocking oppressions, acquire strong positive (positively disruptive) force — under the right conditions. One does not, of course, value Hitchcock's or von Sternberg's or Scorsese's work for the neuroticism itself, but for what it produces when brought into contact (or collision) with other factors, other material: a *Vertigo*, a *Scarlet Empress*, a *Raging Bull*. For this reason it might be considered a pity that Cronenberg so completely dominates his own work, writing as well as directing: there is little room for fruitful collision, interaction, permutation. It will be interesting to see what he makes of *The Dead Zone* (the novel being very interesting in itself).

There is one way in which Cronenberg's work may be extremely interesting to which I (as a mere immigrant) may not be properly attuned: the argument that it is peculiarly Canadian, that it crystallizes a particular national angst. This has a certain credibility: Canada has, on the one hand, a continual dread of cultural colonization by the United States and, on the other, the pervasive American dread (being already effectively colonized) of any alternative form of social organization other than patriarchal capitalism.One can well see that a response to this might logically be the impotence, negativity, fear of change but contempt for the status quo of Cronenberg's films. It does not, however, seem a very *helpful* response (though, again, viewed in this way the films take on a certain value as documentation).

A Joyless World

It is interesting that Cronenberg's work has received so much critical attention and recognition during a period in which it is so alien to the cinema's dominant trends: interesting, because the vicissitudes of bourgeois criticism can generally be explained, not in terms of any "critical objectivity," or set of established, time-hallowed aesthetic criteria, but in relation to the changing social climate. Why, in the age of Lucas and Spielberg, the age of a willing regression to infantilism, the age of reassurance and the "restoration of the Father," is Cronenberg — whose films seem to be the precise opposite of such a cinema — suddenly a name to be reckoned with?

When I first saw *Shivers* (under its original title, *The Parasite Murders*) at the Edinburgh Film Festival about ten years ago, the unanimous reaction among people I talked to was disgust. Edinburgh has traditionally been the left-wing film festival; it was dominated at that time by *Screen* magazine, who organized seminars that were right at the forefront of contemporary theory. We were still in the aftermath of May '68 and its related events over the Western world. Even "bourgeois humanists" like myself were beginning to become politicized and ideologically aware. We believed not only that a "liberated society" was possible, but even that it might be within sight. Now, a decade later, a few of us are still trying to cling on to a

Crimes of the Future is marked by a pervasive homoeroticism

radicalism the society around us (predominantly cynical and reactionary) appears to regard as increasingly ridiculous.

My point is that opposites are often, also, complementary. If Cronenberg's films are the contrary of *E.T.*, the *Rocky* series, the *Star Wars* series, they are also the other side of the coin. Our dominant cinema tells us that we shouldn't wish to change society because it's just great as it is; Cronenberg's movies tell us that we shouldn't want to change society because we would only make it even worse. From a political viewpoint, we are confronted not with opposites but with two variants on the reactionary. If Spielberg is the perfect director for the eighties, so, in his way, is Cronenberg.

What follows is a recapitulation, with additions, of what I wrote in *The American Nightmare*: the additions are a paragraph on *Rabid* and a brief account of the modifications occasioned by viewings of the five films I had not then seen. I want to preface this with one retraction. In *The American Nightmare* my remarks on Cronenberg were followed by a passage on *Halloween* that began by suggesting that John Carpenter is a more interesting and engaging artist than Cronenberg. Carpenter's subsequent work has revealed this as a critical aberration: the confusions I noted in his early work have never been resolved or interestingly developed, and his work overall conspicuously lacks precisely that "artistic authenticity" I have acknowledged in Cronenberg's. Faced with the choice of re-seeing *Videodrome* or any of Carpenter's movies, I would choose *Videodrome*.

*

Shivers, *Rabid* and *The Brood* were the films with which I got to know Cronenberg's work, and it remains convenient to begin with them: they are so closely connected, sharing an identical basic plot structure, as to be seen as a loose trilogy. Their basis is this: a man of science invents something (an aphrodisiac, a new technique of skin-grafting, a new method of psychotherapy) that he believes will benefit mankind and promote social progress (in *Shivers* and *The Brood*, explicitly a form of liberation); he uses a woman as the (chief or sole) guinea-pig for his experiments; the results are unpredictably catastrophic, escalate way beyond his control, and eventually produce a kind of mini-apocalypse. (*Scanners* and *Videodrome* share much of this plot structure, confirming its centrality to the Cronenberg oeuvre, but introduce two important modifications, both of which serve to make the films less actively objectionable: the chief experimentee/victim is no longer a woman, and the form of science involved, the ambition of the scientist, has far less progressive connotations, so that the "awful warning" the films offer is less unacceptable.)

Shivers can be read as Cronenberg's response to the notion of sexual liberation.[1] As the parasites proliferate through the apartment building, all the taboos of bourgeois sexual morality — promiscuity, female aggressiveness, age difference, homosexuality (both male and female), incest — are systematically overthrown. The film identifies this with the spread of disease, and views it with unmitigated horror and disgust. The parasites themselves combine strong sexual and excremental overtones: shaped like phalluses (and one invades a woman in a bath via her vagina), they are coloured like turds. Disgust is indeed the film's dominant and pervasive tone: by the end it has coloured the presentation of every human physical activity, becoming a kind of obsessional aversion therapy for such things as kissing and eating. Cronenberg (in the 1979 panel discussion at the Festival of Festivals) claimed that this disgust is not really sexual — it is disgust with "mortality" itself, with the fact that the human body is prone to disease, grows old, decays. As an "explanation" of the films, that strikes me as fairly ludicrous: it totally fails to account for the sexual nature of their imagery, and it merely substitutes another form of negative and unhelpful morbidity for the one the films insistently project. I pointed out the oddity of the ending of *Shivers* long ago, in my *Film Comment* report from Edinburgh: when all the apartment dwellers have succumbed to the parasites and set out to infect the rest of the world, all signs of disease have disappeared. No reason is given for this; of course, the author of a work of horror or science fiction has every right to ask us to accept a fantastic premise, but I think she or he is then obliged to follow its logic and not arbitrarily alter its data. The absence of disease can, however, give rise to the question, what, then, is finally so terrible about this invasion? If these people are now neither sick nor unhappy, why can't what they are offering the world be seen as liberation after all? What is even odder than this anomaly is that Cronenberg now seems ready to argue that this is a legitimate reading of the film: it can, of course, only be a reading *against* it, the specific signifiers and generic pressures combining to

---

1. Harkness, with what may seem to many callous opportunism, finds my remarks on *Shivers* given "a darkly Cronenbergian irony" by the AIDS epidemic. If this has any point in relation to the film, it is presumably to imply that *Shivers* is somehow validated by its prophecy "coming true." A film (of whatever genre) must be judged according to such features as tone, attitude, imagery; a work of science fiction is no more validated by "coming true" than it is invalidated if it doesn't. To suggest that *Shivers* is some kind of anticipatory film about an actual human tragedy can only make it appear even more distasteful than it already is.

express a totally unambiguous horror at what is happening. And what, in any case, could we possibly make of a film that dramatized liberation like *that*?

Perhaps I should make it clear (in view of Cronenberg's suggestion that my dislike of his work is somehow bound up with "justifying my sexuality") that I am not in the least accusing *Shivers* of being anti-gay or anti-lesbian: it is anti-everything, and if there is one thing it cannot be accused of, it is discrimination. One may feel, however, that the film reserves a special frisson of horror for the release of an active, aggressive female sexuality, and this is pursued much further in *Rabid*. Here, as the result of a skin-graft experiment, Marilyn Chambers develops an all-purpose sexual organ in her armpit: a vagina that opens to let out a nasty sharp little phallus that drains her victims' blood and gives them rabies. (The sexual connotation of her encounters is, I think, quite obvious: she is seeking release or satisfying a "hunger." It is true that the film presents her as a victim (and the victim of a misguided male), but I don't think that radically affects the issue: the horror the film is playing on is the dread of the release of what Freud called the woman's "masculinity," which our culture is so concerned to repress.

If *Shivers* evokes *Invasion of the Body Snatchers*, *Rabid* evokes *Night of the Living Dead* (at the same time anticipating, in its urban settings, *Dawn of the Dead*) — even down to its final images of Marilyn Chambers's body being thrown into a garbage truck. The comparison is instructive. Both films show social breakdown, with human beings converted into predatory monsters; both are entirely pessimistic. But there is an essential difference between the premises of the two films, with marked ideological consequences. Romero's ghouls are the embodiment of established values/dominant norms; from the beginning of the film, and consistently throughout, they are linked specifically to the tensions and conflicts within the bourgeois patriarchal family. The problem for the survivors, then — merely implicit in *Night of the Living Dead* but magnificently developed in the sequel — is to extricate themselves from these values and create new ones, new forms of relating. Nothing comparable is even implicit in *Rabid*, where the catastrophe is caused by an attempt at progress and takes the form of released female activeness, dramatized as horrific and disgusting. It is important to distinguish clearly between pessimism and negativity, two very different phenomena that are often confused. Our current social/political situation gives one few grounds for optimism, and it is scarcely surprising that many of the finest contemporary works of art (the operas of Sallinen, for example) are deeply pessimistic (though not at all negative).

The Brood develops this attitude to female activeness ("masculinity'') much more explicitly; it is also interesting in that "science" here becomes psychotherapy, directly concerned with the release of repressed energies. Again, the central victim/predator is a woman, Nola (Samantha Eggar); again, the film engages with one of our culture's major radical issues and treats it in the most reactionary and negative way possible. Cronenberg's defence of the film (that he saw Nola as just an individual character, not an archetype) strikes me as merely another instance of his extraordinary ideological innocence. It is impossible to make a film without involving oneself in the network of contemporary social relations, and without revealing one's own position within that network. The choice of "individual case" that one makes is, precisely, the dramatization of that position. *The Brood* is concerned with the oppression of women, the repression of the woman's "masculinity," the secret, internalized rage that this repression produces. It then proceeds to attribute this not to patriarchy but to the fact that Nola's father was weak: it was all the fault of an aggressive mother. The implication is clear: patriarchal dominance is "natural," any deviation from it will result in disaster. The misguided psychotherapist (of course) succeeds only in making things much, much worse: he finds a means whereby the repressed rage can be externalized and released, in the form of Nola's monstrous, murderous children. The scene of childbirth gives us one of Cronenberg's most remarkable images: the unborn child, a huge excrescence on Nola's body, has the appearance of an enormous penis, a vivid literal enactment of Freud's perception that, under patriarchy, the child is the woman's substitute phallus. The implication, again, is quite clear (and highlighted by the film's immediate historical context of the growth of radical feminism): at all costs, women's repressed "masculinity," activeness and rage *must* remain repressed — their release would be catastrophic.

If Cronenberg's films are reactionary, they are so in a quite unusual way: they are not reactionary in the simple, easily comprehensible way of *Rocky*, *E.T.* or *Poltergeist*, they do not reaffirm "establishment" values — except perhaps negatively, by default. When what we call "normality" appears in the films, it is presented as unattractive and joyless. In fact, the films seem unable to affirm anything, and unable, at the same time, to offer any very helpful analysis of the oppressiveness of our social institutions. It seems very odd that Harkness should describe him as a "visionary": in the sense in which I have always understood the term — the "vision" of a Blake or a Janacek, in which the furious protest against oppression is accompanied by intimations of a possible transcendence, the coming of the New Jerusalem, or the "transfigured city" of the Janacek *Sinfonietta* — Cronenberg is as far from being a visionary as any artist one can think of. The world of his films is not only a world without joy, it is a world in which there is no *potential* for joy. The films lack any sense of the tragic (though Marilyn Chambers in *Rabid* achieves a certain pathos): nothing of value is lost, because nothing has value. It is this total negativity that gives the films their interest (I would describe it as a "clinical" interest), but it is also their crippling limitation. It accounts for the uniform drabness, the lack of energy, the fact that, while frequently repulsive, the films are almost never exciting or frightening (which perhaps explains the rather meagre box-office response).

*

It remains to discuss the modifications to this view of Cronenberg necessitated by viewing his other five feature films: the two early "experimental" movies (*Stereo* and *Crimes of the Future*); the would-be "commercial" *Fast Company* (it was in fact an unmitigated box-office disaster); and the two films released since *The American Nightmare* was published. The modifications are slight.

Fast Company can be disposed of very quickly. No one (as far as I know) makes any claims for it whatever, and it is indeed utterly conventional. Indeed (some nudity, sexual explicitness and coarse language apart, plus the fact that it is in colour) it seems virtually indistinguishable from the numerous "B" movies I used to see when I was a kid, in the thirties and forties: one feels, nostalgically, that it should have starred Richard Arlen, Wayne Morris and Barton Maclane. On that level, it's not bad. Its interest within the Cronenberg oeuvre lies in its professional competence. This is not, of course, to suggest that Cronenberg's other films are *in*competent, which would be silly. What *Fast Company* does is prove that he can make a decent, ordinary little movie. The term "conventional" can have connotations that are not necessarily negative: if *Fast Company* has a certain energy that the typical Cronenberg films lack, this doubtless derives precisely from the conventions of classic Hollywood cinema. The existence of the film underlines the fact that the peculiar distinction of the "real" Cronenberg films — their very peculiar flatness and drabness — is a matter of artistic choice. Accordingly, the film increases one's respect for Cronenberg — one's awareness of the authenticity of his work.

The two "avant-garde" movies, on the other hand, come initially as something of a shock. Not that they are by any means incompatible with the subsequent films (indeed, *Crimes of the Future* should be seen as their prototype); what is startling is their explicit and pervasive homoeroticism. Cronenberg (in the interview in this book) attributes this to the presence in both films of Ron Mlodzik; yet, according to the credits, Cronenberg himself wrote, directed and edited both films (Mlodzik is credited solely as an actor). If one switched off the soundtrack of *Crimes of the Future* (the loss would not be great), one might easily assume that the main body of the film had no ambition beyond chronicling a series of somewhat kinky gay pick-ups, with the participants perversely interested in each other's feet: one is interrupted by a jealous lover, another is brought to a halt by the second man, who is understandably pissed off by the extremely limited manner of intercourse.

Stereo should perhaps be read as marking, at the outset of Cronenberg's career in feature films (I have not seen the shorts that precede it), a crucial moment of hesitation. The Cronenberg structure (the attempt at progress that goes disastrously wrong) is already there embryonically. Yet the film has an openness and uncertainty that I don't find in any of the subsequent works. What is especially remarkable is the way it moves towards (a) an explicit lecture on

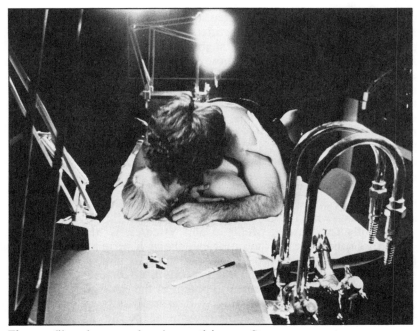

The one film where people enjoy eroticism — *Stereo*

"omnisexuality" of quite extraordinary radical import (heterosexuality and homosexuality are both "perversions," extended bisexuality — with socially constructed "masculinity" and "femininity" quite broken down — the preferred and logical norm) and (b) the one scene in Cronenberg (the "conventions" of *Fast Company* excepted) where people actually appear to enjoy eroticism — the bisexual "threesome" with two men and a woman. I don't want to make any great claims for the film (the Cronenbergian enervation is already the dominant feature); but I think it *does* suggest a direction his work might have taken, and didn't.

Crimes of the Future is much more insistently homoerotic, but it contains no equivalent to the three-way love-making scene of *Stereo*: here, already, sexuality has become perverse, pleasureless, and associated with disgust and disease. It is symptomatic that Ron Mlodzik, who is quite an attractive presence in the earlier film, is here completely devitalized. The two films' chief claim on the attention of aficionados of the "experimental" film is doubtless their play with words and images: the verbal narration and the visual representation seldom neatly coincide — the spectator has to work to piece things together. But it seems uncertain whether the things in question *can* really be pieced together in any satisfactory way: the science-fiction pretensions of the soundtrack often seem more a pretext for the visual kinkiness than an intellectual justification of it. This sense of discrepancy seems to me to recur, in slightly different forms, in the later films also. Mr. Harkness (whose assessment of my intelligence appears roughly to coincide with mine of his) reprimands me for not noticing that Cronenberg's films are "about science." If one manages to reach this perception, apparently, it becomes unnecessary to examine their tone and imagery. In fact, there seems to me throughout Cronenberg's work a dislocation between the intellectual pretensions (what the films *say* they are about) and the repulsive and obsessional imagery (what they actually *do*). The gulf between the two is far from being breached in *Videodrome*.

Two developments (in relation to the preceding "trilogy") need to be noted in *Scanners*: 1. The woman moves from the film's centre to its periphery (with the result that Jennifer O'Neill, who played so wonderfully for Hawks, Mulligan and Visconti, is here completely wasted). Cronenberg, in the interview, shows a certain sensitivity to feminist attacks on his work, and perhaps this change is his tacit acknowledgement of its vulnerability on this score. The dread of female activeness, which seemed so potent in the three previous films, here quite disappears. 2. Arguably — I am really uncertain about this — this relegation of women to the margins of the film makes way for the return of the homoeroticism that seemed to disappear after

Crimes of the Future, in a hideously perverse form: the climax of the film has two men systematically destroying each other's bodies through an exertion of will, a process presented with much relish.

Videodrome is interesting in respect to this, as its imagery once again plays with bisexuality, again in a quite repulsive way: one might say that the phallus that Marilyn Chambers developed in her armpit in *Rabid* gets its echo and "answer" in the vagina James Woods develops in his stomach in *Videodrome*. I think the general consensus that it is Cronenberg's best film to date is probably correct: its science-fiction premise is more interesting than usual, and more interestingly developed. There remains the question of identifying the real impulse behind the film, the problem of the "excessive" imagery — with its marked sexual overtones — which the premise neither demands nor justifies. The film wraps itself in so many ambiguities that it is very hard to read (a number of critics have adopted the line of "I don't understand it, but I love it"): ambiguities centred especially on the two women, and on the question of the "New Flesh" into which James Woods may or may not be about to be reborn when he commits suicide at the end of the film. It is presumably this "New Flesh" that is taken by Harkness to justify the term "visionary"; yet the film offers one absolutely no grounds for reading it positively. The treatment of human physicality throughout the film continues to suggest revulsion as the dominant attitude, and the whole paraphernalia of means by which the "New Flesh" is to be produced (if it is) carries entirely negative, sinister connotations.

I have suggested that — all the way from *Stereo* to *Videodrome* — Cronenberg's work is haunted by the spectre of bisexuality. It takes many different forms: the feminized men of *Crimes of the Future*, the horrified fantasies of transplanted sexual organs in *Rabid* and *Videodrome*, the dread of female activeness. Only in *Stereo* (which gives the impression of being much more a collaborative enterprise than the subsequent films, with the actors given an unusual degree of freedom) is bisexuality allowed any positive connotations. It has been a major tendency of psychoanalytical theory since Freud to suggest that it is on the repression of our innate, constitutional bisexuality that the gender roles (the clear-cut division of "masculinity" and "femininity") that oppress us all are constructed. Conceived positively, the "New Flesh" could only be androgynous.

What follows is an attempt to treat an allusive and elusive movie with a generosity of perspective that is equal to the film's own range of achievements. *Videodrome* is in many respects an anachronism, and it seems only fitting to discuss what it departs from before measuring the extent of its departure. If this results in a kind of scatter-shot analysis, or the occasional foray into confusion, I have succeeded in at least one respect, by addressing *Videodrome* on its own frequently chaotic and slippery terms. The article opens with a consideration of the challenges the film presents to both the discussion and consumption of commercial cinema, then it attempts to situate *Videodrome*

Cronenberg Tackles Dominant Videology

Geoff Pevere

in an ideological context. Finally, by comparing it to another remarkable film with which it bears close structural and intellectual affinities — Martin Scorsese's *The King of Comedy* — I hope to indicate precisely why *Videodrome* was worth all this fuss in the first place.

The categorical elusiveness of this film makes not only its lukewarm critical reception somewhat more understandable but also explains its poor showing at the box office. For the mass of movie consumers, familiarity is a primary condition of pleasure. Any rejection of formula will result in a frustration of expectations that is likely to drive audiences away, to borrow a phrase from Sam

Goldwyn, in droves. Nowhere are verdicts made more swiftly and mercilessly than in the arena of popular taste. Considered purely as a "horror" movie (the tag encouraged by advertising strategists, the popular press and the growing reputation of writer-director Cronenberg himself), *Videodrome* invariably comes up short. If suspense is a condition of horror, and if this is conventionally generated by the audience's privileged perspective in relation to narrative events (i.e., knowing that a potential victim *is* a potential victim), then the relentlessly subjective and hallucinatory structure of *Videodrome* must prevent any secure and anchored relationship between itself and its audience from developing. Throughout, the viewer remains as frantically disoriented as the protagonist, a cable-TV station owner suffering from video-induced hallucinations. Moreover, to sensibilities raised on Hollywood narrative patterns, the most challenging (and possibly threatening) aspect of *Videodrome* is its refusal to resolve itself, to tidily tie the loose threads of the story together and snip off the stray ends. In terms of structuralist criticism, this is the concept of the open text. The narrative, by raising more questions than it answers, and by challenging prevailing notions of what constitutes a good story, announces its origins in artifice and (in theory) encourages the viewer to engage in active reading rather than passive consumption of the text. At the end of the final reel, *Videodrome* remains as stubbornly open and malignant as the angry, throbbing wound borne on the abdomen of the bewildered hero.

This is not to suggest that the film could or should not be discussed in terms of its relationship to more familar forms of genre or popular narrative. Obviously, any judicious evaluation of its merits must take the film's connections to conventional narrative modes into account. Where this effort to contextualize *Videodrome* will invariably fall short, however, is in the application to it of a set of absolute evaluative standards. The fact is, the prescribed and generally accepted structures for what constitutes acceptable narrative and generic practice are too narrow to contain a work like *Videodrome* without bending it entirely out of shape. As long as a qualitative, consumerist, dollar's-worth emphasis dominates the vast machinery of public discourse on cinema, any films that challenge or elude the confined standards of the marketplace are likely to be shut out of that marketplace, stamped Rotten, shipped out of town and banished to the garbage heap of social irrelevance. Occasionally, if the product exudes a certain exotic aroma, it will be stamped Art, or maybe Import, and made available only to exclusive shops catering to exclusive clientele. Either way, the product remains largely unobtainable. (Martin Scorsese's *The King of Comedy*, which shares strong intellectual and ideological affinities with *Videodrome*, committed the same "crime" of having ambitions more expansive than current standards of criticism could contain. Reviewers were largely bewildered, and audiences stayed home.)

So *Videodrome* is a lame horror movie, but is that all there is to it?

If the film must be subjected to some kind of qualitative evaluation of its merits, it seems more sensible to honour it for its scope and resonance — for its break with the terms of compartmentalized criteria, rather than for its adherence to them. Finally, if *Videodrome* it to be deemed "good" (and certainly the operative assumption here is that it is), it must be thought so because of this very multiplicity. What it isn't matters just as much as what it is.

Of the more common grounds for discussing popular movies, *Videodrome* is most likely to be subjected to the following (listed in order of broadening perspective): first, as the product of a national cinema, a discussion that might seek to place the film in the context of a particular and identifiable framework that can somehow be designated as Canadian; or the film might be discussed as it most frequently is, in terms of its relationship to a particular pattern of narrative rules known as genre — in *Videodrome*'s case, as a science-fiction/horror movie; nuzzled close to this discussion is the one concerned with the film as the expression of a particular "vision" or "personality." This, of course, is the persistent and still pervasive auteur theory, which bestows merit on films following the search-and-recovery of consistent thematic preoccupations across the body of a particular filmmaker's work.

Cronenberg is something of a dream for auteurist criticism, because he's the kind of filmmaker for whom the theory seems custom designed. He writes as well as directs his films. He maintains close proximity to a particular genre, and he repeatedly returns to variations on similar narrative situations, which permit a strong thematic consistency throughout the films.

Certainly the most nebulous terms for an evaluative discussion of Cronenberg's work (and fortunately the least common, given the tenacity of intellectual snobbism regarding pop culture) are those set by a consideration of its aesthetic worth, its status as a "work of art." While this is the most relative and ideologically determined type of evaluation, it should not be dismissed because finally any judgement based on some object's "artfulness" is always valuable as a barometer of prevailing popular attitudes, if not as a widely applicable set of standards (one country's genius, after all, is another's Jerry Lewis). While this doesn't address the thorny problem of aesthetic evaluation in any purposeful way, it does dovetail nicely with the final, and most accommodating context for discussing Cronenberg and *Videodrome*: as a product of ideology.

If ideology is understood as the prevailing system of values governing a community at a particular point in time, *Videodrome* must then be viewed as the result of a convergence of factors (moral, social, sexual, psychological) operating more or less simultaneously. Because these factors are both interdependent and fully distinguishable, like links on a chain or the roots of a tree, a discussion of a film as an ideological product allows for — and *necessitates* — dealing with all terms for discussing movies, since each represents another value system. Each is a vital signal on the tangled switchboard of ideological discourse. Thus, the comments of the most facile television reviewer are of equal value with an academic treatise, because either is an indispensable mechanism supporting a common system.

Regarding *Videodrome*, then, we should not be considering what it's worth, but more crucially where it fits. What is its ideological situation? Answering this question, to the extent that it is answerable, will entail a consideration of *Videodrome* in shifting lights: as horror movie, Cronenberg film, national product, art object and pop-culture event. Obviously, a thorough charting of any film's ideological context — let alone one as slippery as this — could easily fill a volume of its own. This article is merely a preliminary survey. It will pound the stakes, so to speak, on which others may build.

Although neither simple nor direct, connections can be made between *Videodrome*'s position in ideology and its failure to win audiences. In more than one respect it is anachronistic, and its ideological stance is both radical and challenging. As a horror movie, it came too late, when the popularity of the "splatter" cycle of pessimistic, explicitly violent *noirs* horror films had all but run down. Also, the mystifying, hallucinatory narrative structure departed radically from the linear, who-gets-it-next formula of most contemporary scary movies. (Even as an allegedly self-conscious and intellectual practitioner of the genre, Cronenberg — and particularly with *Videodrome* — stands alone. Of the other monster-makers most frequently credited with brains — De Palma, Carpenter, Romero, Hooper, Craven, Cohen — none approaches Cronenberg in either intellectual audacity or the apparent need to show it off.) By altering many of the familiar sensation-sparking devices of the gore-for-gore's-sake splatter movie, *Videodrome* encourages a rechanneling of viewer concentration away from purely visceral kicks to a consideration of the smart stuff beneath — well, theoretically, anyway. Usually the response to such meddling with conventions will be bafflement ("What is this crap?"), or worse, boredom ("Who cares, anyway?"). In suppressing certain vital aspects of the genre and in employing others only in a superficial, purely structural way, *Videodrome*

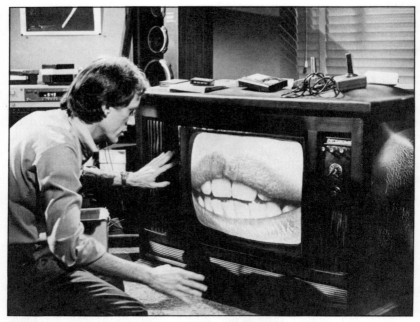

Videodrome — a portrait of a society inundated by the media

"uses" the horror film like a clothing designer uses a mannequin: as an efficient and convenient model on which to hang some dynamite new threads. Using the genre as a body on which to display certain sociological observations, Cronenberg has found an ideal clothes-horse in the horror movie. Moreso than the actual mode of delivery, however, precisely what *Videodrome* delivers to receptive viewers on the conceptual level is what grants the film both its intellectual credibility and its peculiar position in ideology.

Prior to situating *Videodrome* ideologically, however, other factors making up the overall ideological framework in which it operates — and to which it responds — must be considered. For this, we must digress from the designs of "pure" structuralist analysis and step outside the text itself. This is done simply to look at *Videodrome* as a convergence of extra-textual factors — namely, as the product of a particular filmmaker with a unique set of sociological and intellectual associations of his own and finally as the product of a particular attitude and response to specific socio-historical developments that, while not exclusive to Cronenberg or *Videodrome*, are remarkable enough to warrant extensive commentary.

On the eve of 1984, David Cronenberg has become the best known, most written about, hotly disputed and all-around "important" director of feature films ever to emerge from English Canada. Historically and culturally speaking, the controversy and notoriety were wholly foreseeable: not only do the films repeatedly present a vision of a world where agents of an autocratic technology seek out and destroy any traces of assertive individualism, but Cronenberg's work also bears the stamp of an unpopular Orwellian conservatism, which views the onward march of science and technology as signalling a corresponding decline of all that is natural, romantic and, in a word, human. In no other Cronenberg film have these sentiments been more strikingly and extremely represented than in *Videodrome*, a highly literalized rendering of a society so spattered and shot through by media crossfire that television can actually reach out and penetrate hapless viewers — and itself spray very human-looking guts when smashed open.

In another respect, Cronenberg's escalating reputation is decidedly ironic. While the director is engagingly candid about his nationality and its possible influence on his work and temperament ("I don't have a moral plan," he told *Village Voice* critic Carrie Rickey, "I'm a Canadian"), his films seem to have no relation at all (unless it is a subversive one) to either the benignly bland stereotype of the English Canadian national character or the conventional view of English Canadian cinema. (As originally circumscribed by critic Peter Harcourt, English Canadian cinema is a "mode" of expression that "implies more than it says," and is characterized by dramatic emptiness and moments of quiet contemplation.)[1] It is difficult to imagine fitting the edgy, kinetic and visceral cinema of David Cronenberg very comfortably into the image of acquiescent, pensive "Canadianness" that some cultural gatekeepers have devised. In fact, the frantically aggressive nature of a typical Cronenberg movie could suggest something altogether different, and possibly more perceptive, about the psychological determinations of the elusive English Canadian "national character." Considered as integers of a collective sensibility, Cronenberg's films suggest that the accommodating, thoughtful Canadian exterior is a veneer that has been maintained only at the cost of a great and ever-increasing repression of psychosexual impulses. The potentially volatile results of such prolonged psychological pressure-cooking are graphically illustrated in the cinema of David Cronenberg, where Canadians literally explode from the pressure of being what they are. Certainly, if Cronenberg is to be

1. Peter Harcourt: "Introduction" in *Canadian Film Reader*. Edited by Seth Feldman and Joyce Nelson. Toronto, Peter Martin Associates, 1977.

considered as the product of a national sensibility, the concept of what constitutes this sensibility must be expanded or radically reconsidered, so as to be tolerant of possibly "negative" characteristics. Otherwise, the conspicuousness of Cronenberg's exception from the national cultural picture will increase proportionately with his international stature.

Videodrome is both typical and exceptional as a Cronenberg movie. An auteur by any other name, Cronenberg has addressed the implication of particular concepts, themes and situations throughout his work, and *Videodrome* recapitulates most of the Big Ones: the Struggle between Mind and Body (the violent, TV-induced hallucinations of cable-TV station owner Max Renn, which may or may not be occurring in the physical world); the nefarious threat posed to humanity by various manifestations of an Unholy Alliance between Science and Big Business (embodied in *Videodrome* by Spectacular Optical, a "global corporate citizen" that "manufactures cheap eyeglasses for Third World countries and missile-guidance systems for NATO," and which is scheming to obtain a monopoly over minds with a brain-altering, *tumour-inducing*, TV signal). Finally there is the broadest and most pervasive of Cronenbergian preoccupations: the Transformation of Mental Activity into Physical Matter.

In the techno-physiological world of *Videodrome*, where wires and nerves are hopelessly tangled in a single, messy knot, this notion undergoes a further refinement (and a logical one, considering that *Scanners*, in which thoughts could quite literally kill, was the last word on the subject of ideas-as-matter). *Videodrome* posits the existence of a dialectic of sorts between mind and media. Once again, thought can be physically transferred, but only because the blank screen of the cathode-coddled brain is open to infiltration by creeping, rampant broadcast signals, which occupy the mind, take the controls and (horrors!) proceed to dictate the victim's experience of reality. In other words, *Videodrome* demonstrates that, if thoughts can escape from the brain, new thoughts can be just as easily crammed back in. The film's most graphic and outrageously funny moments occur when the operatives of Spectacular Optical programme Max's hallucinations by inserting panting videocassettes directly into a gaping slit in his abdomen. The process of Mind becoming Matter is shown in *Videodrome* to be reversible, and TV is lethal because it quite literally penetrates your brain and fucks with it.

Perhaps in response to those sufferers of intellectual myopia who see no irony in his excess and only madness in his method, *Videodrome* is Cronenberg's most brazenly satirical film. Now *really*, it seems to plea from behind a mask of indulgent grossness, how can you take this seriously? The extremism of the film, in both concept and execution, could indicate only a pronounced self-consciousness or a criminal heavy-handedness. Apart from the graphically visualized metaphors for intercourse between man and machine, consider the clues offered by the DC-comics use of names as eponyms: Dr. Brian O'Blivion (guru of the Cathode Ray Mission), Nicky Brand (a masochist), Barry Convex (Spec Op big cheese) and, of course, the electronic, mind-melting arena of "Videodrome" itself.

But to simply defend something as satire and leave it at that is insufficient because satire does not exist without a referent — that which is satirized. Thus, the question to be asked is: *what* is the object of *Videodrome*'s satire? Seeking the answer — if there is any single answer — will begin to make the film's ideologically subversive situation clearer.

Videodrome is the product of a mentality (which one hesitates to designate simply as Cronenberg's since that implies a degree of intention, of self-conscious design, which is impossible to determine, and makes no difference anyway) made queasy by the apparent ease and acquiescence with which the masses, as represented by dominant media, embraced the surge in communications technology that occurred from the midseventies to early eighties. With this surge came a popular resurgence of scientific idealism, or the romantic celebration of technology for its own sake. Prior to the late seventies, it had been twenty years since the possibilities of a fully harmonious, technologically integrated future had been as tantalizingly suggested by the tools at hand in the present. During the early eighties, among other developments, computers moved into the home, and video games took a bigger bite of the North American entertainment dollar than movies ever did. Of the ailing motion-picture medium itself, the most popular and profitable forms were those that either celebrated technology (present or possible), made extensive use of it, or both. It was a time when mindless fantasy and special effects ruled the box office.

Obviously, this scenario was likely to strike panic in the hearts and minds of the bookish, auteur filmmakers of David Cronenberg's ilk. For not only did the mass, indiscriminate consumption of technology have disturbing intellectual and sociological implications (as the machines burrow deeper into the soul of the public, the precious human factor is displaced), but there must also have been a certain professional panic among a few maverick directors as well, in the order of: does this mean I don't work if I don't have rocketships? Fortunately, it was the former, intellectual response that showed most strongly on the screen. Curiously, the reaction to the popular passion for technology, which was a long-standing preoccupation of a particular wing of science-fiction literature (particularly in the

Swiftian, post technological satires of Philip K. Dick), was slow in coming to the movies. But this hesitancy isn't all that remarkable, really, considering that the industry was virtually rescued from bankruptcy by the popular appetite for purely technological stimulation. Also, aid to the industry arrived in the form of the surge in revenues occasioned by the latest high-tech appliance to occupy the living room: the videocassette recorder. Thus, for the brainier auteurs to lash out with a display of moral indignation over the mass phenomenon of machine worship — when this phenomenon had just saved the industry's neck — wouldn't have been very...well, brainy.

However, the backlash, such as it was (as tiny as it was inevitable) eventually came. At first it came timidly, but with mounting indignation. Early signs of dissent can be detected in Coppola's *The Conversation* (1974), a post-Watergate techno-tragedy chronicling a surveillance expert's belated moral awakening.[2] *Dawn of the Dead* (1979), directed by George A. Romero, astutely drew a connection between an emotionally void, intellectually numbed consumer society and rampaging zombie cannibals. In *Being There*, Hal Ashby's gentle electronic-age variation on the Cinderella legend, a mentally deficient gardener, whose every social response has been absorbed from the TV at the foot of his bed, winds up being courted by fawning financiers who consider the idiot a serious contender for U.S. president.

By 1983, no end to the apparent affair between man and machines was in sight, and two of the most radical responses to rampant technocracy and media downpour were released with a month of each other: Martin Scorsese's *The King of Comedy* and David Cronenberg's *Videodrome*.

Superfically, these films bear little resemblance to each other. Scorsese's film is a harrowing black comedy concerning the abduction of a famous talk-show host by a predatory, celebrity-stalking fanatic. *Videodrome* is a science-fiction/horror movie about a cable-TV station owner's discovery of a corporation's plot to possess the minds of the masses by inducing tumours in docile, defenseless brains. The obvious connection, of course, is TV, and though this is a sufficiently resonant issue in itself, it serves here as only a passageway linking the films on a deeper, more penetrating level. What launches *The King of Comedy* and *Videodrome* into the same ideological orbit is a shared perception of television's function as a social institution. Futhermore, it is the common recognition of this institution's purpose and position in dominant social structures, as well as the thoroughness with which they explore the effects of this, that give both films a truly resonant

2. This is ironic considering Coppola's later surrender to purely mechanical magic shows in *One From the Heart* and *The Outsiders*.

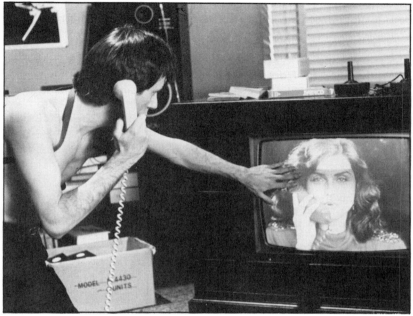

Videodrome — what is real and what is imaginary?

intellectual affinity. Fundamentally, both deal with TV as a conditioning force whose principal function is to reduce everything processed through it to a state of infinite, pulpy sameness. A greater leveller than death itself, television is depicted in these movies as the Cuisinart of information-disseminating institutions, capable not only of swallowing dog food and nuclear war in the same gulp but of spewing it all back as part of an unceasing, uniform flow. To the box, and to those who watch it, it's all the same stew.

But this is nothing new. What really distinguishes *Videodrome* and *The King of Comedy* is their taking of this fundamental — albeit uncommon — acknowledgement of television's meltdown function a vital — albeit logical — step further. In depicting protagonists whose every act and motivation is determined entirely in response to TV, both films situate the tube as the source of all action occurring in the narrative, thereby making even principal characters mere agents set in motion by the medium. What this implies is nothing less than a dialectic, a fusion, between the electronic media and its consumers. Television, in the context of both movies, is as much a *producer* as a product of the society it represents. Rupert Pupkin, the kidnapper/

comic hero of Scorsese's film, sees television as an arena of legitimization: as not simply the only place that matters, but as the only place *of* matter — the only place where things are "real." But Rupert is only the most extreme (if inevitable) product of a society where all, from cons to G-men, conduct their lives as though permanently stuck in front of a live studio audience. To the people living in *The King of Comedy*, shtick is everything. In *Videodrome*, media prophet Brian O'Blivion (whose disembodied, TV-entombed image suggest a perfectly conceivable hybrid of Marshall McLuhan and L. Ron Hubbard) puts the matter somewhat more succinctly, if mystically, as he tells Max of the only possible condition of a society that willfully subjugates its own conscience to the will of an artificial one:

> The battle for the mind of North America will be fought in the video arena, the "*Videodrome*". The television screen is the retina of the mind's eye. Therefore the television screen is part of the physical structure of the brain. Therefore whatever appears on the television screen emerges as raw experience for those who watch it. Therefore television is reality and reality is less than television.

Moreover, the formal organization of both films reflects the thematic concern with the conditioning function of TV. Most commercial narrative cinema depends on the maintenance of an omniscient, third-person perspective for coherence. In addition to binding the various units of narrative action into an impression of linearity, the third-person perspective orients the viewer and facilitates identification with particular figures and actions in the story. Obviously, the successful operation of any visual narrative depends on the viewer's fluency in reading certain systems of signification. Thus, there has developed in popular cinema an elaborate, standardized system of signs, a language, in other words, that serves to satisfy audience expectation and ensure viewer pleasure by speaking in a way that everyone can understand. Flashbacks, for example, will be perceived as such only if indicated by such bracketing devices as a rippling screen or a slow dissolve. These conventional mechanisms for viewer identification and pleasure are largely absent from *The King of Comedy* and *Videodrome*. Instead, both films inscribe the thematic concern with TV as ideological institution in their formal structure. Both skate freely across the conventional barriers between objective and subjective representation. Max's dilemma in *Videodrome* becomes ours, as viewers: that is, to figure out just how much of what goes on is "real" and how much is imagined. (If there's ever any real difference.) Similarly, in *The King of Comedy*, we are given no indication, by way of familiar narrative road signs, when we arrive in the TV-fertilized subjectivity of Rupert Pupkin, nor are we given any clues as to the length of our stay. (The "overnight sensation" epilogue, for example, is particularly troublesome in this respect. When one attempts to ascribe some kind of "objective" context to it, it can be just as easily understood as an expression of Rupert's desire as any "real" event.)

While both *Videodrome* and *The King of Comedy* radically challenge prevailing systems of signification, in terms of both form and content, it could be argued that they also subscribe to a reactionary and somewhat alarmist view of the electronic media. True, both films view TV as a serious and pervasive threat to everything humanity holds most valuable about itself (primarily, the integrity of the individual). But to challenge the films solely on this account is to ignore the full repercussions of the positions they adopt, and the extent to which both rigorously follow through their own implications. Certainly, the suggestion that TV is somehow bad is a banal and easily digested message by now, but to move beyond that obviousness and to demonstrate the *active* role played by the media in ordering our perceptions of what is real and possible (and thus its role in dictating the terms and possibilities of "reality" itself) is to take up a radical position with regard to the function of the electronic media in society. In ostensibly different ways, and while drifting on the fringe of the monolithic institution of commercial narrative cinema, both *Videodrome* and *The King of Comedy* assume such a position. Considering the potential risks involved in such presumptuousness (box-office failure is only the most obvious one) and the intellectual ingenuity required to pull it off, theirs is no mean feat.

Obviously, the last word on *Videodrome* has not been spoken, here or anywhere else. While the grounds for most forms of conventional movie analysis have proven too restrictive to pin an actively anti-conventional film like *Videodrome* down, the telescopic nature of an ideological approach suffers, conversely, from its own inclusiveness. Often, though it touches different aspects of the beast it studies, it cannot call an elephant an elephant. In attempting to situate *Videodrome* in an ideological context, which invariably entails much preliminary scouting of the surrounding territory, this discussion has sacrificed precision in favour of perspective. Consequently, the film may not seem any more apprehensible now than before. But this by no means invalidates the discussion, as its ultimate value — like the film's — must also be sought in a broader context.

What the discussion of popular-culture products in ideological terms can achieve is by no means insignificant. In order to be of any pertinent or lasting value, any examination should, among other things, seek: to change the way in which films are viewed in this society; to illustrate the need for a critical discourse on commercial cinema that is not strangled from the outset by its own assumptions or the pressures of the marketplace; to appreciate a text that does not conform to any arbitrary set of evaluative standards; to deal with cultural products that not only challenge these standards but also that do so with a resonance that reaches the basic values of social organization — a cultural product such as David Cronenberg's *Videodrome*. What is needed, finally, is a mode of critical discourse capable of appreciating something for what it isn't as much as for what it is.

I. The Author of His Work

"You have to go all the way through it, Nola. All the way through it to the end."
The Brood (1979)

The Image As Virus

The Filming of "Videodrome"

Tim Lucas

dialogue!"

Mark Irwin is right. The words appear to possess a talismanic significance for David Cronenberg, the thirty-nine - year - old Canadian writer director,

"But we'll have to all the way through it, Max. All the way through it to the end."
Videodrome, 3rd Draft (1982)

"Imitation is the sincerest form of... Television."
Steve Allen

"Two films later," the cinematographer exclaimed to himself, as he strolled through an aisle separating the cubicles of the Cathode Ray Mission set built for his current project *Videodrome*, "and we're still shooting the same piece of

whose previous work in the genre (*Shivers*, *Rabid*, *The Brood* and *Scanners*) has given him a paradoxical reputation for pushing screen violence and individual artistry as far as they will go. His movies are distinguished by their fluid uniformity of vision — they share an abiding concern with family, whether actual or metaphorical; the Cartesian schism of Mind and Body; and the challenging of mortal barriers by artists and scientists — and, taken together, they create one of the truest oeuvres the fantastic has ever known. This recurrent bit of dialogue (the former spoken by Oliver Reed, the latter — before it was scrapped — by Sonja Smits) seems, in scripted context, to be as much directed at Cronenberg's own creative powers as to his characters; their echoing suggests an incantation used by a struggling author to urge his imagination over the next hurdle.

For Cronenberg and the horror genre itself, his sixth feature, *Videodrome*, is a new frontier. While his first two films focused on the exclusively *sexual* transmission and perpetuation of horror, *Videodrome*, like his most recent work, branches ominously out into the *whole* human system — Mind and Body — but this times cleaves Mind into the Real and the Imagined. As for its value to the genre, *Videodrome* specifically underlines the influence of a sprawlingly technological world on our human senses and makes a bold attempt to describe how this cultural escalation might shift the shape of one's subconscious, where all horror begins.

The horrific potentiality of television (partly Cronenberg's topic here) has not exactly gone unexplored by horror and science-fiction films. Back in 1955, when Hollywood was waging an apparent life-and-death war against the frenzied popularity of TV, Joseph Newman's *This Island Earth* presented the "Interociter," a TV screen that fired deadly beams at its unsuspecting viewers and also a dying planet presided over by a feeble leader called "The Monitor." Since then, of course, audiences have sided against the camera eye of HAL-9000; admired the blaspheming madness of Peter Finch as he probed the limits of news broadcasting in *Network*; and, most recently, witnessed the medium's annexation to the Supernatural in *Poltergeist* and *Halloween III: Season of the Witch*. Among the precursors of *Videodrome*, certainly the closest to Cronenberg's conception is Bernard Tavernier's *Deathwatch* (1981), based on D.G. Compton's novel *The Unsleeping Eye*, which also matches a television show featuring actual deaths with paranoiac corporate control. But whereas Tavernier attends one woman's escape from its clutches, Cronenberg's hero is compelled to investigate the repulsive phenomenon of Snuff TV as a means of finding answers to and analyzing his own fascination with televised sex and violence and becomes physically addicted to it and, ultimately, deranged.

Videodrome, as an idea, actually began "about ten years ago," according to its author, with a screen treatment entitled *Network of Blood*. "It had to do with a private network subscribed to by strange, wealthy people who were willing to pay to see bizarre things on television," Cronenberg recalled. "It did involve an independent TV hustler, like Max Renn (James Woods), who accidentally plugged into the network and tried to find out what it was. That was always an interesting premise to me but, on its own, it was not possible to do more than explore the most obvious aspects of it.'' Much later, Cronenberg had the additional notion of making a first-person film that would show to an audience the subjective growth of the hero's madness. ''Our own perception of reality is the only one we'll accept, it's all we have to go on and, if you're going mad, that is still your reality,'' he reasoned. ''But the same thing, seen from an outside perspective, is a person acting insane. The two ideas clicked together. That was one of the ideas advanced by John Donne and the Metaphysical Poets, the taking of two disparate ideas and yoking them together to come up with something totally new.'' The allusion could be considered a pretentious one were *Videodrome* not a truly metaphysical movie, but it *is* concerned with ultimate causes and the underlying nature of things. ''To delve deeper into the impulses where the film began,'' continued Cronenberg, ''I can only say that I've always been interested in dark things and *other* people's fascinations with dark things, and the idea of people locking themselves in a room and turning a key on a television set so that they can watch something *extremely* dark and, by doing that, allow themselves to explore their fascinations.... *That's* closer to the bone in terms of an original impulse.''

The *Network of Blood* treatment was written ''during a slow period'' about the time Cronenberg was attempting to place another, *Orgy of the Blood Parasites*, which, in 1975, became his first feature, *Shivers*. Cronenberg began his first draft of *Videodrome* in late January 1981. Perhaps understandably, Cronenberg did not want to unveil any fragments of his rough draft publicly (for, to quote his literary mentor Vladimir Nabokov, to do so would be like ''passing around samples of one's sputum''), but its nature reveals a great deal about his creative process, so integral to an understanding of his art. While writing his rough drafts, Cronenberg accepts as a given that they will resemble his final product in only the most basic way and allows his mind to move in any direction it desires, pushing at the limits of what is possible to render onscreen until those limits are broken; it is at this point that he feels truly in touch with his imagination. By granting his imaginative powers an absolute free rein, it is granted the freedom to explode, backfire, frighten *him*. In the first draft of *Videodrome*, Max Renn combats his hallucination by chopping his Flesh-gun off at the wrist and, from the stump, there growns a fleshy ''potato-masher''-style hand grenade that explodes. There is a kissing scene in which Max's and Nicki's faces melt together into a single object that dribbles down, crawls across the floor and up the leg of an onlooker, and melts *him*. And the most horrible murder featured in the finished film — the cancer-engulfing

Max rips away the screen to find — Nicki

death of Barry Convex — originally happened to five other characters, as well. "My early drafts tend to get extreme in all kinds of
ways — sexually, violently and just in terms of weirdness," Cronenberg described. "But I have to balance this weirdness against what an
audience will accept as reality. Even in the sound mix, when we're
talking about what sort of sound effects we want for the hand moving
around inside the stomach slit, for example; we *could* get really weird
and use really loud, slurpy, gurgly effects, but I'm playing it
realistically. That is to say, I'm giving it the sound it would really
have, which is *not much*. I'm presenting something that is outrageous
and impossible, but I'm trying to convey it realistically."

II. The Trouble Is Not on Your Set

"Be regular and orderly in your life, like a bourgeois,
   so that you may be violent and original in your work."

Gustave Flaubert

Since so few horror directors author their own scripts, and even fewer screenwriters specialize in the genre, watching Cronenberg navigate his way through the filming of his concept is a rare sight, to say the least. During the two visits I paid to the set in December and March, I observed as Cronenberg thought and rethought, wrote and rewrote a *few* pivotal scenes. (On the last day of filming, in fact, after a full working day that collected only one take, Cronenberg announced to the crew that he hadn't yet written the film's ending to his satisfaction, that to film it as it was tentatively scripted would not be right, and he opened — with considerable fearful wincing — a champagne bottle of Christmas cheer.) The most pivotal of these, in terms of where a specific scene could alter or clarify the future course of the plot, was perhaps the moment when Max Renn stalks Bianca O'Blivion through the Cathode Ray Mission with his Flesh-gun. Bianca rushes behind a paper screen partition (one of the defining elements of the monitor cubicles there), which Max rips away. Over a six-month period, Cronenberg inserted many things behind that screen — from Nicki Brand to a video image of Nicki Brand.

The first Nicki Brand sequence was the culmination of a sensual trick Cronenberg had initiated and ultimately discarded, in which Max's perceptions of Nicki and Bianca blur together into interchangeable women; the two women were revealed, in this first sequence, to be business partners of a sort. Max tears the screen and finds Nicki, seated authoritatively beside a computer board, wearing an outfit of Biancan conservatism. Nicki explains:

> We knew that you were "Videodrome"'s next target. We planned to intercept you, use you to dig deeper into "Videodrome." I came to Brian O'Blivion five years ago. I studied with him. And I saw what "Videodrome" did to him. I also saw what it could be. In the right hands. . . . Your right hand, Max. I can see what it's become. It may have started out as a hallucination, but now it's real. You're the new spring line. Isn't that exciting?

The scene, present as late as the script's third draft, continues as Max discovers the Flesh TV broadcasting an image of Bianca O'Blivion, her spinsterish hair now loose and languidly tumbling over her shoulders, wearing Nicki's red dress (as seen on the "Rena King Show"), and baring one shoulder to reveal Nicki's own Swiss Army knife scars:

> BIANCA (ON TV)
> But we'll have to go all the way through it, Max. All the way through it to the end. We can't stop where you are now. . . stuck in the middle. Not us, not Bianca, Max and Nicki. The road to excess leads to the palace of wisdom.

Then her TV image was to cut to the flesh-screen of the set extending into a gun that fires and fells Max.

Asked about the symbiotic relationship between Bianca and Nicki in earlier drafts, Cronenberg said, "I was toying with that, yes, but it was not clear and not developed or anticipated enough to work. I don't mind ambivalence or ambiguity in a film — in fact, I think it's *necessary* — but confusion is never necessary."

In post-production, Cronenberg rewrote the scene so that Max, tearing the screen, was confronted by the weeping tele-image of Masha; the videotaped footage was left over from a scrapped effects sequence in which the Flesh TV was to rise, with Masha's image on it, out of the soapy waters of Max's bathtub. The desired effect was that Max would turn against Convex and his Spec Op goons to avenge Masha's death — "They killed me, Maxie," she cries; "I wasn't supposed to tell you about Brian O'Blivion" — but their relationship, in the final analysis, had not been fleshed beyond a casual business relationship. It wasn't until Cronenberg screened a preview print to an audience in Boston in April 1982 that he saw the absolute necessity of bringing Nicki Brand back into the picture, of resolving her character, at the relatively negligible cost of resolving Masha's, and photographed new video footage of Deborah Harry for the film's last scene *and* refilmed this scene (using ex-disc jockey Art Austin as James Wood's stand-in) to show Max tearing the screen away from the Flesh TV, showing Nicki's death on "Videodrome." This explained her sudden disappearance after flying off to Pittsburgh and elevated Max's sense of outrage, aloneness and spirituality in the subsequent scenes, which save his suicidal finale from feeling too defeatist. It was to Cronenberg's puzzle an extraordinary elegant solution. "It felt so right that it felt inevitable," Cronenberg said, "but not so inevitable that I'd thought of it before!"

As for the shipboard suicide that ends the film, it was Cronenberg's intention also to continue the film briefly beyond it, into the "Next Phase," as Nicki's video-image calls it. Before the decision was made to end the scene with the bang of Max's gun, Cronenberg described his envisioning: "After the suicide, he ends up on the "Videodrome" set with Nicki, hugging and kissing and neat stuff like that. A happy ending? Well, it's *my* version of a happy ending — Boy meets Girl on the "Videodrome" set, with the clay wall *maybe* covered in blood (but I'm not sure). Freudian rebirth imagery, pure and simple." Mark Irwin outlined the never-filmed sequence for us cinematically: "He'll shoot himself in the head and go — boom! — out of frame, and we'll cut to his head hitting the clay wall, and the camera will track back and there he is, happy in front of the fireplace with his pipe and slippers and Nicki hopping all over him! Another film for the whole family!''

These descriptions are, in actuality, euphemistic (to say the least) of a sexual crescendo the likes of which have not been seen in Cronenberg's work since the joyously and venereally infected finale of *Shivers*. Cronenberg preferred us not to excerpt from the sequence in question, which depicted Max and Nicki (and, in a separate draft, Bianca) on the ''Videodrome'' set, nude and making love. Nicki reveals to Max a new abdominal slit of her own, and Bianca has one, too, and the three of them probe one another's slits with their hands, which slip out bearing strange, mutated sexual organs emitting even stranger lubrications, ending the film on a note of moist, exploratory feasting. Mutated sex-organ appliances — both male and female — were required and Rick Baker, too engulfed by other responsibilities to design and manufacture them, subcontracted the duty to his friend Greg Cannom (*The Sword and The Sorcerer*). Cannom's foam-latex appliances arrived from Los Angeles in late December and, after viewing an impromptu test of making them breathe and spurt viscous fluids in the EFX Workshop, Cronenberg vetoed the scene altogether. The quality of Cannom's work wasn't to blame; if anything was to blame, it was the accumulation of circumstances. Deborah Harry had contracted stomach flu from which the whole crew had suffered at one time or other during the shoot, the production was behind schedule and rapidly nearing its Christmas deadline, and Cronenberg felt he couldn't execute the scene to his own standards, citing such similar ''liquid, alien sex scenes'' as those in Nicolas Roeg's *The Man Who Fell to Earth* as ''to me, basically unconvincing.''

*

Filmmaking is, for Cronenberg, a truly interior process — at least when he's writing, which in this case was constantly. Watching this interior process from an observer's stance, after a couple of days, became for me creatively frustrating. Standing among the cubicles of the Cathode Ray Mission, where Toronto's derelict class is charitably fed through the retina, I remembered how Cameron Vale in *Scanners* was introduced as a derelict. ''One of these days, I'll have to ask you what derelicts mean to you,'' I warned the director, who was wandering about the set between shots and looking vaguely reflective. ''Sure,'' he granted. I thought he was about to wander right away, but he stayed put. ''Okay,'' I piped up, ''what *do* derelicts mean to you?''

''All of the fabled American artists became derelicts,'' he exaggerated, but continued to cite specifics, ''Walt Whitman, Melville. Maybe me, someday.'' Then it was time to continue shooting.

III. Cutting the Cord

"Word begets image and image is virus...."

William Burroughs, *Naked Lunch*

On May 24 and 25, Deborah Harry returned to Toronto to film the videotape insert shown on the Flesh TV in the condemned boat, in which she reassures Max Renn that "Death isn't the end." Originally, during post-production shooting, James Woods acted the scene from a script that depicted him conversing with his own televised image:

SC.A-85 INT. NIGHT. CONDEMNED BOAT
Max walks into the condemned boat. He sits in corner. Max looks up. The TV set is there. Max's own image is on it.

MAX

I was hoping you'd be back.

TV MAX

I'm always here when you need me.

MAX

I'm confused. I don't know where I am now. I'm having trouble finding my way around.

TV MAX

Well, I think we've gone about as far as we can go with the way things are. I think it's time for a change, don't you? Time to go on to the next phase.

MAX

What phase is that?

TV MAX

I don't know, but I'm excited to find out, aren't you?

MAX

I guess I am. How do we do it?

TV MAX

Watch. I'll show you. It should be easy.

TV Max stands up and puts Flesh-gun to his head.

Cronenberg felt that the scene of a troubled man talking to himself was "too claustrophobic" and that he "needed Nicki — or Max's *image* of Nicki — to come around again" to close the picture on a note of dissonant spirituality — that in suicide lies hope. Lines for

Deborah Harry were written around the above preexisting dialogue, replacing the concept of the "TV Max." Also filmed on the two pick-up days (which uncommonly reunited all the necessary members of the principal photography crew) was the footage in the Cathode Ray Mission in which Renn is shown Nicki's death on "Videodrome" and (in a clever, last-minute script manipulation) is reprogrammed by Bianca O'Blivion against Convex and the other usurpers of her father's signal. These new pieces combined to make *Videodrome* ideally lucid, emotionally disturbing and surprisingly spiritual.

In my review of *Videodrome*, published in the April/May 1983 issue of *Cinefantastique*, I was able to record only my rawest impressions of the movie — a considered rave. To leave it at that would be an injustice to the subtlety of Cronenberg's accomplishment, because *Videodrome* is a film that operates on comparatives, juxtapositions and paradoxes that ought to be noted here.

First, the film's Renaissance motif; Cronenberg initially pursued it as "a visceral thing; it wasn't a calculated move at all," but in hindsight he can view his instinctive movements with greater clarity. "O'Blivion's milieu was rather Medieval, as you see; his room has a distinct Middle Ages flavor," Cronenberg told me. "There was a time in the Middle Ages when the era was thought of as the Dark Ages, and the Renaissance was then the rebirth of everything worthwhile. Later, of course, it was realized that there was much that was rich and sustaining in the Middle Ages. Therefore, I think it probably pleases Convex and his people to view their actions as a Renaissance of sorts, as the preparatory stage of the world's moral rearmament, as the development of a new regime — under Spectacular Optical — of harmony and goodness. As Bianca says, "They want to go much further with my father's concept, and in different directions that he would've wanted.""

The neoreligious atmosphere of the Spectacular Optical convention's decor emphasizes the organization's piety, and their adoption of Lorenzo de Medici as patron figure and use of his two quotations — "The eye is the window of the soul" and "Love comes in at the eye" — underline their radical misinformation. The first quotation actually comes from Leonardo da Vinci, and the second — to get really radical — is the second line of W.B. Yeat's poem "A Drinking Song." "They're misinformed and don't really care," Cronenberg explained. "They're very cynical about using whatever suits them."

Cronenberg was also conscious of the echoing of Max Renn's name in *Ren*aissance and in *Loren*zo de Medici, and that Harlan's affected nickname for Renn (*patron*, meaning boss) is reflected in Medici's described nature as "famous Renaissance spokesman and patron of the arts." Most importantly, I realized, the Renaissance motif is resolved with Max's suicide that, Nicki reassures him, will result in his own spiritual rebirth: "I've learned that death isn't the end," she promises. This lends the viewer a sudden insight, and looking back over the entire film, he sees rebirths evident everywhere: Professor O'Blivion's rebirth into videotape, machine's rebirth into man, man's rebirth into machine, Harlan's rebirth in Max's perception of him from comrade to villain, et cetera.

While the Spectacular Optical company is an openly and proudly subversive influence, *Videodrome* is itself brilliantly subversive in its own sense of structure. Early on in the film, when Max enters a seedy hotel to meet Shinji Kuraki of Hiroshima Video to audition "Samurai Dreams" for Civic TV, he passes in the corridor a drunken man pounding violently on a door and pleading/demanding his lover to grant him entry. "For fuck's sake," he cries, "let me in! C'mon, for *fuck's* sake!" The obscenity is accentuated by the sudden anger in his voice and the fact that he hits the door especially violently when shouting it, subliminally establishing an awareness of the tangled natures of sexual and violent behavior. The man is pleading for entry, but demonstrating violence to insinuate himself into the woman's domain. The scene reminded me that the word "fuck" is synonymous with the German word *ficken*, meaning "to strike, or hit." (When I mentioned this to Cronenberg, he expressed an interest but no surprise.) Even earlier, while perusing an assortment of stills from "Samurai Dreams," Renn gets some pizza sauce on one of them, again subliminally establishing the connection of bare skin to red streaks, flowering shortly thereafter in the first glimpse of the "Videodrome" show; this comes across even stronger in the script, which emphasizes that "the stains won't come off." When Nicki Brand burns her breast with a flaming cigarette tip, it isn't this act that provides the horror of the scene but that she then hands the cigarette to Max and offers him the other breast; there is a shot of Max, deciding, and a quick cut to the next scene before we see his acceptance or denial of the moment. The scene forces the audience, tricked into Max's point of view by the first-person angle of the narrative, to make his decision *for* him in their own minds, thereby learning something potentially revealing about their own natures. Similarly, the extreme horror of Barry Convex's death is incomprehensibly magnified by the ear-piercing shriek of feedback issuing from his dropped microphone; it emphasizes that the anarchy of the moment is total, that no one is in control, the the child born of a new technology is screaming at the horrific fate of its murdered stepfather.

The Image As Virus by Tim Lucas is a brief excerpt of material to be published in the October issue (vol. 14 no. 2) of *CINEFANTASTIQUE* magazine, P.O. Box 270, Oak Park, Illinois 60303. The issue is devoted to the filming of *Videodrome*, and includes a preview of Cronenberg's new film, *The Dead Zone*.

The Interview   William Beard and Piers Handling

Can you tell me about your early life?

My father was a writer, a columnist for the *Toronto Telegram*. He wrote the stamp column for about thirty years. He also wrote short stories for a Canadian magazine called *True Detective*, I think. He was always writing for magazines, *Reader's Digest* or one of those things. My mother is a pianist; she was an accompanist — she played for ballet groups and choirs. We always had books in our house. There were walls made of books, literally; they were piled so high there were corridors made of books, thousands of them. And that's basically the atmosphere I grew up in, which was to say very understanding, very accepting of all the arts.

I read very widely, especially novels. I specifically remember at the age of ten beginning to write what I thought was a novel. It turned out to be only a couple of pages long, but as far as I was concerned it was a novel. So I aspired to write very early. I was interested in underground novels — William Burroughs, Henry Miller and some of the people that T.S. Eliot introduced to North America.

At the same time you were developing an interest in the sciences?

Reading and science mingled together very nicely. I hadn't understood that I was supposed to be schizophrenic about it. I had cats that I loved, so I was interested in animals. A natural interest in nature and animals developed into an interest in biology and biochemistry. It went hand in hand with the reading, and it of course led me to science fiction, but not as an end street or anything. It was just one of many things I would read. And I always went to the movies, too, because when I was a kid there was no television. And movies were where you got your walking and talking imagery of life. I went to see everything — whatever happened to be playing at the neighbourhood theatre, everything from cartoons to westerns to heavier stuff.

I was not raised as a film buff. It was not until I was in my twenties that I focused on film. As I got older I remember I went to the Toronto Film Society. I became interested in European films, and I guess in those days that qualified me as a bit of a film buff, except that I did not think of myself as one. To me it was just the same as being interested in obscure novels. I remember seeing *Last Year at Marienbad* at the Little Cinema,[1] and the lady selling tickets tried to

---

1. The Little Cinema was one of Toronto's first art-house cinemas.

talk me out of it so she could go home early. She said, "Well, you know it's in French," as though this would dissuade me from seeing it. Anyway, I was the only one who was watching it. But still there was no career motivation or anything like that, whereas when I was reading novels I was always thinking of myself as a potential novelist, so my approach to that was slightly different.

As a teenager you submitted a story to a fantasy magazine, didn't you?

I was sixteen. I had been writing stories and sending them to magazines. I was into short-story writing as a first attempt to get something published. I used to read *Writer's Digest* and various magazines that focused more or less on the professional writer. And when I was sixteen I got a nice letter from the editor of *The Magazine of Fantasy and Science Fiction* telling me that this story came quite close to being published. Please send us more. As it turned out, I don't think I ever wrote another short story after that until I got to university, and I certainly never sent any off for publication. But I was very pleased, to say the least, that I had gotten something back besides a form rejection letter.

When you went to university you decided to study the natural sciences. Was it a problem choosing which area you wanted to go into?

It wasn't really, especially at the end of high school. I had a science teacher in North Toronto Collegiate who really wanted me to go into the sciences. He thought it would be a shame if I didn't. And I also had English teachers who were sure that I would go into English, so the split was suddenly made very real at that point, by the educational system I think more than anything else. But I always knew that you didn't have to go into English language or literature to write. I thought I could go into the sciences and write, as Isaac Asimov and several other scientists, who were also well-known science-fiction writers, had done. And that's why I went into science in my first year.

I understand you lasted only a year.

Spiritually, I did not last more than a couple of months. By the end of the year I was not going to classes. I was hanging out in the Junior Common Room of University College at the University of Toronto, talking to everybody in the arts.

What made you think about film as something more than just a passing interest?

I just never thought of myself making a film. I had shot 8mm footage of car races — another one of my many obsessions as a kid — but it never occurred to me to make a fiction film or anything like that. There was no encouragement to in the society that I lived in —it was not something anybody did. Then a group of students at the university made a feature film. It was quite astounding for me to see *Winter Kept Us Warm*, which starred people like Iain Ewing, Henry Tarvainen, Janet Amos, Joy Tepperman and Jack Messinger, ² who is in *The Dead Zone*, and had roles in some of my other films including *Stereo, Crimes of the Future* and *Rabid*. The main thing was not that it was made by people I knew, because I did not know David Secter, ³ but that it had actors who were friends, and that is what connected me with the filmmaking process. I was suddenly fascinated, and the movie was not a bad movie. I thought I could do better. So that's really where it started, and it was astounding for me to realize that human beings made movies.

So it was not film per se that got you interested, it was also people around you making films. It was connected to your life as something real to you as opposed to watching some extraordinary film from another culture.

2. Iain Ewing directed a dozen or so independent films between 1967 and 1975, including two feature-length works, *Kill* (1968) and *Eat Anything* (1970). He also acted in a number of films. Henry Tarvainen became a theatre director of some repute. Janet Amos is now the director of the Blythe Summer Festival, and Joy Tepperman, now Joy Fielding, is a novelist.

3. The director of *Winter Kept Us Warm*, David Secter, was a fourth-year English student at the University of Toronto when he made this film. It was a considerable success and had screenings at a number of international film festivals. Secter, however, only made one other feature, *The Offering* (1966), before disappearing from the film scene.

That's exactly right. And more than just Canadian, because I don't know that I had ever seen a Canadian film at that point, to be quite frank. I don't think I had, although I had seen a lot of stuff on CBC that impressed me at the time like *Pale Horse, Pale Rider*, and there were things on television that really affected me. It still didn't feel immediate to me in the sense that I had access to the machinery. I just did not feel at all encouraged to go to the CBC and say, "I really want to be involved in this. I've seen some wonderful things."

It has to be immediate, doesn't it?

And it takes someone your own age or someone close to you to suddenly say, "My God, I can do this — it's exciting." And that's exactly what happened.

Was there a community of people making films in Toronto at this time?

Well, I was one of the ones who started it. I mean, Bob Fothergill, Iain Ewing, Ivan Reitman and I started the film coop. We based ourselves in Cinecity,[4] at Film Canada,[5] which was Willem Poolman's crazed brainchild, and which had a very long and profound influence on all of us. It connected us with very arty films and also with New York underground films. That was really where we found our access to films.

Cinecity showed all kinds of films. When it was not New York underground or L.A. underground, it tended to be European. That's not to say I did not see movies showing at other theatres. I'm sure I did. I'm sure I saw the American films that were popular, but the really exciting stuff for me was all the Hungarian, Polish, Czech films, Miklos Jancso. And I'd go to Cinecity where they had screenings of films that Poolman was looking at to see whether or not

---

4. Cinecity was another of Toronto's art-house cinemas, which no longer exists. It was responsible for showing a number of the most important European films of the period.

5. Film Canada was a distributor of avant-garde films in the late sixties and early seventies.

he was interested in distributing them for Film Canada. It also made us all feel like insiders as opposed to outsiders. And when you start to feel that you are an insider it helps with your sense of power. You feel you can actually do something rather than be just a spectator.

*

When did you decide to make your first film?

The first one was called *Transfer*, and it was really an attempt to make a film based on my reading about how you make a film using the encyclopedia and *American Cinematographer* magazine. I hung around Janet Good's company[6] and talked to the cameramen who would float by there and learned how to take care of the camera. When I felt I was ready, I went out and made this little seven-minute film, which I wrote and shot and edited and recorded sound, and I did everything else. I shot it with an Auricon. It was a two-character sketch. Urjo Kareda,[7] in the paper — I think it was the *Globe* — accused me of stealing the idea from Mike Nichols and Elaine May, because he said it was very similar to a sketch that they had done. I wrote a letter to the paper saying I had no knowledge of the sketch, and he wrote me a private letter apologizing and saying that because one of the actors knew all the Nichols and May sketches, he assumed that... It was nice to be compared with them, anyway.

It was about a psychiatrist who is pursued by his patient wherever he goes, because the patient feels that their relationship is the only one he's ever had that meant anything to him.

It prefigures the relationship that Mike has with Raglan in The Brood. *Mike can't live without Raglan. Raglan is the perfect father figure.*

6. Janet Good and her Canadian Motion Picture Equipment Company has been a true friend to the young independent filmmaker in Toronto. Innumerable emerging filmmakers borrowed equipment from her to make their films, deferring payment until later dates, if at all. Her contribution to the film scene should not be overlooked.

7. Urjo Kareda, coincidentally, was another denizen of University College's old Junior Common Room at the same time Cronenberg found intellectual stimulation there.

That's interesting. You are absolutely right, but I hadn't thought of that before. But, yes it would.

You described it as being a very arty film.

Arty in that I tried visual dislocation. Most of it takes place in a snowy field, and they're eating on a table set up out in the field without any sort of logical or realistic attempt to explain why they would be doing that. There is a surrealistic element, which did not quite match the psychological humour in the film. Whether it works or not I have no idea, but certainly technically it was pretty lumpy.

Was your next short film, From the Drain, *very different from* Transfer?

It is definitely more like a Samuel Beckett sketch. Thinking about it now, it had that element. There are two guys sitting in a bathtub with their clothes on and no water in the tub. They begin to talk, and the first line is, "Do you come here often?" And as they talk, you begin to realize that they're veterans of some bizarre war that you don't really know anything about. It involves biological and chemical warfare. And finally a plant comes out through the drain and strangles one of them, and the other takes his shoe and throws it in a closet that is full of other people's shoes. So it's obvious that somewhere along the line there is a plot to get rid of all the veterans of that particular war so they won't talk about what they know.

Were you beginning to evolve your own style, moving away from some of the conscious influences, perhaps?

Well, I did not really ever feel that I had any conscious influences in film. I have mentioned this before, and it's very true. When I wrote I was thinking of Nabokov, of William Burroughs and maybe Beckett, God knows who else, and I did feel very pushed and pulled by my influences there. This is one of the reasons why film was very liberating. Despite the fact that I had seen everybody who is normally considered a huge influence — Fellini, Bergman and Antonioni — I suppose I was just consuming them rather than studying them. I never

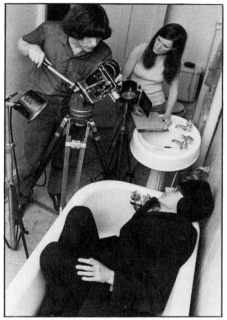

Early days — Cronenberg shooting *From the Drain*

felt that I was influenced by anybody. It is actually a very liberating thing to honestly be able to say and feel that. I know because when I was writing I found it very destructive to wonder what Nabokov would think about this, and look at it and suddenly think, this is just sort of imitation Nabokov.

So *From the Drain* was an evolution just in the sense that I was becoming a little bit more technically adept and finding my way around the technology and the rhythms of editing and all that.

What happened to these films? Did they have local screenings?

They were shown at Cinecity. The Cinethon was a great event in my life. It was an all-night-and-into-the-morning screening of underground films. It was a marathon event. It was very exciting because a lot of filmmakers came up. I think Kenneth Anger and Ed Emshwiller introduced their films. I remember emerging to have croissants and coffee in the morning and saying, "This is art!" At about five in the morning the sun was just coming up, and we came out for a break and went back into the theatre for another four hours of films. My film was shown amongst all the others.

And the kind of response you got encouraged you to keep on making films?

(*Laughs*) No, I did not think I got a very good response at all.

Did you know when you started to make Stereo *that it would be a much longer, more ambitious piece of work?*

I don't know if I knew that or not but I must have because I shot it in 35mm. That meant, though, that I could not do sync sound. I had to make that decision, and at the time I could not afford to do both. It was either going to be 16mm with sync sound or 35mm. I wanted to try 35mm because it had a terrible mystique for all underground filmmakers who were either working in Super 8mm or 16mm. I decided to come to grips with that, and the technology and the content fused together. It is very hard to say at this point what influenced what. Whether I wrote off sync sound and therefore decided to do something about telepathists that would all be internal, I can't remember. But I felt it was time to try something a little more substantial.

All your first four films were very private films that you wrote, scripted, edited, shot, and produced. Why did you choose not to work with a group of people?

I think my general background as a would-be writer made me isolationist. I suppose it's a very Canadian thing to do. But I felt very private about the work I was doing, and the projects I was thinking of were just not communicable to anyone else. It never occurred to me to get help other than from a few friends, and the actors were also friends and acquaintances. They were not professional actors.

When you look back at Stereo, *what do you find in it that relates to your other films?*

Interestingly enough, both *Crimes of the Future* and *Stereo* were influenced by Ron Mlodzik, who was the lead character in both of them. And Ron was, and undoubtedly still is, a very elegant gay scholar, an intellectual who was studying at Massey College. So there are elements in those two films that you might not see in my later films. That's my response to Ron Mlodzik and his sort of medieval gay sensibility, which I like a lot. His Catholicism was very medieval and so was his sense of style.

When I showed *Stereo* in Montreal, after the screening a young man came up to me and started to proposition me. I told him I was flattered that he should want me to go to bed with him because he just liked my movie, but I wasn't gay. He was shocked. He was sure after seeing *Stereo* that I was gay. So I attributed that to the translation of Ronald Mlodzik's presence in *Stereo* and *Crimes of the Future*. How

Behind the camera shooting *Stereo*

that translates to the other films I'm not sure. It's still very illuminating about my own sensibility though, simply because I chose to use
Ron as a sort of lead player in those films. So how directly that
connects with my own sexuality or not, it certainly connects very
directly with my aesthetic sense of his space and his presence in those
films. In that sense it is fairly illuminating, and that's the one element
I'm not sure is immediately visible in my other films, when you try to
see the roots of them in *Stereo* and *Crimes of the Future*. There are
certainly many, many other things. I think it is fairly obvious, and I
suppose the less obvious things are my sense of space and editing and
a few other things.

There is a strong sense of architecture in these films — using physical
space to express certain things within characters or certain things
about environment.

One of the primary things you have to deal with when you're directing
— and I think it's something you forget to worry about when you
become more adept at directing, except for certain scenes that present
problems — is just dealing with space, dealing with how you show
what when and how much of it. That translates technically into what
size of lenses you use, and what kind of camera move you employ,
and how far back you are, and what size closeups you use. Since I was
a very pure filmmaker at the time I suppose that was one reason those
considerations were more strikingly apparent in those films. It is pure
filmmaking in that sense. It is less obliquely concerned with space and
time and images and rhythm and how they relate to certain kinds of
sounds and certain kinds of silences, which is something that you're
totally afraid to do in commercial films — go to a completely dead
soundtrack. But I had no fear at the time.

I remember when the Backstage cinemas opened, and all the pub-
licity said they were going to run art films. I took *Stereo* to show to
the guy who was running the theatre. Ten seconds went by, twenty
seconds went by, thirty seconds went by, and the guy said, "Where's
the sound? Something wrong with the sound?" "No, no, it's
coming." He got up and walked out. That's it. He never heard any
sound. That I sould be so absurd as to present to him a film with an
absolutely dead soundtrack was enough for him to say, "I'm not
going to show this film in my theatre." But I didn't care, and that's
another sense in which it was pure filmmaking. I was dealing with the
most basic, vital elements of film.

The architecture suggests order but the behaviour of the characters in front of the camera suggests the opposite — total chaos.

Yes. That has always fascinated me as well. Here is an order that masks impending chaos. Toronto in the fifties had a certain kind of stifling order. This was the Eisenhower era, which masked something very delicious, which turned out to be partially chaos but also turned out to be partially just raw energy. There was a lot of sexual energy being repressed by society then, but also artistic and creative energy, not in my own household, but in school and society. The massive architecture suggests order and calm and eternity, when in fact the poor human beings who have to live inside that society are inflicted with many other things that don't have much to do with those concepts. I think I was trying to come to terms with the balance between the two of them, although I wasn't suggesting that this order must be totally stripped down, and we have to live in chaos. If you're a Red Brigade terrorist I suppose it would be very cathartic to say that and to believe it — that you must tear down all the old order and live in eternal chaos — but I never believed that and still don't. On the other hand there is something stifling about a certain kind of monolithic order and established social structure.

There is no real rebellion in Stereo *and* Crimes *of the* Future.

Not overtly, no. Although in *Crimes of the Future* you do have a man who never appears, who has been overturned and who reincarnates himself to return as a little girl. I guess it's not really rebellion, but it's certainly not a bad trick. I think open rebellion is not generally something that interests me cinematically. It's the balancing act that you have to do that is intriguing.

You have just described Antoine Rouge reincarnating himself as the little girl at the end of Crimes of the Future *as a nice trick. Could you expand on this?*

It's a trick I'd like to be able to do. Well, *Crimes of the Future* is quite a complex little film, and you could interpret it in many ways if you wanted to. The plot of the film, which Ivan Reitman once told me could have been a big commercial success if I'd only done the movie straight, dealt with a society, and presumably a world, in which there were no women. They have all died because of a cosmetics malfunction. If the men in the world were going to have any female-ness at all, they were left to try to find it within themselves. So if you wanted to view the film psychologically, or let's say in a standard Freudian psychological way, the film is about men coming to terms with the female part of their sensibility without it necessarily affecting their sexuality, coming to terms with those things that we consider to be female — attributes like gentleness and warmth. The ultimate version would be that a man should die and re-emerge as a woman and be completely aware of his former life as a man. In a strange way this would be a very physical fusion of those two halves of himself. That's what the movie is about.

The ending of *Scanners* is very similar to the ending of *Crimes of the Future*. It deals with the reincarnation of a person who is now a combination of two people, and it is expressed through the eyes and through a closeup of his face.

Crimes of the Future is an obscure movie, but there you are — I was less concerned that it be immediately apparent what the film meant than I was when I made *Scanners*. Even though many, many people were confused about the ambivalent ending of *Scanners*.

*

What turn did your career take after Crimes of the Future?

I was trying to figure out what to do next. The gap between *Crimes of the Future* and *Shivers* was partially filled by my spending almost a year in the south of France writing and making some television fillers for the CBC with a Beaulieu camera I bought there.

I also got a Canada Council grant at that point. Really for the longest time I stayed away from the camera even though every time I went into Nice and saw this nice little Beaulieu in the window of the camera store, I drooled over it.

I went to the Cannes film festival and I was appalled by it. Here I was living in Tourettes, a little town of 800 people and no traffic, and I suddenly came down to Cannes, having made these relatively obscure films and with no desire to really promote them commercially and understanding that they were very limited in terms of their circu-lation. Suddenly coming down to the Cannes film festival, with all the Lamborghinis and the Rolls Royces and the three-storey cut-out of

James Bond on the Ritz Carlton appalled me. I also did not know how to cross the streets because I had just forgotten about traffic. Eight months of medieval life will do that to you — no refrigerators, no stoves. And then I fled Cannes immediately. I could only stay there for half a day, and I was just overwhelmed.

I went back to Tourettes, and then when I was up there I thought, well, if I want to continue making movies the only way I'm going to do it is to do it commercially. I thought it would have to be a professional endeavour in the sense that I would have to make money to live on from making movies. I did not really want to do that kind of movie anymore as a hobby. Even Michael Snow to some extent makes some money from his movies. So I said, well, I'm going to have to come to terms with the Cannes film festival if I'm going to make movies. I forced myself to go back there. I think I slept in the CFDC office in the Carlton one night.

And in fact I started to enjoy it because...it depends how you approach it. I mean if you take it with a sense of humour and a little bit of cosmic distance, Cannes can be terrific. If you go there with your little film tucked under your arm and you think art, you're going to be swamped and repelled. The two visits to Cannes were entirely different. Even though the festival was the same, I was very different. And I realized that, yes, I was willing to do what was necessary to make commercial movies.

When you started to think about making a commercial film, did you automatically think of a horror movie?

No. I wasn't thinking about commerce in that sense. I thought in terms of making a movie instead of a film. I would have a crew that was paid for by a producer who was in it because he felt the film would make money and who had plans to distribute it. To me the difference was that I would no longer be shooting the film myself. I would no longer be able to make it totally in private without any consideration whether they liked what I was doing or not. That was the big difference. I figured the genre and the subject matter would take care of itself and it did. So it was not as though I said, "Hmmm, horror films, that's interesting."

There must have been a moment when it occurred to you that what you were going to do was make a horror film?

Cronenberg and Allan Migicovsky rehearse a scene in *Shivers*

Only when I started to type. Up until that moment I did not know
what it was going to be.

What is obviously different about Shivers *is the increase in violence
and the explicitness of sexual activity. Of course that's also what
makes it "horror" as opposed to something else.*

That's definitely something I wanted to do. Why it should have come
at that point I don't know, but as you well know there are a lot of
underground films that are very sexual and very violent. There are a
lot of underground films that could never be shown. But certainly
symbolic violence was everywhere in underground films, partially I
think because the people who felt they were undergrounders had a
certain rage and anger. I mean, Kenneth Anger's name is no mistake.
That would express itself in my early films. There is a certain violence
in *Stereo* and *Crimes of the Future*.

It is more suppressed.

It is, but both those films are about repression as well. In that sense making *Shivers* was a very liberating and very cathartic experience for me. It was not at all degrading and some people have suggested that I've sold out. I'm sure Bob Fulford would have that view, having given *Stereo* a very nice review and then walking in to see *Shivers*. I invited him to see *Shivers* because I thought somebody who liked *Stereo* would like this. And it was my naivety, but I felt that the films were very connected, and he obviously did not see it that way.

How do you deal with the fact that as soon as you have parasites crawling around, with blood on the screen, the audience that was appreciative of you before suddenly disappears?

First of all you do get another audience. There are a lot of very explicit horror films around that I'm not even interested in because a slaughterhouse is not what I want to see. So I never think of my films as that, although obviously for some people this is a very fine distinction. I remember people who said that all rock-and-roll songs are the same and they really meant it. They could not distinguish amongst them, but to those of us who were fans of rock-and-roll it was laughable to say that. So I suppose it depends on your perspective, but for me all the arguments for off-camera violence and suggestion were irrelevant.

The very purpose was to show the unshowable, to speak the unspeakable. I could not have those parasites happen off-camera because nobody would know what was going on. It's one thing when somebody raises a knife to someone else's chest and then off-camera you hear "swoosh"; you know what's going to happen, you understand it. I was creating things that there was no way of suggesting because it was not common currency of the imagination. It had to be shown or else not done. I mean, you could not have someone looking off-camera saying, "My God, parasites are coming out of his mouth." In truth it seemed absolutely natural to do what I did. And to people who look to Hitchcock as the master of restraint, I'd say you have to look at him in the context of his personality and of his time, and you also have to look at *Frenzy*, too, which has a couple of very nasty scenes. The man did them — he wanted to, no one was forcing him. The times were such that he was allowed to do that, and so I say even with Hitchcock it's not so cut-and-dried.

Shivers *and* Rabid *both release a chaos on the world, but in somewhat different ways. How do you view the release of chaos?*

I'm looking at these things for the first time actually, but I tend to view chaos as a private endeavour as opposed to a social endeavour. That's undoubtedly because I was born and raised in Canada. I'm sure if had I been born and raised in some other country I would not think of chaos strictly in terms of private chaos. Mort Sahl was recently criticizing modern comedians like Steve Martin because they deal only with personal madness rather than social issues. I guess I see, just making that connection now, that the chaos that most appeals to me is very private and very personal. And what happens is that you have these little pockets of private and personal chaos brewing in the interstices in the structure of general society, which likes to stress its order and control, and that's the collision you see. We were talking about *The Year of Living Dangerously* and in that

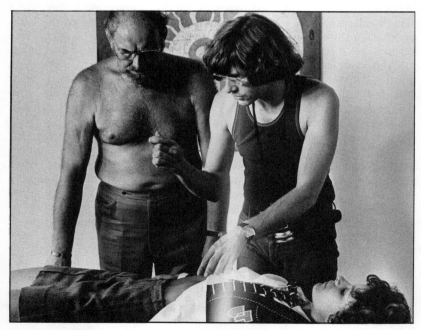

Cronenberg explains what he wants Fred Doederlein to do to Cathy Graham in *Shivers*

film chaos was considered in a completely different way: how do individuals maintain order and rationality in the midst of social and political chaos?

This is something I haven't quite thought about in such terms before, but I think what that connects to directly is my sense of myself, which is ultra-traditional. Obviously the understanding of myself as an outsider came later, because I am an artist, for one thing. People have certain sensibilities and never quite feel that they are securely embedded in their social context. They always feel that the slightest little thing is going to jar them loose, and they're going to be hopping around. I did not have a very strong sense of myself as being a Jew. I still don't really, because I wasn't raised that way. I did not understand it and had to be educated into it.

I'm not particularly insecure or paranoid, but I understand it very well. I always thought that I would much more likely be put in jail for my art than for my Jewishness. But it becomes a moot point. I have to tell you that a friend, Peter Rowe, saw *Videodrome*, came up to me, said that he really liked it, and added, "You know, someday they're going to lock you up," and walked away. (*laughs*) That did not help, you know. But I suppose underneath I always have a feeling that my existence as a member in standing of the community is in grave jeopardy for whatever reason. That's a personal chaos — it's as though society has suddenly discovered what I really am, what is really going on inside, and wants to destroy it.

The chaos in Shivers *and* Rabid *is not a personal chaos, it's really a social chaos.*

Yes and no. To the extent that those films happen in my mind the chaos is very private. I'm not really playing games with you. I think of it that way. My personal experience of society is not what is in *Rabid*, where people are running amok on the streets. I've never experienced that. So in a very real sense it's just another example of interior, as opposed to exterior, chaos.

In *Shivers* and *Rabid* the chaos arises from very small, private, personal experiments in science. As it starts to filter out and make its presence known, society turns on it and tries to attack it. That's where the conflict comes from. For example, in *Rabid* I'm not positing a city in conflict. The conflict comes from the woman and the disease, and society attempts to destroy that. So until her advent the society is well ordered.

But by the end of Shivers *the chaos is not private at all. In fact, there is a suggestion that the chaos is going to extend beyond the boundaries of the apartment complex.*

I know, but we're still talking about a group of twenty people going out into the city of Montreal, and that still feels very private to me. In other words, think of the imagination as a disease. There are societies in which imagination is considered a disease. Your art is at the service of the state — that is what art is. So true imagination, which is free-ranging and knows no bounds and knows no censorship, is a disease to be stamped out, to be repressed.

So Shivers *and* Rabid *actually express a form of social alienation because the consciousness that is imagining them has the sense of being an outsider, and consequently there is a slightly paranoid attitude towards society.*

That's right, but the paranoia is justified by what happens. This is like imagination as disease — it depends on your point of view. This is something that Robin Wood has never understood — that the ending of *Shivers* was for me a happy ending. I think he really does not understand whose side I'm on in those two films.

If there is a joyous release at the end of Shivers, *certainly the release is not joyous in* Rabid, *nor is the ending of* Rabid *joyous. Yet you're dealing with the same concept of releasing all this suppressed energy, all this surplus rage.*

That's right, because I'm very balanced — I'm cursed with balance, which is to say I immediately see all sides to the story at once. And they are all equal, they all seem to have equal weight. You could tell the same story three times, each time with a totally different tone — one is happy, one is tragic, one is melancholy or funny — and they would all be true. They would all be aspects of the same phenomenon. That can be a curse, maybe it's very Canadian, too. This has been noted by some critics like Carrie Rickey, who humourously said that my political stance, since it seems to come down on all sides at once or none at all, seems to be very Canadian. And that's true, there is a certain point when that can be paralyzing: it stops you from action, you don't move. If you shove one way, even if it's the wrong way, at least what you get is motion. And it's certainly true that Americans, if nothing else, have moved, even wrongheadedly, but they'd rather move than stand still, which is not the same as what happens in Canada. In Canada we'd rather stand still.

How much does this have to do with the fact that you're moving from a collective protagonist in Shivers *to more of a focus on the individual in* Rabid*?*

I think that's an interesting point. Something might seem funny when you're seeing a group of people slipping on banana peels, but when you get closer and see that someone is breaking his head open it's suddenly not so funny. In a sense both situations are real but the vantage point is different. I don't think they are contradictory. I think *Shivers* posits that disease has a positive aspect. The parasite takes a little blood, but so what — you've got lots to give and in the meantime it does this for you and that for you. Why not give it a chance? You know, that approach to disease.

And *Rabid*, says, yes, but if you really take this personally all the way to the end, what happens? What are the consequences on a personal level? And then it's suddenly not so funny, and it's a little hard to carry it all the way to a happy, funny ending. It has a lot to do with how I was feeling when I wrote it. That's not facetious at all. You don't approach these things from a schematic philosophical distance. You approach it from the inside out in order for it to have the energy to work. It has to come from the inside, and you invent the rationale and the philosophy afterwards.

I try not to be that conceptual about it to begin with; filmmaking is a very instinctive act, no matter how verbal it is or how rational some characters in it might be. The creator is working very much on instinct, always.

Don't you think in Shivers *that the audience automatically identifies with the doctor who wanders through the emerging chaos. This is underlined by his growing relationship with the nurse. When finally both of them become infected, there is something human that has been lost, so it's not a joyous release.*

The crew on *Shivers* — Robert Saad behind the camera, Cronenberg is the third from the right.

But you're wrong. You're right and you're wrong. There's a repressed sexual something going on. He's a saint, don't forget. He doesn't really get close to her, to kiss her, until the disease has introduced itself. If this is civilization and its discontents, this is a disease of the id arising. What it destroys is the socially acceptable way of a man and a woman coming together, but it replaces that with a very bizarre, strange, alien mode of coming together.

The standard way of looking at *Shivers* is as a tragedy but there's a paradox in it that also extends to the way society looks at me. Here is a man who walks around and is sweet — he likes people, he's warm, friendly, he's articulate and he makes these horribly diseased, grotesque, disgusting movies. Now, what's real? Those things are both real for the person standing outside. For me those two parts of myself are inextricably bound together. The reason I'm secure is because I'm crazy. The reason I'm stable is because I'm nuts. It's true, it's palpable to me.

So what I'm saying to you is that you're right. Certain audiences won't accept *Shivers* at face value, *but* there is a devil in the film.

Each of my films has a little demon in the corner that you don't see, but it's there. The demon in *Shivers* is that people vicariously enjoy the scenes where guys kick down the doors and do whatever they want to do to the people who are inside. They love the scenes where people are running, screaming, naked through the halls. They like these scenes, but then they might just hate themselves for liking them. This is no new process. It is obvious that there is a vicarious thrill involved in seeing the forbidden.

There is real horror when the kiss happens.

Yes, I think you should feel that as well, but I think all these things push and pull at the same time. *Shivers* does not lend itself to an easy schematic breakdown which I think is the sign of a good film. The characters experience horror because they are still standard, straight-forward members of the middle-class high-rise generation. I identify with them after they're infected. I identify with the parasites, basically. Your argument is turned upside down if I say, of course they're going to react with horror on a conscious level. They're bound to resist. I mean, they're going to be dragged kicking and screaming into this new experience. They're not going to go willingly. But underneath, there is something else, and that's what we see at the end of the film. They look very beautiful at the end of the film. They don't look diseased or awful, they're well dressed.

*

Your films seem to take a classic Freudian stance towards the structure of the personality in the sense of a balancing of the forces of the conscious and the unconscious mind. The unconscious mind is something that can't really be liberated with any confidence whatso-ever. It has to be watched. Is it possible to interfere with this mechanism at all. How do you feel about that philosophically?

I think it *must* be interfered with despite the fact that the consequences are sometimes horrific. You have to live a life that balances between safety and disaster. I don't think the aim of life is to find a niche that is totally safe and secure, because I think that's death, really. On the other hand I don't personally want to live in the

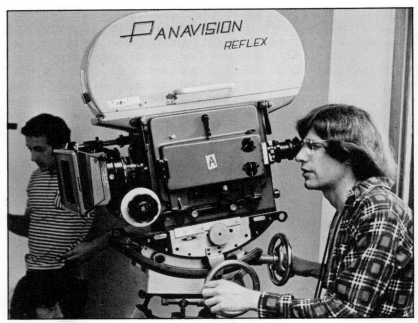

Lining up a shot

midst of chaos and disaster. I don't want either one, and therefore it means that you're constantly balancing.

When the unconscious is released in The Brood, *it has to be destroyed.*

The film deals with the unconscious of one specific person and so that does not mean I think her destruction is the inevitable result of releasing the unconscious or the subconscious. But in this case it's the unconscious of a woman who is enraged beyond reason and control and it is therefore destructive. But it's specific. It's tempting, but it's dangerous to assume that everyone in the film stands as an archetypal creature. This is something that drives me crazy with critics. On the one hand they want the characters to be individuals who are unique and real, and on the other hand they want to interpret them as archetypes who stand as the filmmaker's emblem for a whole mass of people. You can have it both ways, but it's unfair to demand it.

If I am creating Nola, the ex-wife in *The Brood*, as a very specific crazed person, she does not necessarily stand for all women, all mothers. This is a specific story I am telling. It also enrages me when women's lib groups and so on attack *Videodrome* because Debbie Harry burns her breast with a cigarette. They jump to the conclusion that I am reinforcing the stereotype of women enjoying pain. I don't say that, I don't mean that. I am saying that this specific character whom I invent pretends at least to enjoy pain and uses that to seduce Max Renn into a bizarre relationship. It's much more complicated.

Do you think The Brood *and* Scanners *deal with more defined moral absolutes than your previous films?*

I don't think consciously, anyway, in terms of the struggle between good and evil. Martin Scorsese thinks I don't know what my movies are about. He said, "I read your interviews, but it's obvious you don't know what they're about, but that's okay, they're still great." Scorsese does deal with good and evil in very proto-Catholic terms, and I'm sure that what he meant was that when he saw my films he saw the same struggle being played out. I don't see it quite that way, because I really don't see the lines drawn in those terms.

That's my curse, you see. I can't believe in the devil because I would have to believe in a purely evil being, and I don't feel that I've met anybody I could consider evil. I have difficulty thinking in terms of good and evil. I'm sure if I had been raised a Catholic I would have no trouble, because those issues are raised at a very early age. So I don't consciously think in those terms and I certainly don't think in terms of moral absolutes, because I know what happens when you try to find a moral absolute. It's very difficult to come up with something that will hold for all men in all societies in all times. It's very hard whether it's murder or incest — whatever is taboo. It always varies — you can always come up with extenuating circumstances and my demon is that all sides appeal.

Do you feel that of all the films Scanners *is the one that does polarize good and bad? I thought about* Scanners *in terms of* Star Wars, *with Cameron Vale as a Luke Skywalker figure.*

Wasn't it strange that Darth Vader turns out to be his father. Afterwards I said, "God, it is the same plot." Mind you, for both of

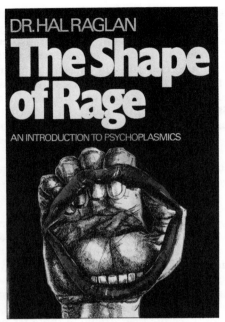

"The Shape of Rage" book cover that
Carol Spier designed for *The Brood*

us, this is not a new plot; the same plot exists in *Scaramouche* — the
question of paternity. Are you really royalty or are you a derelict?
Polarization occurs I think because of the genre, because an action
movie concerns two opposing groups and people caught in the middle.
This is another Hollywood cliché of course. When you present a
complex group of people, or two groups of people, the people in
Hollywood want to know — and I must say they're not wrong,
because most audiences also want to know — who are the good guys
and who are the bad guys. If there are too many twists and turns, and
all the characters seem to be both good guys and bad guys at the same
time, there is a certain dramatic conflict that gets lost in the
confusion, and it's a tricky thing to handle.

   In *The Brood*, Raglan is the one whom the viewer first thinks is
going to be totally bad, and it turns out that he's not. That's
confusing in a positive way — it shakes you up a little bit. Nola is
unredeemingly bad, and yet she has moments when she cries, when
she's a little girl, when she's shattered, and in those moments her evil
is mitigated somewhat because you say, well, she's mad, she's

enraged, but maybe she does have reasons to be, and maybe her rage has gone beyond reasonable bounds, but that's one of the characteristics of rage — it's the shape of rage.

This is a behaviourist question. Is a person evil if you go back to his roots and see how he was made to be evil? Does his evil still feel the same? If we had seen Hitler as a little baby, he was probably a cute kid — who knows, maybe not. But if you saw him being battered and hammered psychologically you'd say ultimately he still has to be destroyed because he is still evil. But is he pure evil? And the answer is maybe not, and then you say, well, why do we feel we want to find pure evil? Because it simplifies things if you can actually say this person is the embodiment of evil. Then it's really easy to decide to destroy the person.

Now, in movies we get lots of evil characters who are unredeemingly evil — in James Bond movies for instance. But I don't think you find anybody who's that simple in real life. I think I try to deny my audience's desire to see someone who is born evil. I don't believe in it.

Do you think the husband in The Brood *feels remorse when he kills his wife? In a way he becomes as extreme as she is.*

I think so. You see that in his drive home after rescuing his daughter. He's telling the kid it's going to be all right, but he does not believe it, and it's not true, as well. He's staggering and, of course, he's a murderer. Given what a bland and straight guy he is, there is no way a person like that is going to suddenly be able to come to terms with himself as the murderer of the mother of his child, no matter how grotesque she might have been.

Most people have considered murdering someone, whether or not they were kidding or serious. In a way killing someone is the ultimate human experience. Especially in the twentieth century. Why were people fascinated by Vietnam vets? It's because they experienced that incredible chaos where morality was stripped away, and they were allowed to kill. Then they had to come back to real life, to organized society where murder is prohibited. One of the first things people want to know when they hear that someone was in Vietnam, whether they say it or not, is did you kill anybody, did you kill women and children? Were you involved in one of those horrible bloodbaths? I do, and I don't think I'm alone in that.

That's one of the reasons why people are fascinated by the Nazi era, and this fascination is as strong as it ever was right now. It's all because suddenly there was a society that set itself up to completely reorganize the moral order, using people as objects, experimenting on people, killing people. That's one of the reasons it's fascinating to people — because it's terrifying — but it was invented by people. It's something people are capable of doing.

Would it be fair to say that in some way that's a good capsule description of the basis of your work? You tend to be fascinated by the suspension of order, the suspension of normality whether it's moral or whether it's physical.

I think that's very true because I feel disorder is always very close, which is one of the reasons I suppose I feel like an outsider. When I am feeling like an outsider it's simply because I think I'm more aware of the presence and closeness of chaos than other people are. This

Cronenberg, Samantha Eggar and Oliver Reed work out a moment in *The Brood*

feeling of myself as an outsider includes the awareness that everyone else could have that feeling very easily if they just looked at what's happening in a certain way. And in fact everyone else might have that feeling. I don't think I'm the kind of person who makes himself special by saying that I am outside. I think it actually is a part of everyone's life. It's like Sartre's philosophy, it's like his book *La Nausée*: something is there ready to hit you or anybody. But if it does not hit you, then it does not exist. But the moment it hits you, it's overwhelming and incredibly potent, and you don't ever quite recover from being hit.

There is a sense of community in Scanners *that contrasts with* Stereo, *which also sets up a community but subverts it.*

Well, either I'm just feeling more optimistic about all that or I'm exploring to see what it would be like, in the same sense that you get a chance to rehearse your own death when you do a film. Every time I kill somebody, it's really a rehearsal for my own death. I think many of the things that you do in a film are rehearsals or experiments rather than statements of belief. I don't think you can overemphasize that, certainly not in my case. These things are not always conscious.

I do think there is an urge for critics to find an element of belief or attitude in a series of films. I'm not saying you could be wrong, but I just want you to be aware that I am sometimes very consciously experimenting with a philosophy that I don't necessarily hold. I am experimenting with it through my characters to see how it fits. I am experimenting with a kind of death; I am experimenting with a kind of life; I am experimenting with a kind of relationship, and to me that's when a movie becomes part of the process of life rather than a hole into which you disappear for six months and emerge into real life.

For me Videodrome *is a film about a rehearsal for death in the same way as Fassbinder's* Veronica Voss *is. Perhaps* Scanners *is a rehearsal for life and* Videodrome *the converse of that. In* Scanners *there is a potential for life beyond the end of the film.*

Well, how about this? How about some of these films being a rehearsal for a life after death or a transmuted life — a life that is transformed into something else. That has occurred to me, as well.

On the set of *The Brood* — Cronenberg, Oliver Reed and Samantha Eggar

There is an overtone of a dream about Videodrome.

Yes, you could accept O'Blivion's statement at face value that there is nothing real outside our perception of reality, therefore whatever we are perceiving is real. On that level, there is no hallucination in the film whatsoever. It's all real, equal on its own terms.

I was trying to make a film that was as complex as the way I experience reality. I think it's very ambiguous, charged with all kinds of energy, and very complex. But I wanted it to be like that because to me that's the truth. It could have been a very straightforward movie like a James Bond film. I thought that's what it was going to be when I started to write it, but it just went off into this other direction, which got me much more excited. I knew that making the movie was going to be dangerous and complex. I knew that it wasn't going to be an easy one to sell or buy for a lot of people. But I may never get another chance to make an expensive movie that does that because obviously it's difficult for a lot of viewers. I can understand that. I can't even tell you that if I walked in to see *Videodrome* off the street I would like it.

The film constantly comes back to questions such as, there's something wrong here, where does the fault lie? Or what is the source of the problem? On one hand the source of the problem is something that comes from outside — it's the video signal, or perhaps it's our culture. On the other hand, it's something that comes from inside. It's something that Max feels when he gets involved with Deborah Harry, and there is a collision between the two opposites. Either there is individual responsibility or there is social responsibility, but the film seems to be more about personal responsibility.

Or perhaps you find that once you go deeper and deeper into what social responsibility consists of, you inevitably end up examining personal responsibility. You don't have one without the other. If you're trying to consider something pure and innate as opposed to just culturally relative, then you just say, when in Rome you do as the Romans do and you call it morality, and you leave it at that. But if you want to get to something more absolute you can't stop there. You have to dive deep into yourself, and that can be very perilous.

Another question Videodrome *asks is, who is in control? Is anybody in control? Everybody you see seems to be a victim.*

That is also what I believe. Most movies that posit a villain have, for simplicity's sake, to posit a villain who is in control of his destiny. He wants to do evil. In fact I don't believe that anybody is in control.

That's what McLuhan was talking about when he said the reason we have to understand media is because if we don't it's going to control us. We don't have to anthropomorphize the media and say they will control us. In fact the media does not have a brain. It is technology, there is no brain attached, there is no person. What it means is that things are out of control. They are certainly out of human control. They are in the control of fate and happenstance. And unless we understand what is going on, right to the most extreme edge, we don't even have a prayer of controlling it — we're just fumbling around in the dark. I actually think that is the way the world works, that we are in fact fumbling around in the dark. Nobody's in control. There is only the appearance of control, or on the part of individual people the delusion of control.

I think O'Blivion felt he was in control, but he's dead, and these are only his tapes. He managed to rationalize what happened to him to his own satisfaction, but I don't know if he's right or not, and I don't know if he would prefer to still be alive.

It's the same as Luther Stringfellow in *Stereo*. He is not there, but his presence is there. He's mentioned all the time. He has set up the experiment, he thinks he knows what is going on, and yet you can see that what is actually happening is not what he thinks is happening, so he's not in control. He set things in motion.

In fact now that you mention it, most of my films have a slightly absent, if not totally absent, professor-scientist. I wouldn't call it a father figure exactly, because it's something else, but it's certainly a professor figure. They think they know what they're doing, but they don't really knew what they're doing. It's in almost every film I've made.

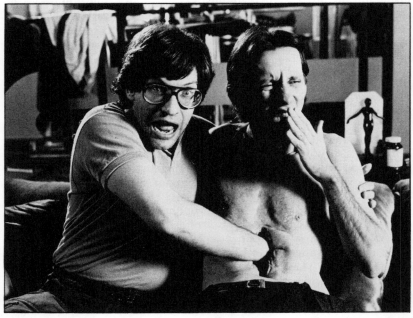

Director and star clown on the set of *Videodrome* — Cronenberg and James Woods

If the world is out of control, what can the individual hope to accomplish? Is there any potential to establish more control over our lives, or are you a fatalist?

I don't think I'm fatalistic. I think we were born not to be fatalistic — now you figure that one out. We are condemned to be free. We have to continue to try to wrest control from the world, from the universe, from reality, even though it might be hopeless. I think we have to do that, and I think that the more inventive and the more extreme we are, the better off we are. There is a part of me that really feels that, but I know that is a dangerous route to take, so I am also exploring the dangers of going that particular route.

Max explores that route in Videodrome, *and it ends in suicide.*

But does it? I think he commits suicide. However, I also believe that Max has come to think that he can create his own reality by force of will. When his inner voice in the form of Debbie Harry on this breathing television set tells him not to be afraid and to go on to the next phase — it's going to be extreme, it's going to be strange, but it's the only way — he believes that he's doing this. So he is not killing himself in the state of mind that most suicides kill themselves. He has recreated himself. Ernest Hemingway thought he was going to be reincarnated after his suicide and it would be interesting to know if he was.

Is the "New Flesh" as totalitarian and as dangerous an ideology as Convex and Harlan's neo-Fascist sense of the world?

I don't think it has to be. When you mention genetic control immediately everyone thinks, ah yes, it began with the Nazi experiments on midgets and twins, and it is now being carried out in the States with cloning and genetic engineering and all of that. You immediately think of right-wing control, although to tell you the truth, I don't make much distinction between extremes of right and left.

The most accessible version of the new flesh would be that you can actually change what it means to be a human being in a physical way. We've certainly changed it in a psychological way since the beginning of mankind. And we have in fact changed it in a physical way as well. We are different physically from our forefathers, partly because of what we take into our bodies, and partly because of things like glasses and surgery and so on. But there is a further step that could happen, which would be that you could grow another arm, that you could actually physically change the way you look — mutate, all of these things.

These physical mutations are there in the films. In Videodrome *Max Renn develops a kind of a vagina, and in* Rabid, *Marilyn Chambers acquires something that is like a penis. There is an interchangeability happening between the sexes.*

Yes. You realize how important sexuality is to the human race, in terms of art, culture, society, psychology, everything. My instinct tells me that an enormous amount of sexuality, and everything that springs from that is our society, is a very physical thing. Human beings could swap sexual organs, or do without sexual organs as sexual organs per se, for procreation. We're free to develop different kinds of organs that would give pleasure, and that have nothing to do with sex. The distinction between male and female would diminish, and perhaps we would become less polarized and more integrated creatures to the extent that there is, generally speaking, a male sensibility and a female sensibility.

This takes me back to *Crimes of the Future*, because I was fooling around with those concepts then, very unconsciously, but it all makes perfect sense now. In other words, I'm not talking about transsexual operations. I'm talking about the possibility that human beings would be able to physically mutate at will, even if it took five years to finish that mutation. Sheer force of will would allow you to change your physical self. I think that there would be a diminishing of sexual polarity, and there would be a reintegration of human beings in a very different way.

Both the characters with these sexual mutations are killed in Rabid *and* Videodrome, *though.*

They are different in terms of how negative their endings are, but I do think that it would be a perilous journey to undertake. I mean it's dangerous. Certain morality tales end badly because they are there to illustrate to the reader how dangerous certain things are.

You think you know what is going on, or at a certain point you make a decision to find out what's going on and allow yourself to be absorbed by it. But you're never really sure what you're going to get out of it. I suppose it's like taking a drug. You've heard that this drug is addictive. You think that you are not an addictive personality. You will try this drug, but you don't really know what will happen. You don't know that you will not end up like everybody else or worse, or will you? I mean you just don't know.

Would you say that overall there is a move in your work away from objectivity towards a greater amount of involvement, an identification, or at least a willingness to feel with your characters?

I don't know. That's true, and yet a lot of people found the Jimmy Woods character in *Videodrome* very unsympathetic.

I don't think it's relevant whether he's sympathetic or unsympathetic.

Well, that's nice to hear. I agree with you, but try to say that in Hollywood. Everybody from the bellboy to the guy in the elevator, the taxi driver, the producer and the head of whatever studio has always got one line: "I don't think the lead character is sympathetic enough." I wonder if anybody has *ever* had a script meeting where somebody did not say that. No one seems to question whether it makes a damn difference or not, whether *Taxi Driver* would have been better if Travis Bickle were a little more sympathetic. Who cares? Certainly you want involvement, but identifying with a character or having the character be cute and sympathetic are not absolutes of any narrative art. It's not a must, but for a lot of people in the film business in Hollywood it is an absolute must. You don't have a picture if you don't have that.

*

Your films have come under a lot of criticism, especially from critics like Robin Wood, who has called your films reactionary.

Well, you can interpret anything in the light of a particularly dogmatic stance, whether it's Freudian or Marxist or whatever. You can rigorously apply these standards to any work or person or thing or newspaper or article, and then judge the artifact as wanting or not wanting.

But is that really the function of criticism? I don't think so. Let's say that all of that is true. It only is bad if you're Robin Wood and you are justifying your own sexuality through your criticism. I think that's exactly what he's doing. When your work becomes an apology for an event or a turn in your life then I think you have invalidated yourself as a serious critic. This is not to say that one can't read him and be entertained or be given insights, but why should I be beaten over the head with what he has written about me in *The American Nightmare*. What he says is: these are good filmmakers who are on the side of progressiveness, and these are bad filmmakers who are reactionary. I don't think that is what art is about, and I don't think that's what criticism is about.

The critics that I have admired most are a lot less schematically inclined. I suppose that's because I don't base my life's value and work's value in any ideology.

But don't you agree that as an artist there are certain things you will reflect in terms of the society that surrounds you in an ideological way, whether it's conscious or unconscious?

Absolutely, and I am certainly a product of my environment, but I don't devalue people of a different ideology, and I don't look at a work of art that comes from somewhere else and say, unfortunately this is reactionary and should be suppressed, which is really what I object to in Robin's criticism. There is a very strident moral imperative being broadcast from his work that is really saying, despite the fact that this piece of film of Larry Cohen's is awful, it is admirable and should be seen because it proposes what I think is right for human beings to do in society. Now that is very twisted.

I think criticism has moved away from an individual, humanist response and become much more interested in exploring the underlying ideology and patterns that are at work in the cinema.

Shooting the grisly special effects death of Barry Convex for *Videodrome*

That's fine except I think criticism has gone through that phase many times before at different times in different countries and I think it's a shame. I don't read propaganda. Other than for historical reasons, why would anybody want to watch a propaganda film? A truly propagandistic film is repulsive to watch. I have a very specific response: I know I'm seeing interesting historical artifacts, but I find it is very difficult to respond to such a film as art. And what happens, too, when that social context changes, which usually does, certainly within one's own life time. Suddenly the guys who used to be neo-Nazis are Zionists. I mean, it happens.

There are a number of scenes in your films that involve the humiliation of women. In Shivers *nurse Forsythe's mouth is taped shut, and* Videodrome *portrays Nicki Brand as a woman fascinated by sexual sado-masochism. Is there any reason why similar forms of sexual punishment aren't meted out to males?*

Well, I think it certainly has to do with the fact that I am male, and my fantasies and my unconscious are male. I think I give a reasonable amount of expression to the female part of me, but I still think that I'm basically heterosexual male. And so if I'm saying, let loose the social bonds and see what my sexuality is at its darkest and its most insane and its most amoral — not immoral, but just amoral — if I'm going to get into scenes of bondage and torture and you name it, I'll show a female instead of a male. I've talked about admiring *Naked Lunch* and wanting to do a movie of it. One of the barriers to me of being totally one hundred per cent with William Burroughs is exactly that. Burroughs' general sexuality is homosexual, and it's very obvious in what he writes that his dark sexual fantasies happen to be sodomizing young boys as they're hanging. Well, to be quite frank, I actually can relate to that to quite an extent. I really understand what's going on. But if I were to fantasize something similar, it would be more like the parasite coming up the drain, and it would be attacking a woman, not a man. Now to say that's sexist is politicizing something that is not political. It's *sexual*, not sexist — that's just my sexual orientation. I don't necessarily hold with theories of democracy: I have no reason to think that I have to give equal time to all sexual fantasies whether they're my own or not. Let those people make their own movies — leave me alone to make mine.

Marilyn Chambers was a well-known female sex-object, and you were aware of that fact when you cast her in Rabid. *What's the connection in your mind between her sexuality and her predatory activities in that film?*

Well, of course you get nailed both ways by women's lib groups and so on. If the woman is a victim, the outcry is against portraying women as victims. If the woman is aggressive, the outcry is against showing the woman as a predator. And yet, at the same time, I don't think anyone is suggesting that a movie that shows anybody as either a victim or a victimizer should not exist — to say that is to deny a lot of things in the world.

I feel censored, in a strange way, I feel that meanings are being twisted and imposed on me. And more than meanings — value judgements.

*

Is your sense of alienation and being an outsider disappearing?

I doubt it. I think it's the reverse. The older you get, the more children you have, the more accepted you become in your society and the more a part of the establishment you become, the more tenuous the grip on your "insideness" is. I suppose some people might be fooled into thinking that they are invulnerable. I think anyone who is an artist knows. You don't think Scorsese still thinks he's living on the edge of his art and his life even though he is a famous filmmaker who is honoured and recognized. He knows very well how close to the edge he is.

But the feeling isn't one of being an outsider surely, because you know you're not an outsider anymore.

Well, I don't agree. I am. I'm just much more in disguise.

But that's also in the films. Scanners *and* Videodrome *both deal with derelict characters — Cameron Vale and Max Renn.*

I think you're absolutely right. Basically your awareness of yourself is driven even deeper because the layers or veneer of civilization become thicker and thicker, but inside you *know*. You always know.

It's a game you can never win. You start out thinking you're on the outside and that you are alienated, and you end up knowing you're alienated, on the outside.

There's a strength to be taken from that. There is also a certain sadness and frustration at the same time.

Does The Dead Zone *fit into this?*

Well, you know the story of *The Dead Zone*? It's basically similar to *Scanners*. You have someone who thinks he is a normal, well-entrenched member of society — low profile, nothing special, an okay guy who teaches at school. There was an incident in his past when he was hit in the head (with a hockey puck in my version; in the

Shooting *The Dead Zone* — Mark Irwin behind the camera

book it's an actual fall on the ice). There was some little suggestion that he had a bit of a flash forward but as a kid he would not have remembered that, he totally repressed it. He thinks he is a normal person. In fact he has the seeds of being a visionary, which might as well be the archetype for an artist, the same as the scanner was. At a certain point in his life that comes out, and it destroys his life as he had known it. He tries to find another life that will accomodate his abilities as a prophet. He is of course a total outsider for most of the movie, and certainly most of the book as well. He is an outsider even though he looks like a normal guy, but he knows he's not. He's cut off from the life he thought he had as his birthright as a normal human being. His girlfriend, his mother, his father, the town he was living in, the school that he taught at, are all gone suddenly.

Do you emphasize the subjectivity of the story line? I read that a lot of the evidence that he has this insight are removed in your version. Consequently one might believe he is just somebody having visions, and he goes out to shoot somebody, as opposed to somebody who genuinely does know.

I think on a very straightforward dramatic level, people will believe his visions are real and therefore will believe he is justified in going to kill this potential presidential candidate. We also have scenes as they were in the book that show Stillson, the political candidate, as a bad guy. Emotionally you will go along with it — there is some proof of other visions that Johnny has that have turned out to be true, so you'll totally believe it, I think. But the demon in *The Dead Zone* is exactly what you're talking about, which is that in fact nothing that Stillson does in the movie would be enough to condemn him to death. You see him leaning on a newspaper editor, bribing and threatening, but everybody does that in politics. That's not enough to have him killed, and finally you begin to realize that all you're left with is Johnny's belief in his vision.

In that respect, it connects with Max in Videodrome *going out and shooting people because of things that are happening inside him.*

As I say, I haven't really twisted the book around. You have him realizing that the daughter of his nurse is in danger because her house is on fire. Sure enough the house is on fire. It is too big a cheat to make it totally subjective. There is no way of knowing. And yet he still takes it upon himself to kill somebody, based totally on a vision that he has, with absolutely no objective proof at all that it could happen.

Apart from Fast Company *this is the first time you've done something in which you did not actually conceive the story yourself and write the script. Did it make a difference at all?*

Because I had done *Fast Company* before, and because I hadn't written the two tape shows I did for the CBC, either, it was different but familiar-different. I did not try to impose myself on the subject matter. I just had to assume that through the accumulation of the thousands and thousands of details that go into making a film, I would be there and obviously I chose to do the project. I've been

A moment of relaxation — father and son

offered a lot of things in the last ten years, and this was the first one I had accepted.

Did you feel passionate about it?

Yes. It's different when it's not your own — there is no question about it — but gradually it becomes your own and suddenly you can't tell the difference, in a strange way. The process at the beginning was very different. But I was involved in structuring the script and the characters from the beginning, so I felt very involved. There is a certain last little distance you can't go because it is not yours. I would not have written *The Dead Zone*, and yet I'm sure you'll see many similarities to *Videodrome* and *Scanners*.

After I did *Videodrome* I was ready to do a movie I had not written. I was not ready to write anything, and why that should have been I don't know. So I was happy to do it, and now I really want to write something. That's what I'm going to do next. I have an agreement with Universal to write an original script.

May 1983

Filmography Established by D. John Turner

1966

TRANSFER

7 minutes, 16mm, colour
Director/screenplay/photography/editing: David Cronenberg. Sound:
Margaret Hindson, Stephen Nosko.
Cast: Mort Ritts, Rafe Macpherson.
Shot on location in Toronto in January 1966.
Cost: $300

1967

FROM THE DRAIN

14 minutes, 16mm, colour
Director/screenplay/photography/editing: David Cronenberg.
Cast: Mort Ritts, Stephen Nosko.
Shot on location in Toronto in July 1966.
Cost: $500

1969

STEREO

63 minutes, 35mm, bw, 1.85:1
Production company: Emergent Films. Producer/director/screenplay
photography/editing: David Cronenberg. Production aides: Stephen Nosko,
Pedro McCormick, Janet G.M. Good. Narrators: Glenn McCauley, Mort
Ritts. Laboratory: Pathé Humphries of Canada Ltd. (Toronto)
Cast: Ronald Mlodzik, Jack Messinger, Paul Mulholland, Iain Ewing, Arlene
Mlodzik, Clara Meyer, Glenn McCauley.
Toronto from early August to November 6, 1968.
Première: National Arts Centre, Ottawa, June 23, 1969.
Cost: $8,500

1970

CRIMES OF THE FUTURE

63 minutes, 35mm, colour (Kodak 5254) 1.85:1
Production company: Emergent Films Ltd., with the participation of the Canadian Film Development Corporation. Producer/director/screenplay/editing: David Cronenberg. Production assistant: Stephen Nosko. Titles: Jon Lidolt. Laboratory: Film House Ltd. (Toronto)
Cast: Ronald Mlodzik, Jon Lidolt, Tania Zolty, Paul Mulholland, Jack Messinger, Iain Ewing, William Haslam, Ray Woodley, Stefen Czernecki, Rafe Macpherson, Willem Poolman, Donald Owen, Udo Kasemets, Bruce Martin, Brian Linehan, Leland Richard, Stephen Zeifman, Norman Snider, William Wine, Kaspers Dzeguze, Sheldon Cohen, George Gibbins.
Shot on location in Toronto from August 1969 to February 10, 1970.
Cost: $15,000

1971

While living in France, Cronenberg directed, scripted and shot three fillers for television:

TOURETTES
LETTER FROM MICHELANGELO
JIM RITCHIE SCULPTOR

1972

Upon returning to Canada Cronenberg directed, scripted and shot another six fillers for television:

DON VALLEY
FORT YORK
LAKESHORE
WINTER GARDEN
SCARBOROUGH BLUFFS
IN THE DIRT

SECRET WEAPONS

(for *Program X*)

30 minutes, 16mm, colour
Production company: Emergent Films Ltd. for the Canadian Broadcasting
Corporation. Executive producer: Paddy Sampson. Associate producer:
George Jonas. Director: David Cronenberg. Screenplay: Norman Snider.
Narrator: Lister Sinclair.
Cast: Barbara O'Kelly (*motorcycle gang leader*), Norman Snider (*the
scientist*), Vernon Chapman (*the bureaucrat*), Ronald Mlodzik, Bruce Martin,
Tom Skudra, Moses Smith, Michael D. Spencer, G. Chalmers Adams.
Shot on location in Toronto from June 6 to August 31, 1971.
Telecast: June 1, 1972

1975

THE PARASITE MURDERS

87 minutes, 35mm, colour (Kodak 5247) 1.85:1
Production company: DAL Productions Ltd., with the participation of the
Canadian Film Development Corporation. Executive producer: Alfred
Pariser. Producer: Ivan Reitman, John Dunning, André Link. Director/
screenplay: David Cronenberg. Photography: Robert Saad. Sound: Michael
Higgs. Editing: Patrick Dodd. Music: Ivan Reitman. Production manager:
Don Carmody. Continuity: Diane Boucher. Boom: Jean-Claude Matte, Jim
Thompson. Sound assistant: Len Blum. Sound supervisor: Dan Goldberg. 1st
assistant cameramen: Rick Maguire, Yves Drapeau. 2nd assistant cameraman:
Paul Gravel. Key grip: John Daoust. Assistant grip: Jim Lawler. Electrician:
Tom Sawyer. Assistant electrician: Dexter Pattie. Gaffer: John Sawyer. Best
boy: Jean-Paul Houle. Stunts: Les Frères Fournier. Make-up: Suzanne Riou-
Garand. Make-up assistant: Louisette Champagne. Art Assistant: Rose Marie
McSherry. Special make-up and creatures created by: Joe Blasco. Assistant to
Joe Blasco: David Ditmar. Stills: Attila Dory. Rerecording: Nolan Roberts.
Production secretaries: Josette Perrotta, Irene Litinsky. Production assis-
tants: Stewart Harding, Cliff Rothman. Laboratory: Les Laboratoires de
Film Québec (Montréal).
Cast: Paul Hampton (*Roger St. Luc*), Joe Silver (*Rollo Linsky*), Lynn Lowry
(*Forsythe*), Allan Migicovsky (*Nicholas Tudor*), Susan Petrie (*Janine Tudor*),
Barbara Steele (*Betts*), Ronald Mlodzik (*Merrick*), Barrie Baldero (*Detec-
tive Heller*), Camille Ducharme (*Mr. Guilbault*), Hanka Posnanka (*Mrs.
Guilbault*), Wally Martin (*doorman*), Vlasta Vrana (*Kresimar Sviben*),
Charles Perley (*delivery boy*), Al Rochman (*Parkins*), Julie Wildman (*Miss
Lewis*), Arthur Grosser (*Mr. Wolfe*), Edith Johnson (*Olive*), Dorothy Davis

(*Vi*), Joy Coghill (*Mona Wheatley*), Joan Blackman (*mother in elevator*), Fred Doederlein (*Emil Hobbes*), Sony Forbes (*man in garbage room*), Silvie Debois (*Benda Sviben*), Kirsten Bishopric (*daughter in elevator*), Nora Johnson (*laundry woman*), Cathy Graham (*Annabelle*), Robert Brennen (*boy*), Felicia Shulman (*girl*), Roy Witham (*bearded man*), Denis Payne (*man in elevator*), Kevin Fenlow (*man in elevator*).
Shot on location in Montreal from August 21 to September 14, 1974.
Released: Ten theatres in Montreal (English version in three, French version in seven) October 10, 1975.
Other titles: SHIVERS (in English Canada and the U.K.)
THEY CAME FROM WITHIN (in the U.S.)
FRISSONS (French version in Quebec and France)
Cost: $179,000

THE VICTIM

(for *Peep Show*)

30 minutes, 2" VTR, colour
Production company: Canadian Broadcasting Corporation. Executive producer: George Bloomfield. Producer: Deborah Peaker. Director: David Cronenberg. Screenplay: Ty Haller. Photography: Eamonn Beglan, Ron Manson, John Halenda, Dave Doherty, Peter Brimson. Audio: Brian Radford, Bill Dunn. Videotape editing: Garry Fisher. Art director: Nikolai Soloviov. Assistant designer: Gavin Mitchell. Costumes: Suzanne Mess. Set decoration: Robert Parker. Special effects: George Clarke. Technical producer: Joe Parkinson, Merv Curley. Lighting director: Aylmer Wright, Bob Schmidt. Sound effects: Olive St. Sauveur. Music consultant: Ed Vincent. Switcher: Ken Livermore. Video: Syed Bokhari. Story editor: Anne Frank. Production assistants: Jeanette Soloncoe, James Swan. Service producer: Duncan Lamb. Casting: Clare Emery. Unit manager: Sandra Fox. Production coordinator: Jim Innes.
Cast: Janet Wright (*Lucy*), Jonathan Welsh (*Donald*), Cedric Smith (*man on park bench*).
Shot on location in Toronto and in the CBC studios from August 16 to 18, 1975.
Telecast: January 22, 1976.

THE LIE CHAIR

(for *Peep Show*)

30 minutes, 2" VTR, colour
Production company: Canadian Broadcasting Corporation. Executive pro-

ducer: George Bloomfield. Producer: Eoin Sprott. Director: David Cronenberg. Screenplay: David Cole. Photography: Eamon Beglan, George Clements, Tom Farquharson, Peter Brimson. Set Design: Rudi Dorn. Audio: Roland Huebsche, Bill Dunn. Set decorator: Robert Parker. Lighting: Aylmer Wright, Bob Schmidt. Technical producers: Joe Parkinson, Dick Ewing.
Cast: Richard Monette (*Neil*), Susan Hogan (*Carol*), Amelia Hall (*Mildred*), Doris Petrie (*Mrs. Rogers*).
Shot on location in Toronto and in the CBC studios from October 22 to 28, 1975.
Telecast: February 12, 1976.

1976

THE ITALIAN MACHINE
(for *Teleplay*)

30 minutes, 16mm, colour
Production company: Canadian Broadcasting Corporation. Executive producer: Stephen Patrick. Director/screenplay: David Cronenberg. Photography: Nicholas Evdemon. Sound recording: Tom Bilenky. Editing: David Denovan. Music consultant: Patrick Russell. Art director: Peter Douet. Assistant director: Michael Zenon. Continuity: Diane Parsons. Unit manager: David Barlow. Sound editing: Lock Johnston. Rerecording: Len Abbot. Lighting: John Dixon. Set decoration: Alan Hayes. Design coordinator: Torben Madsen. Costumes: Hilary Corbett. Makeup: Mario Cacioppo. Casting director: Gail Carr. Story editor: L.S. Mirkin.
Cast: Gary McKeehan (*Lionel*), Frank Moore (*Fred*), Hardee Linehan (*Bug*), Chuck Shamata (*Reinhardt*), Louis Negin (*Mouette*), Toby Tarnow (*Lana*), Geza Kovacs (*Ricardo*), Cedric Smith (*Luke*).
Shot on location in Toronto from April 8 to 14, 1976.
Telecast: December 2, 1976.

RABID

91 minutes, 35mm, colour (Kodak 5247) 1.85:1
Production company: Cinema Entertainment Enterprises Ltd. (for DAL Productions Ltd.), with the participation of the Canadian Film Development Corporation. Executive producers: André Link, Ivan Reitman. Producer: John Dunning. Associate producer: Dan Goldberg. Director/ screenplay: David Cronenberg. Art director: Claude Marchand. Photography: René Verzier. Sound: Richard Lightstone. Editing/2nd unit director: Jean Lafleur. Music: Ivan Reitman. Production manager: Don Carmody. Assistant production manager: Sarah Dundas. 1st assistant director: John

Fretz. 2nd assistant director: Phil Desjardins. Continuity: Tatania Mihailoff. Boom man: Jim Thompson. Sound supervisor: Dan Goldberg. 1st assistant camera: Denis Gingras. 2nd assistant camera: Jean-Jacques Gervais. 2nd unit cameraman: Louis de Ernsted. Key grip: John Daoust. 2nd grip: André Ouellette. Grip: Marc de Ernsted. Gaffer: John Berrie. Best boy: Jean-Paul Houle. Prop master: Jean Lavigne. Prop assistant: Andrew Deskin. Set construction: Romeo Turcotte. Wardrobe: Erla Gliserman. Wardrobe assistant: Carolynne Roberts. Key makeup: Mireille Recton. Makeup assistant: Heather Allan. Special makeup design: Joe Blasco Makeup Association. Special makeup artist: Byrd Holland. Special makeup effects assistant: Kathy Flynn. Special effects: Al Griswold. Assistant special effects: Joe Elzner. Stills: Joel Sussman. Wrangler: Claude Moreau. Assistant editor: Debra Karen [Debbie Karjala]. Assistant sound editor: Patrick Dodd. Sound assistant: Len Blum. Post-sync recording: Austin Grimaldi. Rerecording: Joe Grimaldi. Medical technical adviser: Susan Thompson. Production assistants: John Caradonna, Caroline Zeifman, Norma Bailey, Jaki Carmody, Patricia Cahill. Casting and 2nd makeup: Sharron Wall. Laboratory: Les Laboratoires de Film Québec (Montréal).

Cast: Marilyn Chambers (*Rose*), Frank Moore (*Hart Read*), Joe Silver (*Murray Cypher*), Howard Ryshpan (*Dr. Dan Keloid*), Patricia Gage (*Dr. Roxanne Keloid*), Susan Roman (*Mindy Kent*), J. Roger Périard (*Lloyd Walsh*), Lynne Deragon (*nurse Louise*), Terry Schonblum (*Judy Glasberg*), Victor Désy (*Claude LaPointe*), Julie Anna (*Rita*), Gary McKeehan (*Smooth Eddy*), Terrence G. Ross (*farmer*), Miguel Fernandes (*man in cinema*), Robert O'Ree (*police sergeant*), Greg Van Riel (*young man in plaza*), Jérôme Tiberghien (*Dr. Karl*), Allan Moyle (*young man in lobby*), Richard Farrell (*camper man*), Jeannette Casenave (*camper lady*), Carl Wasserman (*camper child*), John Boylan (*young cop in plaza*), Malcolm Nelthorpe (*older cop in plaza*), Vlasta Vrana (*cop at clinic*), Kirk McColl (*desk sergeant*), Jack Messinger (*policeman on highway*), Yvon Lecompte (*policeman*), Grant Lowe (*trucker*), John Gilbert (*Dr. Royce Gentry*), Tony Angelo (*dispatcher*), Peter McNeill (*loader*), Una Kay (*Jackie*), Madeleine Pageau (*Beatrice Owen*), Mark Walker (*Steve*), Bob Silverman (*man in hospital*), Monique Belisle (*Sheila*), Ronald Mlodzik (*patient*), Isabelle Lajeunesse (*waitress*), Terry Donald (*cook*), Louis Negin (*Maxim*), Bob Girolami (*newscaster*), Harry Hill (*Stasiuk*), Kathy Keefler (*interviewer*), Marcel Fournier (*cab driver*), Valda Dalton (*car lady*), Murray Smith (*interviewer*), Riva Spier (*Cecile*), Denis Lacroix (*drunken Indian*), Sherman Maness (*Indian*), Basil Fitzgibbon (*crazy in plaza*).

Shot on location in Montreal from November 1 to December 5, 1976.
Released: Twelve theatres in Montreal and the province of Quebec (English version in two, in Montreal; French version in ten), April 8, 1977.
Other title: RAGE (French version in Quebec and France).
Cost: $530,000.

1979

FAST COMPANY

91 minutes, 35mm, colour (Kodak 5247) 1.85:1
Production company: Michael Lebowitz Inc. (for Quadrant Films Ltd.), with
the participation of the Canadian Film Development Corporation. Executive
producer: David M. Perlmutter. Producers: Michael Lebowitz, Peter
O'Brian, Courtney Smith. Director: David Cronenberg. Screenplay: Phil
Savath, Courtney Smith, David Cronenberg [and uncredited, John Hunter]
from an original story by Alan Treen. Art director: Carol Spier. Photo-
graphy: Mark Irwin. Sound: Bryan Day. Editing: Ronald Sanders.·Music: Fred
Mollin. Production manager: Caryl Brandt. Production coordinator: Sherry
Cohen. 1st assistant director: Jim Kaufman. 2nd assistant director: Jim Lang.
Continuity: Margaret Hanly. Boom men: Christopher Tate, Ken Pappes.
Focus puller: Robin Miller. Clapper/loader: Gary Armstrong. 2nd unit
camera operators: Robert Holmes, Allan Jones, Jon Anderson. Key grip:
Maris Jansons. Grip: Lee Wright. Gaffer: Roger Bate. Best boy: Bob
Holmes. Property master: Peter Lauterman. Property assistant: Dave
McAree. Costume designer: Delphine White. Wardrobe assistants: Madeleine
Stewart, Wendy Partridge. Makeup: Jan Newman. Special effects: Tom
Fisher. Special effects crew: Peter Von King, John Thomas. Still photo-
grapher: Rick Porter. Assistant sound editors: David Street, Arnie Stewart.
Dialogue and effects editor: Terry Burke. Racing effects editor: Bruce
Carwardine. Rerecording: Gary Bourgeois. Production assistants: Isabelle
Foord, Richard Mead, Bob Murphy. Canadian casting: Gail Carr. Additional
casting: Bette Chadwick. Laboratory: Alpha Cine Service Ltd. (Vancouver).
Cast: William Smith (*Lonnie "Lucky Man" Johnson*), Claudia Jennings
(*Sammy*), John Saxon (*Phil Adamson*), Nicholas Campbell (*Billy "The Kid"
Brooker*), Cedric Smith (*Gary "The Blacksmith" Black*), Judy Foster
(*Candy*), George Buza (*Meatball*), Robert Haley (*P.J.*), David Graham
(*Stoner*), Don Francks (*"Elder"*), David Petersen (*Slezak*), Chuck Chandler
(*Edmonton track announcer*), Cheri Hilsabeck (*hitch-hiker*), Sonya Ratke
(*hitch-hiker*), Michael Bell (*Chuck Randall*), Douglas Main (*TV newscaster*),
Patricia Goodwin (*new Miss Fastco*), L. Peter Feldman (*security guard*),
Graham Light (*track official*), Fred Hodgson (*TV camera crew*), Michael
Ouellette (*TV camera crew*), Trevor Yacyshyn (*hot rodder*), Robert Hill (*hot
rodder*), Jerry Knowles (*track starter*), [and uncredited, Neil Dainard].
Shot on location in Calgary and Edmonton from July 21 to August 29, 1978.
Released: Three theatres in Edmonton, May 18, 1979.
Cost: $1,200,000.

THE BROOD

91 minutes, 35mm, colour (Kodak 5247) 1.85:1
Production companies: Les Productions Mutuelles and Elgin International Productions, with the participation of the Canadian Film Development Corporation. Executive producers: Victor Solnicki, Pierre David. Producer: Claude Héroux. Director/screenplay: David Cronenberg. Art Director: Carol Spier. Photography: Mark Irwin. Sound: Bryan Day. Editing: Alan Collins. Music: Howard Shore. Production manager: Gwen Iveson. 1st assistant director: John Board. 2nd assistant director: Libby Bowden. Continuity: Nancy Eagles. Boom man: Tom Mather. 1st assistant camera: Robin Miller. 2nd assistant camera: Greg Villeneuve. Key grip: Maris Jansons. Grip: Carlo Campana. Gaffer: Jock Brandis. Best boy: Bob Gallant. Property master: Peter Lauterman. Property assistant: Tom Reid. Set dresser: Angelo Stea. Assistant set dresser: Michael Fruet. Construction manager: Bill Harman. Wardrobe: Delphine White. Wardrobe assistant: Granada Venne. Makeup: Shonagh Jabour. Makeup assistant: Inge Klaudi. Special makeup: Jack Young, Dennis Pike. Special effects: Allan Kotter. Still photographer: Rick Porter. Location manager: David Coatsworth. Assistant picture editor: Carolyn Zeifman. Post production coordinator: John Board. Sound editor: Peter Burgess. Assistant sound editor: Jeremy MacLaverty. Dialogue editor: Brian Holland. Assistant dialogue editor: Lois Tupper. Rerecording: Joe Grimaldi. Canadian casting: Canadian Casting Associates. Los Angeles casting: Hilary Holden. Laboratory: Medallion Film Laboratories Ltd. (Toronto).
Cast: Oliver Reed (*Dr. Hal Raglan*), Samantha Eggar (*Nola Carveth*), Art Hindle (*Frank Carveth*), Cindy Hinds (*Candice Carveth*), Henry Beckman (*Barton Kelly*), Nuala FitzGerald (*Juliana Kelly*), Susan Hogan (*Ruth Mayer*), Michael Magee (*Inspector Mrazek*), Joseph Shaw (*Dr. Desborough, coroner*), Gary McKeehan (*Mike Trellan*), Robert Silverman (*Jan Hartog*), Nicholas Campbell (*Chris*), John Ferguson (*creature*), Felix Silla (*creature*), Larry Solway (*Resnikoff, lawyer*), Rainer Schwartz (*Dr. Birkin*), Mary Swinton (*Wendy*), Jerry Kostur (*construction worker*), Christopher Britton (*man in auditorium*).
Shot on location in Toronto from November 14 to December 21, 1978.
Released: Chicago, Detroit, Cleveland, etc. (400 theatres), May 25, 1979.
         Toronto, June 1, 1979.
Other titles: CHROMOSOME 3 (French version in France)
             LA CLINIQUE DE LA TERREUR (French version in Quebec).
Cost: $1,400,000.

1980

SCANNERS

103 minutes, 35mm, colour (Kodak 5247) 1.85:1
Production company: Filmplan International Inc., with the participation of the Canadian Film Development Corporation. Executive producers: Pierre David, Victor Solnicki. Producer: Claude Héroux. Director/screenplay: David Cronenberg. Art director: Carol Spier. Photography: Mark Irwin. Sound: Don Cohen. Editing: Ronald Sanders. Music: Howard Shore. Production manager: Don Buchsbaum. 1st assistant director: Jim Kaufman. 2nd assistant director: Mike Williams. 3rd assistant director: Anne Murphy. Continuity: France Boudreau. Boom: Gabor Vadnay. 1st assistant cameraman: Robin Miller. 2nd assistant camerman: Greg Villeneuve. Key grip: François Dupéré. Grips: Maris Jansons, Michel Periard. Electrician: Arshad Shah. Gaffer: Jock Brandis. Best boy: Claude Langlois. Property master: Jean Bourret. Assistant propsmen: Ernie Tomlinson, Michel Comte. Set designer: Alfred. Assistant art director: Barbara Jones. Sculptors: Tom Coulter, Peter Borowski, Peter Dowker. Set dresser: Peter Bray. Assistant set dressers: Melanie Johnson, Serge Bureau. Construction supervisor: Claude Simard. Stunt coordinator: Alex Stevens. Action vehicles driver: Armand Thomas. Costumes designer: Delphine White. Costumes assistant: Blanche Boileau. Dresser: Renée April. Assistant dresser: Fabienne April. Makeup: Brigitte McCaughry. Special makeup: Stephan Dupuis, Chris Walas, Tom Schwartz. Consultant for special makeup effects: Dick Smith. Special effects: Gary Zeller. Micro effects: Dennis Pike. Special effects assistants: Don Berry, Louis Craig, Jacques Godbout. Stills: Denis Fugère. Production coordinator: Danièle Rohrbach. Unit manager: Jean Savard. Locations manager: Christine Burt. Assistant editors: Chris Hutton, Bob Boyd. Post production coordinator: Bill Wiggins. Sound editing supervisor: Peter Burgess. Sound editors: Charles Bowers, Bruce Nyznik, Peter Jermyn. Assistant sound editors: Terry Burke, Gary Da Prato. Music supervision: LMS Publishing House Ltd. Music editor: David Appleby. Sound rerecording: Donald White. Production assistants: Glendon Light, Nick Rose, Marilyn Majerczyk, Patrick Ferrero, Claire Veillet, Nerses Kolanian, Victor Blazevic, Guy Cadieux, Dominique Landry, Neil Bibby. Casting Toronto: Canadian Casting Associates. Casting Montreal: Daniel Hausmann. Assistant casting: Ginette D'Amico, Muriel Fournier. Laboratory: Bellevue Pathé Québec (1972) Inc. (Montréal).
Cast: Jennifer O'Neill (*Kim Obrist*), Stephen Lack (*Cameron Vale*), Patrick McGoohan (*Dr. Ruth*), Lawrence Z. Dane (*Braedon Keller*), Michael Ironside (*Darryl Revok*), Robert Silverman (*Benjamin Pierce*), Adam Ludwig (*Arno Crostic*), Mavor Moore (*Trevellyan*), Fred Doederlein (*Dieter Tautz*), Sony Forbes (*invader*), Jérôme Tiberghien (*invader*), Denis Lacroix (*invader*), Elizabeth Mudry (*invader*), Victor Désy (*Dr. Gatineau*), Lee Broker (*security*), Louis Del Grande (*scanner*), Tony Sherwood (*scanner*), Ken Umland (*scanner*), Anne Anglin (*scanner*), Jock Brandis (*scanner*), Geza Kovacs (*scanner*), Jack Messinger (*Jack*), Karen Fullerton (*pregnant girl*),

Margaret Gadbois (*middle aged woman*), Terry Coady (*security man*), Steve Michaels (*security man*), Victor Knight (*Dr. Frane*), Malcolm Nelthrope (*escort car driver*), Nickolas Kilbertus (*escort car partner*), Don Buchsbaum (*large man*), Kimberly McKeever (*security*), Graham Batchelor (*Courtney*), Lee Murray (*programmer*), Dean Hagopian (*programmer*), Alex Stevens (*programmer*), Chuck Shamata (*Tony*), Robert Parson (*security*), Bob King (*security*), Samuel Stone (*security*), Barry Kozak (*security*), Rolland Nincheri (*man in subway*), Neil Affleck (*medical student*), Griff Brewer (*elderly man*), Robert Boyd (*security guard*), Michael Dubois (*waiter*), Lillian Horowitz (*passerby*), Jim Kaufman (*scanner N.D.*), Tom Kovacs (*boy friend*), Jorma Lindquist (*security*), William Spears (*technician*), Harriet Stein (*woman's friend*), Paul Stewart (security guard).
Shot on location in Montreal from October 30 to December 23, 1979.
Released: United States (387 theatres), January 14, 1981; Canada, January 16, 1981.
Cost: $4,100,000.

1982

VIDEODROME

87 minutes, 35mm, colour (Kodak 5247) 1.85:1
Production company: Filmplan International II Inc., with the participation of the Canadian Film Development Corporation. Executive producers: Pierre David, Victor Solnicki. Producer: Claude Héroux. Associate producer: Lawrence S. Nesis. Director/screenplay: David Cronenberg. Art director: Carol Spier. Photography: Mark Irwin. Sound: Bryan Day. Editing: Ronald Sanders. Music: Howard Shore. Production coordinator: Roger Héroux. Creative consultant: Denise Di Novi. Production manager: Gwen Iveson. Assistant production manager: Janet Cuddy. 1st assistant director: John Board. Assistant directors: Libby Bowden, Rocco Gismondi. Continuity: Gillian Richardson. Boom operator: Michael LaCroix. Assistant cameramen: Robin Miller, James Crowe. Key grip: Marris Jansons. Assistant key grip: David Hynes. Grips: Christopher Dean, Brian Danniels. Electrician: Gary Phipps. Gaffer: Jock Brandis. Best boy: Douglas (Scotty) Allen. Property master: Peter Lauterman. Assistant propman: Greg Pelchat. Set decorator: Angelo Stea. Set dressers: Enrico Campana, Gareth Wilson, Gary Jack, Ed Hanna. Costume designer: Delphine White. Assistant designer: Eileen Kennedy. Construction manager: Bill Harman. Wardrobe master: Arthur Rowsell. Wardrobe assistants: Maureen Gurney, Mary Partridge-Raynor, Kathy Vieira, Kat Moyer. Makeup artist: Shonagh Jabour. Makeup assistant: Inge Klaudi. Special makeup design and creation: Rick Baker. Special makeup artists: Steve Johnson, Bill Sturgeon. Special makeup assistants: Michael Kavanagh, Mark Molin. Special video effects: Michael Lennick. Stills photographer: Rick Porter. Location manager: David Coatsworth.

Assistant art directors: Barbara Dunphy, Tom Coulter. Craft service: Lydia Wazana. Assistant editors: Elaine Foreman, Michael Rea, Carol McBride. Post production coordinator: Bill Wiggins. Supervising sound editor: Peter Burgess. Assistant sound editors: Gary Da Prato, Beverle Neale, Michele Cook. Dialogue editor: Charles Bowers. Sound rerecording: Paul Coombe, Michael Hoogenboom. Casting: Walker-Bowen Inc. Laboratory: The Film House Group (Toronto).
Cast: James Woods (*Max Renn*), Sonja Smits (*Bianca O'Blivion*), Deborah Harry (*Nicki Brand*), Peter Dvorsky (*Harlan*), Les Carlson (*Barry Convex*), Jack Creley (*Brian O'Blivion*), Lynne Gorman (*Masha*), Julie Khaner (*Bridey*), Reiner Schwarz (*Moses*), David Bolt (*Raphael*), Lally Cadeau (*Rena King*), Henry Gomez (*Brolley*), Harvey Chao (*Japanese salesman*), David Tsubouchi (*Japanese salesman*), Kay Hawtrey (*matron*), Sam Malkin (*sidewalk derelict*), Bob Church (*newscaster*), Jayne Eastwood (*woman caller*), Franciszka Hedland (*bellydancer*).
Shot on location in Toronto from October 27 to December 23, 1981.
Released: Canada and the United States (600 theatres), February 4, 1983.
Cost: $6,000,000.

1983

THE DEAD ZONE

100 minutes [approx.], 35mm, colour (Kodak 5247 & 5293) 1.85:1
Production company: Dead Zone Productions Ltd. Executive producer: Dino De Laurentiis. Producer: Debra Hill. Associate producer: Jeffrey Boam. Director: David Cronenberg. Screenplay: Jeffrey Boam, from the book by Stephen King. Production designer: Carol Spier. Art director: Barbara Dunphy. Photography: Mark Irwin. Sound: Bryan Day. Editing: Ronald Sanders. Production manager: John M. Eckert. Production coordinator: Philippa King. 1st assistant director: John Board. 2nd assistant director: Otta Hanus. 3rd assistant director: Lydia Wazana. Boom man: Michael LaCroix. Set decorator: Tom Coulter. Set dressers: Gareth Wilson, Gary Jack, Tom Reid. Wardrobe designer: Olga Dimitrov. Assistant wardrobe designer: Denise Woodley. Wardrobe master: Arthur Rowsell. Wardrobe: Maureen Gurney. Makeup: Shonagh Jabour. Video and electronic effects: Michael Lennick. Special effects coordinator: Jon G. Belyeu. Special effects: Mark Molin, Michael Kavanagh, Derek Howard, Clark Johnson, Laird McMurray. Stunt coordinator: Dick Warlock. Stills photographer: Rick Porter. 1st assistant art director: Dan Davis. Continuity: Gillian Richardson. Boom man: Michael LaCroix. 1st assistant cameraman: Robin Miller. 2nd assistant cameraman: Donna Mobbs. Key grip: Maris Jansons. Grips: Carlo Campana, Christopher Dean, David Hynes. Gaffer: Jock Brandis. Best boy: Douglas (Scotty) Allan. Property master: Peter Lauterman. Assistant propman: Don Miloyevich. Construction manager: Joe Curtin. 1st assistant editor: Elaine

Foreman. 2nd assistant editor: Michael Rea. Casting director (Canada): Deirdre Bowen. Casting director (U.S.): Jane Jenkins. Extra casting: Peter Lavender. Laboratory: Medallion Film Laboratories Ltd. (Toronto).

Cast: Christopher Walken (*Johnny Smith*), Brooke Adams (*Sarah Bracknell*), Martin Sheen (*Greg Stillson*), Sean Sullivan (*Herb Smith*), Jackie Burroughs (*Vera Smith*), Herbert Lom (*Dr. Sam Weizak*), Tom Skerritt (*Bannerman*), Anthony Zerbe (*Roger Stuart*), Nicholas Campbell (*Frank Dodd*), Geza Kovacs (*Sonny Elliman*), Colleen Dewhurst (*Henrietta Dodd*), Peter Dvorsky (*Dardis*), Barry Flatman (*Walt*), Simon Craig (*Chris Stuart*), Robert Weiss (*Alma Frechette*), Jack Messinger (*therapist*), Jim Bearden (*deputy*), Cindy Hinds (*Natalie*), Bill Copeland (*Secretary of State*), Kenneth Pogue (*Vice-President*), Gordon Jocelyn (*Five Star General*), John Koensgen (*TV anchorman*), Carlos Estevez (*teenage boy with camera*), Chapelle Jaffe (*nurse*), Julie-Ann Heathwood (*Amy*), Raffi Tchalikian (*Denny*), Red Dreger (*George Harvey*).

Shot on location at Niagara-on-the-Lake, Uxbridge, Stouffville and Toronto from January 10 to March 26, 1983.

Release: Set for October 28, 1983.

Cost: $10,000,000.

A Select Bibliography

General

Braun, E. "The Gentle Art of Mind Boggling." *Films*, I/7, June 1981, p. 22-25.

Chute, David. "He Came From Within." *Film Comment*, XVI/2, March-April 1980, p. 36-39, 42.

Czarnecki, Mark. "A Vivid Obsession With Sex and Death." *Maclean's*, February 14, 1983, p. 61-63.

Govier, Katherine. "Middle-class shivers." *Toronto Life*, July 1979, p. 50-51, 56-58, 61-62.

Harkness, John. "David Cronenberg: Brilliantly Bizarre." *Cinema Canada*, No. 72, March 1981, p. 8-17.

——————. "The word, the flesh and the films of David Cronenberg." *Cinema Canada*, No. 97, June 1983, p. 23-25.

Hookey, Robert. "Backtalk ... with David Cronenberg. *Motion*, VI/4&5, p. 16.

James, Noah. "The Horrifying David Cronenberg." *Maclean's*, July 9, 1979, p. 4-7.

Kroll, Jack. "The Beauty of Horror." *Newsweek*, March 9, 1981, p. 73, 75.

McCarty, John. *Splatter Movies*. FantaCo Enterprises, Inc., Albany, 1981. Chapter on Cronenberg, p. 95-108.

Peredo, Sandra. "The Dark Mind of David Cronenberg." *Today Magazine*, February 28, 1981, p. 14-16.

Pringle, Douglas. "New film in Toronto." *artscanada*, 142/143, April 1970, p. 50-54.

Sammon, Paul M. "David Cronenberg." *Cinefantastique*, X/4, Spring 1981, p. 21-34.

Snider, Norman. "Just Two Innocent Canadian Boys in Wicked Hollywood." *Saturday Night*, July 1974, p. 17-22.

Sutton, M. "Schlock! Horror! The Films of David Cronenberg." *Films and Filming*, 337, October 1982, p. 15-21.

The Films (Listed chronologically)

Stereo

Medjuck, Joe. "Stereo." *Take One,* II/3, January-February 1969, p. 22.

Rayns, Tony. "Stereo." *Monthly Film Bulletin*, XXXVIII/453, October 1971, p. 204.

Crimes of the Future

Briggs, Peter. "Crimes of the Future." *Take One*, II/6, July-August 1969, p. 21.
Rayns, Tony. "Crimes of the Future." *Monthly Film Bulletin*, XXXVIII/454, November 1971, p. 217-218.

The Parasite Murders

Chesley, Steven. "It'll Bug You." *Cinema Canada*, No. 22, October 1975, p. 22-25.
Combs, Richard. "Shivers." *Monthly Film Bulletin*, XLIII/506, March 1976, p. 62.
Delaney, Marshall. "You Should Know How Bad This Film Is. After All, You Paid For It." *Saturday Night*, September 1975, p. 83-85.
Edwards, Natalie. "The Parasite Murders." *Cinema Canada*, No. 22, October 1975, p. 44-45.
Lajeunesse, Jacqueline. "Frissons (Parasite Murders)." *Image et son*, 320-321, octobre 1977, p. 113.
Leayman, Charles D. "They Came From Within." *Cinefantastique*, V/3, Winter 1976, p. 22-23.
Link, André. "Delaney's Dreary Denegration." *Cinema Canada*, No. 22, October 1975, p. 24.
MacMillan, Robert. "Shivers ... Makes Your Flesh Creep!" *Cinema Canada*, No. 72, March 1981, p. 11-15.
Sachs, L. "They Came From Within." *Variety*, CCLXXXII/7, March 24, 1976, p. 21.
Schupp, Patrick. "Frissons." *Séquences*, 83, janvier 1976, p. 35.
Shuster, Nat. "Shivers." *Motion*, V/3, 1976, p. 47-48.
Viviani, Christian. "The Parasite Murders." *Positif*, 171/172, juillet-août 1975, p. 68.
Whitman, Marc. "Shivers." *Films Illustrated*, V/57, May 1976, p. 330.
Yacowar, Maurice. "You Shiver Because It's Good." *Cinema Canada*, No. 34/35, February 1977, p. 54-55.

Rabid

Allombert, Guy. "Rage (Rabid)." *Image et son*, 322, novembre 1977, p. 122.
Combs, Richard. "Rabid." *Monthly Film Bulletin*, XLIV/526, November 1977, p. 240.
Hofsess, John. "Fear and Loathing to Order." *The Canadian*, February 26, 1977, p. 14-17.
Irving, Joan. "David Cronenberg's Rabid." *Cinema Canada*, No. 37, April-May 1977, p. 54.
L., R. "Rage." *Cinéma*, 227, novembre 1977, p. 81.

Q., D. "Rabid." *Films Illustrated*, VII/75, November 1977, p. 88.
"Rabid." *Filmfacts*, XX/10, 1977, p. 225-227.
Rolfe, Lee. "David Cronenberg on Rabid." *Cinefantastique*, VI/3, 1977, p. 26.
Schreger, C. "Rabid." *Variety*, CCLXXXVII/8, June 29, 1977, p. 28.
Shuster, Nat. "Canadian Filmview." *Motion*, VI/4&5, p. 15.

Fast Company

Adilman, Sid. "Fast Company." *Variety*, CCXCV/3, May 23, 1979, p. 24.
Beard, Bill. "Fast Company." *Cinema Canada*, No. 58, September 1979, p. 32-33.
Jones, M.J. "Cronenberg On Wheels: Fast Companies (2)." *Cinema Canada*, No. 49-50, September-October 1978, p. 17-19.

The Brood

Braun, E. "The Brood." *Films and Filming*, XXVI/6, March 1980, p. 34-35.
Dowler, A. "The Brood." *Cinema Canada*, No. 58, September 1979, p. 33-34.
Fox, Jordan R. "The Brood." *Cinefantastique*, VIII/4, p. 23.
Francis, Diane. "Fun and games on the terror set." *Maclean's*, July 9, 1979, p. 4.
Guérif, François. "Chromosome 3." *La revue du cinéma/Image et son/Ecran*, 345, décembre 1979, p. 119.
Lucas, Tim. "The Brood." *Cinefantastique*, IX/1, p. 42.
MacCarthy, T. "The Brood." *Variety*, CCXCV/5, June 6, 1979, p. 20.
Milne, Tom. "The Brood." *Monthly Film Bulletin*, XLVII/554, March 1980, p. 44-45.
O'Toole, Lawrence. "Growing bumps in the night." *Maclean's*, June 11, 1979, p. 50.
—————————. "The Cult of Horror." July 16, 1979, p. 46-47, 49-50.
R., F. "Chromosome 3 (The Brood)." *Positif*, 227, février 1980, p. 88-89.
Rabourdin, Dominique. "Chromosome 3." *Cinéma*, 252, novembre 1979, p. 88.
Schupp, Patrick. "Les Monstres de l'été." *Séquences*, 98, octobre 1979, p. 27-32.
T., C. "Chromosome 3." *Cahiers du cinéma*, 306, décembre 1979, p. 58.

Scanners

Braun, E. "Scanners." *Films* I/5, April 1981, p. 36-37.
Cros, Jean-Louis. "Scanners." *La revue du cinéma/Image et son/Ecran*, 360, avril 1981, p. 60-61.
Garsault, Alain. "Scanners." *Positif*, 242, mai 1981, p. 78-79.

Harkness, John. "David Cronenberg's 'Scanners'." *Cinema Canada*, No. 72, March 1981, p. 34-36.

MacCarthy, T. "Scanners." *Variety* CCCI/12, January 21, 1981, p. 26.

Nacache, Jacqueline. "Scanners." *Cinéma*, 269, mai 1981, p. 78-79.

Sammon, Paul M. "Scanners." *Cinefantastique*, X/4, Spring 1981, p. 45.

Schupp, Patrick. "Scanners." *Séquences*, 105, juillet 1981, p. 29.

Siegel, Lois. "Artists of Illusion." *Cinema Canada*, No. 63, March 1980, p. 20-27.

Taylor, P. "Scanners." *Monthly Film Bulletin*, XLVIII/567, April 1981, p. 78.

Testa, Bart. "No Thrills or Chills." *Maclean's*, February 2, 1981, p. 51.

Videodrome

Ansen, David. "TV or Not to Be." *Newsweek*, February 14, 1983, p. 85, 87.

Chute, David. "David Cronenberg's Gore-Tech Visions. *Rolling Stone*, March 17, 1983, p. 33, 36.

──────────. "Journals: David Chute from L.A." *Film Comment*, XVIII/1, January-February 1982, p. 2, 4.

Dowler, Andrew. "Videodrome." *Cinema Canada*, No. 93, February 1983, p. 35.

Hoberman, J. "Tech It or Leave It." *Village Voice*, February 15, 1983, p. 50.

Klady, Len. "Videodrome." *Variety*, February 2, 1983, p. 18.

Lucas, Tim. "Videodrome." *Cinefantastique*, XII/2&3, April 1982, p. 4-7.

──────────. "Videodrome." *Cinefantastique*, XII/5&6, July-August 1982, p. 6-7.

──────────. "Videodrome." *Cinefantastique*, XIII/4, April-May 1983, p. 4-5.

McKinnon, John P. "Videodrome: Insidious Effects of High Tech." *Cinema Canada*, No. 81, February 1982, p. 32.

O'Toole, Lawrence. "A Thinking Man's Nightmare." *Maclean's*, February 14, 1983, p. 63.

Rickey, Carrie. "Make Mine Cronenberg." *Village Voice*, February 1, 1983, p. 62-65.

The Dead Zone

Lucas, Tim. "Dead Zone." *Cinefantastique,* XIII/5, June-July 1983, p. 17.

The Contributors

WILLIAM BEARD holds a Ph. D. from King's College, University of London. He is a practicing film critic, and has contributed over 500 reviews to Alberta's educational radio network. Since 1978 he has been a full-time lecturer in Film Studies at the University of Alberta.

PIERS HANDLING studied history at Queen's University. He established the Publications Division at the Canadian Film Institute, where he edited *Film Canadiana* and began the "Canadian Film Series," before being appointed Associate Director. For the past two years he has taught Canadian cinema at Carleton University. He has written extensively on Canadian film for *Cinema Canada*, *The Journal of Canadian Studies*, *Motion* and *Copie zéro*; edited *Canadian Feature Films 1964-69* and *Self Portrait — Essays on the Canadian and Quebec Cinemas*; and written *The Films of Don Shebib*.

JOHN HARKNESS studied film at Columbia University. His criticism has appeared in *Ottawa Revue*, *The East Villager*, *CineFile* and *Cinema Canada* for whom he worked as a trade reporter. He is currently the film critic of *NOW* magazine in Toronto.

TIMOTHY R. LUCAS has written widely about the films of David Cronenberg and others for *Cinefantastique*, *Heavy Metal*, *The Vladimir Nabokov Research Newsletter* and *Demonique*. He recently completed five years of work on a video-oriented fantasy of his own, a 600 page novel entitled "T.V. Heaven." Currently he is writing a book-length study of Italian filmmaker Mario Bava.

Although a graduate of the Film Studies programme at Carleton University, and a freelance film critic, both in print and on the radio, GEOFF PEVERE really prefers movies to films.

ROBIN WOOD studied English at Cambridge University, where A.P. Rossiter and F.R. Leavis left lasting impressions on him. While teaching English at high school he wrote all his early books: *Hitchcock's Films*, *Howard Hawks*, *Ingmar Bergman*, *The Apu Trilogy*, *Claude Chabrol* (with Michael Walker) and *Antonioni* (with Ian Cameron), and contributed to the film journal *Movie*. *Personal Views*, a volume of essays, was a transitional work that marked his growing commitment to gay activism, feminism, Marxism and the political use of psychoanalytical theory. He has had numerous articles published, most notably in *Film Comment* and he still contributes to *Movie*. He has taught Film Studies at Queen's University, the

University of Warwick, and is presently teaching at York University. He is working on a book dealing with American cinema of the seventies, and is the current film columnist for *Canadian Forum*.

MAURICE YACOWAR is the Dean of Humanities at Brock University, where he also teaches film. He has written extensively on the cinema and his books include: *I Found It At the Movies*, *Tennessee Williams and Film*, *Hitchcock's British Films*, *Loser Take All: The Comic Art of Woody Allen* and *Method in Madness: The Comic Art of Mel Brooks*. He has published in *Cinema Canada*, *The Journal of Popular Film*, *Quarterly Review of Film Studies* and sits on the editorial board of *Cinema Studies*. He is also the regular film reviewer for CBC-FM's "Stereo Morning."

Photo Credits

Nigel Dickson: 1, 80, 87, 98, 114, 136, 149

Rick Porter: 109, 184, 186, 193

David Cronenberg: 165, 167, 180, 188, 198

Cinepix Inc.: 9, 21, 27, 82, 102, 118, 172, 174, 178

New Cinema Limited: 12, 15, 127, 133

New World-Mutual Pictures of Canada: 5, 36, 38, 43, 46, 84, 90, 92, 106, 122, 184, 186

Paramount Pictures Corporation Ltd.: 196

Universal Films: ii, 55, 62, 71, 109, 140, 152, 193

Cinema Canada: 172, 174

La cinémathèque québécoise: ii, 38